This book is to be returned on or before
the last date stamped below.

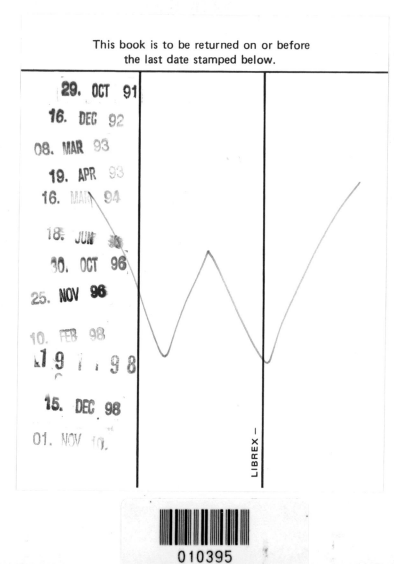

29. OCT 91

16. DEC 92

08. MAR 93

19. APR 93

16. MAR 94

18. JUN

30. OCT 96

25. NOV 96

10. FEB 98

19 7 98

15. DEC 98

01. NOV 10.

LIBREX —

CRUFTS

The Official History

Frank Jackson

Pelham Books

PELHAM BOOKS

Published by the Penguin Group
27 Wrights Lane, London W8 5TZ, England
Penguin USA, 375 Hudson Street, New York, NY 10014, USA
Penguin Books Australia Ltd, Ringwood, Victoria, Australia
Penguin Books Canada Ltd, 2801 John Street, Markham, Ontario, Canada L3R 1B4
Penguin Books (NZ) Ltd, 182–190 Wairau Road, Auckland 10, New Zealand

Penguin Books Ltd, Registered Offices: Harmondsworth, Middlesex, England

First Published 1990
1 3 5 7 9 10 8 6 4 2

Copyright © Frank Jackson 1990

Typeset in 10½/12¼ pt Meridien by
Cambrian Typesetters, Frimley, Surrey
Printed and bound in Great Britain by
Butler and Tanner Ltd., Frome

A CIP catalogue record for this book is available from the British Library.

ISBN 0 7207 1889 9

Contents

Photo Credits

The author and publishers are grateful to the following for permission to reproduce copyright photographs in the book: Thos. Fall page 92; Dave Freeman pages 174, 177, 182; Marc Henrie pages 173, 185; *Illustrated London News* page 45; Kennel Club pages 25, 50, 58, 63, 90, 94, 96, 121, 123, 125, 127, 128, 130, 131, 132, 135, 136, 137, 138, 139, 141, 152, 154, 155, 156, 157, 158, 160, 178; Bill Moores pages 165, 170; *Our Dogs* pages 27, 68, 80, 98, 106, 114, 118; Alan Walker page 176. Every effort has been made to trace copyright owners but in a few cases this has not been possible. It is hoped that any omissions will be excused.

Foreword

By HRH Prince Michael of Kent
President of The Kennel Club and Crufts

1991 sees the Centenary of Crufts Dog Show and I am very pleased to introduce this History of Crufts. The story of the Show, and of its originator, Charles Cruft, is of particular significance now. It is a tale of initiative and enterprise, frequently in the face of significant difficulties. Cruft himself ran the Show, which stood as a tribute to his determination and tenacity, until his death in 1938. It was only after the Second World War that the Kennel Club continued the tradition and assumed management of the event.

Dog showing is a sporting activity encompassing many people and all types and condition of breeds. The number of exhibitors and their dogs runs into many tens of thousands each year but the one activity which is known to everyone, exhibitors and the general public alike, is Crufts Dog Show. It is unique, world renowned and typically British. This history of the Show gives an insight into the character of Mr Cruft and should interest not only the experts in canine activities but all those interested in dogs. I warmly recommend it.

Author's Note

Up until 1974 Cruft's Show always had an apostrophe but this was dropped in that year. In this history we have followed this rule when giving the show its title.

Introduction

I want to see the Beefeaters; and Cruft's Dog Show; and your blood horses, and the Derby.

James Galsworthy (THE SILVER SPOON)

Crufts Dog Show is, without doubt, the most famous dog show in the world. For ninety-nine years it has provided London with a compelling winter event which attracted visitors from all over the world. The show's centenary will be celebrated in Birmingham in 1991 when the eighty-eighth Crufts Dog Show will take place.

Crufts provides, for the many thousands of people whose hobby is breeding and showing dogs, a winter competition which offers unusual excitement. It offers an exhibition which annually attracts over 100,000 spectators and it offers a shop window for the £1000 million complex of industries which are supported by the British interest in dogs. This interest can no longer be seen as a peculiarly British characteristic, interest in pedigree dogs is worldwide.

Crufts is widely regarded as the biggest and best dog show in the world, at various times in its history it has certainly been both. Its reputation rests on a potent mixture of fact and fiction. This book offers, not a detailed portrait, but simply a sketch which attempts to trace the main features of the show's origins and hundred year history.

During the hundred years after the middle of the eighteenth century the Industrial Revolution created changes at a pace which had never previously been experienced, or even imagined. The changes had a profound effect on society's attitudes towards and need of animals. It was out of these changes that interest in pedigree dogs and, ultimately, Cruft's Show were to grow.

Historians have barely scratched the surface of the way in which man's relationship with dogs has developed during the last 12,000 years or so. The relationship is unique but its importance only began to be realised after the Industrial Revolution had threatened its very existence. Even now the importance of the relationship is not fully understood.

If a dog was to write this book he might, without any trace of the irony with which the phrase is usually associated, sign it 'Your Humble and Obedient Servant'. Nevertheless dog is not always humble, or even obedient, and is not always a servant. There have been times when he has been elevated to the position of a God, at others he has been regarded as no more than the ingredient for a stew. He has been a companion, a fellow warrior, a taster for suspect food, a source of warmth and comfort, an early warning device, a sporting companion and a basis for gambling. He has guarded us and our belongings, offered us warmth, a sympathetic and uncritical ear in which to pour our problems and his presence has relieved our loneliness. He has been admired for his strength, his speed, his intelligence, his hunting ability, his courage and his value as a servant. Nor has his beauty ever lacked appreciation. The ancient Sumarians, the Chinese, the Egyptians, the Greeks and the Romans, as well as their descendants, were all capable of admiring the beauty of dogs as something apart from their value as servants.

Breeding and showing dogs is a hobby which has never been more popular, not just in Britain, but throughout the world. The Kennel Club, founded in 1873, is the oldest of the bodies which regulate the world of breeding and showing dogs, and is linked with similar organisations in almost every country in the world. In 1891, when the first Cruft's Show took place, the Kennel Club licensed fewer than fifty shows. Now it licenses over 7000 events each year, the largest attract about 20,000 dogs, the smallest perhaps no more than 20 or 30. They offer an opportunity for dog owners to share and develop their interests and to indulge in friendly competition which reflects their particular aspirations. These competitions, in a way achieved by few, if any, other competitive activities, cater for young and old, for the able bodied and for those with limited mobility, as well, as for all levels of society. There can be few activities which have such a wide appeal.

A detailed history of the development of dog shows has yet to be written. This is the first book even to attempt to sketch the way in which the most famous dog show in the world has developed during its first hundred years. It cannot be expected that being the first will conceal or excuse its inadequacies. These would have been far greater without the help of a number of people. John MacDougall, the Kennel Club Chairman, read and approved the manuscript at various stages. *Our Dogs* gave free access to their archives. Teresa Slowik and Caroline White, from their desks in the Kennel Club Library, helped to complete the appendices. Len Pearce provided access to his obedience records. John Williams offered suggestions and wise counsel. Without Jean and Elspeth Jackson's timely encouragement, criticism and assistance, which took many forms, attempting the task would have been unthinkable.

Frank Jackson
Ashworth Moor, 1990

1. The British Barnum

*I*n 1851 James Spratt, an electrical engineer with a singularly inventive mind, left Canada where he had patented, manufactured and marketed a lightning conductor, in order to promote his invention at the Great Exhibition in the Crystal Palace, London. Perhaps interest in his invention did not come up to his expectations or perhaps Spratt's interest in dogs led him into other channels but whatever the reason, in 1860, he set up a firm, Spratt's Patent Limited, in order to manufacture and market his most recent invention, Spratt's Meal Fibrine Dog Cakes.

In 1852, just a year after James Spratt had left Canada, a son was born to a London goldsmith, said to be 'in a small way of business', whose workshop and home were in Hunter Street, Brunswick Square, Bloomsbury. The boy was Charles Cruft. He was educated at Ardingley College in Sussex, not a school usually associated with the children of fathers in no more than a small way of business and, as an evening student, at Birkbeck College, London. After leaving Ardingley he spent some time working for his father but in 1866 the fourteen-year-old Charles Cruft, who had, by now, decided that the family jewellery business was not to his liking, successfully applied for the post of office boy at Spratts. The appointment was to have almost as much significance for Spratts as it had for Charles Cruft himself. Subsequently Spratt used to enjoy telling how, at the initial interview, the precocious youngster, showing the sort of confidence and prescience which would never desert him, had said 'You know I think this kind of business ought to do very well, I do honestly'.

An electrical engineer and inventor of patent lightning conductors leaving Canada and going into the business of producing dog biscuits is, in itself, a story sufficiently out of the ordinary to satisfy most people but the story has since been embellished, in a manner which has all the hallmarks of the way in which Cruft was later to attract attention to his own endeavours. It is claimed that James Spratt invented dog biscuits after finding a ready sale for a load of condemned ship's biscuits. The ease with which he sold the biscuits led him to produce his own secret and superior recipe for dog biscuits and to go on to make his fame and fortune. There is, in fact, no evidence to show that James Spratt ever sold stale biscuits as dog food, though had he done so he would not have been the first or the last.

He certainly did not invent dog biscuits. The Domesday Book, which records the results of surveys begun in 1085, contains a reference to *ter mille panes canibus* – three thousand cakes of dog bread – being produced in Chintenham, Gloucestershire. The manufacture of food intended for dogs was obviously already established in the eleventh century.

In 1826 the *Sporting Magazine* carried an advert for dog biscuits produced by a Mr Smith. A later issue of the same magazine drew renewed attention to Mr Smith's dog biscuits in a way which remains familiar.

> 'We find that Mr Smith, who has introduced his biscuits on our Magazine cover, has met that encouragement and patronage which we trust will ever follow the endeavours of all who study to promote the pleasures and conveniences of the Sporting World. We have seen a letter from our valuable correspondent, NIMROD, who states:– "I approve of them very much, and shall not fail to recommend them to my sporting friends;" – also, from E. Cripps Esq. whose black bitch, Emerald, won the Ashdown Cup, stating "I must say it is the best food for Greyhounds I have tried".'

If Nimrod, C. J. Apperley, that most snobbish of nineteenth-century sporting journalists, had deigned to notice dog biscuits we may be sure not only that there was something in it for him but that he regarded dog biscuits and their manufacturers as worthy of the notice of his aristocratic sporting readers.

So even though James Spratt and his new office boy were not embarking on an entirely new business there is no doubt that Charles Cruft was absolutely right when he expressed confidence in the future of the business to his prospective employer.

Within a few months of becoming Spratt's office boy Cruft had managed to convince his superiors that if another office boy was taken on he could be better employed devoting himself to selling Spratt's products. Once this had been achieved he then set about convincing James Spratt that it would be better if 'he could go out and see customers instead of waiting for them'. It says much both for James Spratt's confidence in his brash young assistant and for Cruft's ability to recognise and sell the idea which was central to success that Cruft was quickly promoted to the newly created position of travelling salesman.

The firm prospered and quickly outgrew its first, cramped premises in Old Middle Row. New premises were taken at 28, High Holborn, London. These included an old farm house which was said to have been one of the very many places where the peripatetic Queen Elizabeth had rested for the night. The business continued to prosper in its new home with James Spratt supervising the manufacturing process and Charles Cruft energetically selling the product. His energy and ability to peddle

James Spratt came from Canada to set up in business manufacturing dog biscuits.

Spratt's products so impressed his employer that twelve years after leaving his father's jewellery business Cruft was managing the office and sales department of James Spratt's thriving business. Much of the credit for the firm's success has been ascribed to Charles Cruft. It is certainly true that the enterprising twenty-six year-old had already begun to develop methods, not always closely related to the quality of the product he wished to sell, by which he could attract public attention to his wares. He was already an astute publicist.

Throughout his life Charles Cruft was acutely aware of the value of publicity, of the importance of attracting public notice and of exciting public imagination. He was not slow to realise that this was probably a more effective key to success than was the quality of the product itself. His famous shows were usually, though not invariably, well run and well organised but they were probably no better, and sometimes may have been worse, than many other dog shows which took place without making any significant impact on public interest and attention. Nor has the situation materially changed during the last hundred years. Charles Cruft went out of his way to attract the notice of the press and to use this in such a way as to attract the public's attention. He ensured that the press would report that Cruft's Show was the biggest and best, perhaps even the only, dog show in the world, and would do so even when it was nothing of the kind. He was always ready to talk to reporters who knew that they would get a good story from him. If the story was little more than a thinly disguised way of promoting Cruft's Show what did it matter as long as their readers were interested? It was not for nothing that he became known as the British Barnum. Nor is it without significance that he enjoyed comparison with that extraordinary showman.

It would, however, be wrong to underestimate the part played by James Spratt both in the success of his own business and in Charles Cruft's development as an entrepreneur. Spratt already had a long, varied and reasonably successful business career behind him. He was to die in 1878, twenty-seven years after leaving Canada. It was he who had produced and jealously guarded the original recipe from which Spratt's Dog Biscuits were made. He also supervised the manufacturing process and ensured that production met the increasing demand. It was also James Spratt who recognised the young Cruft's talents and who ensured that these were fully used and well rewarded.

From the later years of the eighteenth century and throughout the first half of the nineteenth the world of dog shows produced a number of entrepreneurs and show managers whose names, though now largely forgotten, deserve to be remembered. Warde and Parrington, Shaw and Aistrop, Pape, Reid and Shorthose, and, perhaps above all others, Brailsford and Douglas. Each had made a valuable and individual contribution to the rapidly developing interest in dog shows and show dogs. Their interests in dogs reflected the wide range of interests which dogs, then as now, were able to offer. For John Warde and Thomas Parrington foxhounds mattered most. Pape, Reid and Shorthose were principally interested in gundogs. Jemmy Shaw and Charlie Aistrop might be regarded as converts from the darker side of dogdom involved in fighting and baiting. Initially, at least all were interested only in what were then regarded as sporting dogs. Initial shows offered an opportunity to compare dogs whose main use was in sporting activities. This was to change during the early years of the nineteenth century as interest in pet dogs began to develop.

Not only did these early promoters demonstrate the range of interest which dogs could offer but they also showed that an interest in dogs was not confined to a single thread of our social fabric. Then, as now, interest in dogs cut across all social barriers. Even Charlie Aistrop, whose activities and associates in dogs can hardly be regarded as entirely respectable was, in 1814, invited to take Billy, whose fame derived from having killed five hundred rats in an hour, to Buckingham Palace where he was admired by the Prince Regent's wayward daughter, Princess Charlotte. It is even suggested that Billy was mated to one of Princess Charlotte's Toy Spaniels, though why she should want to use a cross-bred terrier and Bulldog to mongrelise a breed which could already trace pedigrees back to the Toy Spaniels kept by Charles II during the seventeenth century is not clear. Nevertheless legend is adamant that Charlie Aistrop received 10 guineas from the royal purse for Billy's services. Perhaps if Billy could regularly command such a stud fee Aistrop's later refusal of 300 guineas for him becomes more easily understood, though the alleged refusal of a pension for life if he would part with the famous old dog can only be explained by the pride and affection Aistrop must have felt for Billy and which is not at all incompatible with the stern tests to which Billy and others of his ilk were subjected.

From the closing years of the eighteenth century, when formal dog shows seem first to have made their appearance, to the time when Cruft began to take an interest, dog shows had undergone a metamorphosis. Shows for working hounds and the small urban shows for pet dogs continued to be held, just as they do today, but the growing number of shows, which catered for all breeds, taking place all over the country and often attracting their entries from far afield had already given notice that breeding and showing pedigree dogs was likely to become a major recreational activity in Britain. The new shows had not only brought all the different threads of interest in dogs together and so laid the basis for activities which are now to be found being enthusiastically pursued all over the world but they had also produced an entirely new source of entertainment which the public, from all walks of life and of all ages, could enjoy both as participants and spectators. Inevitably this popularity and interest would attract the notice of other entrepreneurs who would develop the ideas and methods pioneered by the early promoters.

One such, and by far the most famous of them all was, of course, Charles Cruft. It might even be said that the influence which he exerted over the development of dog shows from about 1880 until his death in 1938, and even beyond, has led directly to the sort of shows we know today. The course taken by that development might, however, have been very different but for the existence of the Kennel Club which, by the time Charles Cruft appeared on the scene, had developed something of the authority needed to ensure that Cruft's flair for showmanship did not take his show too far down the path which was already being so successfully travelled by the American showman, Phineas T. Barnum. Inevitably there would be times when Cruft's intention to produce a profitable show which would attract public interest would conflict with the Kennel Club's more cautious approach and with their intention to ensure that dog shows would preserve and encourage honest, fair competition based on sound and knowledgeable judgement and would help to improve the quality of pedigree dogs.

Much of the incredible success of Crufts Dog Show was, and over fifty years after his death, remains, the result of Charles Cruft's almost uncanny ability to attract publicity. This ability was at the basis not just of the success of Cruft's Show but of all his other enterprises. However Charles Cruft's interest in publicity was strictly confined to business. He was not only shy of personal publicity but managed to ensure that there was no public intrusion into his private life. During his lifetime he successfully discouraged the press from focusing unwelcome attention on himself or his family and, therefore, away from the shows which would benefit from such attention. Cruft surrounded his private life with a screen which was seldom penetrated and the press, well supplied with material relevant to his shows, were, in those days, content to respect his desire for privacy. A few articles about the man himself did appear during his lifetime and others have appeared since his death but these are often both sparse in detail and inaccurate. Some of the inaccuracies stem from deliberately misleading information supplied by Cruft or his wife. Even Theo Marples, the founder of *Our Dogs*, who had known Charles Cruft at least since the late 1870s and whose stormy relationship with Cruft only slowly grew into a firm friendship was unable, or unwilling, to produce a biography which contained more than a few anodyne facts. Perhaps, astute journalist though he was, he too was merely respecting Charles Cruft's desire for personal privacy.

When it came to business however Cruft was able and willing to use almost any means to gain the publicity on which the success of his efforts depended. Sometimes he seems even to have had an instinctive ability to produce things round which a good story could be woven and which would generate publicity.

One of the clerical procedures he used during his time spent in Spratt's office was to be of great importance to the company but which only someone with an uncanny ability to attract publicity could have anticipated. In order to ease the task of book-keeping Cruft was in the habit of differentiating between private and trade buyers by using a small cross made against certain names in the ledger. This small cross, formalised into a Maltese cross, was later to provide Spratt's with its distinctive trade mark and must rank alongside Bass's triangle as a simple mark whose influence and value has been profound. Charles Cruft was well aware of the importance of providing the public with a memorable and simple symbol by which they could recognise a particular product. For his own show he produced a logo which consisted of a St Bernard's head, one of the breeds for which he had a personal fondness, enclosed in a stylised dog collar, the whole surmounted by a crown. The symbol, virtually unchanged, remains in use today and offers telling evidence of Cruft's remarkable ability to capture and encapsulate public interest in order to further his own enterprises.

The business of selling dog biscuits brought Charles Cruft into close contact with kennels throughout the country as well as providing him with a need to visit the shows at which his customers would be gathered. Undoubtedly he would quickly have recognised the potential for further development which dog shows offered, just as he would also have realised that he could run shows at least as well as the two gamekeepers, Brailsford and Douglas, who, between them seem to have made the running during the third quarter of the nineteenth century as far as show promotion was concerned. The way in which dog shows were being run and, perhaps more especially, the way in which they were presented to the public, must have been anathema to Cruft. Equally the personable young Charles Cruft, who was now about thirty years old, would have impressed the major kennel owners and exhibitors, just as he had impressed James Spratt, with his energy and talent. He was never one to hide his very considerable light under a bushel. It is hardly surprising that it was not long before he was taking a hand in show management.

By this time James Spratt Patent Limited had been sold to Edward Wylan who had moved the business to much larger and less idio-syncratic premises in Bermondsey. With the change in ownership came further promotion for Charles Cruft, first to Chief Traveller and then to Manager of the rapidly expanding business. The manufacture and sale of dog biscuits remained the firm's staple business but under Cruft's management foodstuffs and equipment for other animals were also manufactured and sold. Food for game birds and poultry, as well as accessories for dogs, cats and poultry were added to the list. However, in spite of the demands of the growing business and of his greater responsibility within it, Charles Cruft also found time to become Secretary of the Toy Spaniel Club, thus taking over the reins which had formerly been held by Charlie Aistrop and establishing an interesting historical link.

Cruft also became Secretary of the Pug Dog Club and was involved with clubs and shows for Setters, St Bernards and Borzois. His choice of breeds is interesting. Toy Spaniels were one of the breeds which might be said to have been in at the beginning of urban dog shows. The 1859 Newcastle show and those which came soon after it had demonstrated that gundog owners could be enticed to show their dogs and Cruft's travels as a salesman with a range of goods which now included food for game birds as well as for dogs would inevitably have brought him into contact with the major gundog kennels. One of these was at Clumber Park, where the Clumber Spaniel had its origins. This was the home of the Duchess of Newcastle. She had already interested herself in dog shows and had established a kennel which housed a number of breeds including some of the best Borzois outside Russia. It was no accident that one of the breeds in which Cruft took a particular interest was Borzois.

According to Theo Marples, it was in Europe that Charles Cruft cut his teeth as a show manager. In 1878, and already with twelve years experience of the dog food business behind him and having achieved remarkable success for a twenty-six year old, Charles Cruft was placed in charge of the dog section of the Paris Exhibition. The event was, in some respects, a Parisian answer to the 1851 Crystal Palace Exhibition, which had brought James Spratt to London, and was to provide a springboard for his assistant's fame and fortune. The dog section, benefiting from Charles Cruft's abilities, was an enormous success both with French exhibitors and with the public, who Cruft had ensured knew all about the event and would be attracted to it. The success brought Cruft invitations to act as Secretary to the Dutch Club Cynophilia and as Manager of the livestock sections of the Brussels and Antwerp Exhibitions. During this busy period Cruft was also becoming involved in show management in Britain. For a number of years, he was show manager for the Scottish Kennel Club, running their shows at Kelvin Hall in Glasgow and Waverley Market in Edinburgh. He also ventured further into Scotland to run shows as far north as Inverness, where, to Jimmy Garrow's delight, he was photographed in full Highland dress which he wore 'well and with dignity'.

As well as managing dog shows throughout Britain Cruft acted as manager to the poultry section of the Royal Agricultural Society. At one time or another he was secretary and, with Mons Vandersnecht, co-founder of the Schipperke Club of Brussels, secretary to the Royal St Hubert Society of Brussels, secretary of the Toy Spaniel and Pug Dog Clubs. Charles Cruft was neither without ambition nor the energy to fulfil that ambition.

By 1886 he felt well able to accept yet another suggestion put forward by the Duchess of Newcastle, though he might well have seen the suggestion more in the nature of a royal command. It had apparently occurred to Her Grace that it was about time there was a London show for terriers. It was this and the subsequent seven terrier shows which led to the foundation of the National Terrier Club, of which Cruft was the first secretary, and which, as the series attracted more notice, placed the name of Charles Cruft firmly before the British public and led directly to the first Cruft's Show in 1891.

Let us, for a moment step back from our examination of Charles Cruft's progress as a dog show manager, to wonder why he chose to devote such energy to dog shows. His career with Spratts cannot be said to have been without success or challenge. Many a youngster, even a very ambitious one, might have been more than satisfied with a successful career in a rapidly expanding business. Work as a travelling salesman with Spratts had brought Charles Cruft into contact with a great many dog owners from all walks of life. He must have seen the enthusiasm which dog owners of all sorts had developed for showing their dogs and he could not have failed to recognise the way in which this enthusiasm was increasing the popularity of dog shows. He was probably unimpressed by the way in which British dog shows were being organised and promoted and, at the same time saw, in the potential they offered, the sort of business opportunity which might lead to even bigger things than a successful career as a Spratt's employee.

If Charles Cruft also shared a deep interest in dogs with his customers the decision to run dog shows might be even more easily explained. On this point there is a body of conflicting evidence, at least some of which serves to show how Cruft was at pains to hide his private life and interests. Various authorities, among them James Garrow and Theo Marples, both of whom knew Cruft well, have suggested that he kept Schipperkes, Pointers and Fox Terriers. His wife, on the other hand, who might be regarded as being an incontrovertible authority on the subject, firmly denied that her husband ever owned a dog. Writing in *Mrs Charles Cruft's Famous Dog Book*, published in 1949 as a means of raising funds for Our Dumb Friends League, she said:

> 'Although for more years than I care to remember I have been closely concerned with my late husband, Charles Cruft, in organising and producing each year the greatest Dog Show in the World, it may come as a surprise to you who are reading this book when I unblushingly confess that I have never owned a dog. . . . There was a very good reason for this, for being closely associated with the show side of the dog world I was constantly having to decline offers from breeders of many magnificent animals, so rather than offend anyone my husband and I both made it an iron rule never to accept or even to own a dog in case we were accused of favouring one particular breed. But we were determined to own a pet, so we took the least line of resistance and kept a – CAT!'

There seems to be no good reason to doubt Mrs Cruft's word and explanation though the motives advanced by Mrs Cruft for owning a cat rather than a dog become a little strained when it is realised that Charles Cruft, at one stage in his career, also ran cat shows. Fortunately the matter was, perhaps inadvertently, resolved by Cruft himself. He also wrote a book about dogs, though, for some reason, it was not published until 1952, three years after Mrs Cruft had published her denial that

Cruft ever owned a dog. The book is a simple care and maintenance manual aimed at the novice owner which not only remained relevant at least fourteen years after Cruft could have written it but is still much better than some of the present genre.

In his book* Cruft discusses the choice of a particular breed.

* *Charles Cruft's Dog Book* (W. Foulsham 1952)

> 'I myself have found that a big breed such as, for example a Dane or Alsatian, can be less trouble in a confined space than many of the small breeds, provided there is ample opportunity for exercise, particularly as most big breeds are very docile fellows and will curl up in an incredibly small space – often artfully chosen before the fire, keeping everyone else at a considerable distance'.

That sounds like a statement made by someone with experience of living with large dogs. Indeed Cruft says that his opinion stems from his own experience. But he goes still further in a way which totally resolves any mystery about Charles Cruft as a dog owner.

> 'I must, however, agree with my wife that having my St Bernard in our cottage is rather beyond a joke, to say nothing of what happens on a wet day.'

So while Charles Cruft shows evidence of having lived with Great Danes and Alsatians, possibly in the homes of others, he readily admits to having been the owner of a St Bernard. Mrs Cruft, perhaps out of loyalty to her husband and to a story which they had found it convenient to tell while he was running his dog shows, probably did no more than retell the story they had always told. Charles Cruft, writing a book late in a very long life and knowing that his career as a showman was coming to an end, had no reason to continue to tell the convenient, if untruthful, tale. On the other hand Mrs Cruft might well have told the truth but her husband, never afraid to manipulate the truth, might well have realised that since the best dog books are written by people with practical experience of dogs he should establish himself as a dog owner. Perhaps if Mrs Cruft had claimed to have been a dog owner her book might have been better received. Her husband, however, would have had no compunction in improving the story in order to sell more books.

The probability is that it was Charles Cruft who told the truth in this instance. It seems very unlikely that a man who had spent all his working life with dogs and their owners and who had made his name and fortune out of an involvement with dogs could have remained indifferent to the attractions of dogs. Could he have been so unimpressed by the enthusiasm for which his show catered and by the obvious enjoyment that people found in the company of dogs that he would not want to share that enthusiasm and enjoyment? Charles Cruft's book reads as if it was written by someone who had lived with dogs and who knew both their problems and their benefits from first hand experience.

By 1894 Charles Cruft could look back to three very successful dog shows which had carried his name as well as a series of terrier shows on which he had satisfied himself that he could achieve success as an independent promoter of shows. Inevitably he looked round for other events on which his talents could be exercised. The agricultural societies, some of which had already been running shows for over one hundred years, were prepared to use Cruft as an organiser but there was no room among these events for an independent show promoter intent on private gain. Among shows devoted to other forms of agricultural or domestic livestock none came within sight of the popularity of dog shows but cat shows were a distant second. Perhaps cat shows would provide an additional opening for Cruft's talents and so, with what now seems to be uncharacteristic haste, Cruft decided that he would try his hand at cat shows.

On 7 and 8 March 1894 Cruft's Cat Show took place at the Royal Aquarium, Westminster with Lord Marcus Beresford as President of the new venture and a list of aristocratic patrons which included the names of some of those to whom Cruft looked for support of his dog shows. The Patrons included Her Grace the Duchess of Newcastle, Her Grace the Duchess of Wellington, the Countess of Sefton, the Countess of Warwick and a galaxy of ladies including Lady de Trafford. Among the fifteen patrons were only two men, a sharp contrast to the male dominated world of dog shows. The show offered 'Nearly 50 Special Prizes from 25 guineas, 75 Classes with Prizes from £5' and a panel of four judges which included the two Weir brothers John and Harrison, John Jennings and Miss Gresham.

Fur and Feather was unequivocal in their welcome of the new venture.

> 'Mr Cruft having turned his attention to matters Catty, it was only to be expected that he would eclipse all previous efforts at a Cat Show, and such expectations have not been belied . . . With only some six or eight weeks in which to develop matters, Mr Cruft has succeeded in getting together such a collection of cats as was never before seen, and this has been accomplished with the intervention of his Great Dog Show in that short space of time. What he would have done had the Cat Show claimed his undivided attention from the time of its inception till its close we know not, neither can we imagine. Be that as it may, Cruft's Cat Show has come, and it has come to stay. Its future is secure and henceforth we shall look forward year by year to the Cruftonian event as one of the great features in the Cat exhibition world'.

With over six hundred entries the show was certainly bigger by far than any previous cat show but the entry was a product of a classification which was itself far bigger than anything which had gone before. The generous classification was supported by a list of special prizes and awards which also eclipsed what cat exhibitors had hitherto been accustomed to. Even so, perhaps as a result of the impossibly short time in which the show was organised, Cruft himself seems to have been far less confident about the new venture than were *Fur and Feather*. Even the show's title, Cruft's Cat Show, is strangely muted when set alongside that of Cruft's Great International Dog Show and Exhibition of Sporting Appliances and Fine Arts Society.

The advertising which had preceded the cat show had also been, by Cruft's standards, almost reticent. Nor were Cruft's fears proved groundless. Some classes, even entire breeds, received very few, if any entries, though it was still possible to trumpet the cat show as the biggest ever. Still worse than a disappointing entry was, from Cruft's point of view, a spell of unusually atrocious March weather which deterred the public from supporting the show. Even the press, with the exception of that section which might be said to have had a vested interest in the success of the new venture, gave the show scant attention. Charles Cruft may not have taken the view that the event was a failure, and especially for an inaugural event, but it certainly was not the sort of success to which he had become accustomed or which he expected.

Yet, in the short space of time available to him, he had done wonders.

> 'The masses of red drapery,' enthused *Fur and Feather*, 'the innumerable Japanese lamps, umbrellas, flags, and other ornaments which adorned the walls and roof, to say nothing of the magnificent palms which were largely in evidence about the floor of the building, all helped to give visitors the idea that they were attending some fashionable fancy fair rather than a Cat Show whilst the daintily arranged tables and seats helped to convey an idea far remote from a Cat Show. . . . The disinfecting was beyond all praise . . . after twelve years' experience of the leading cat shows, we have never met anything like it. This perfection was arrived at by the use of Spratt's new pens, fitted with earth drawers, and Mr Carvill's Air Purifier.'

Is it ungenerous to wonder what Cruft received, pure air apart, for promoting Carvill's Air Purifier?

After what Cruft could only have regarded as a lukewarm reception there were doubts that he would venture another, though *Fur and Feather* did its best to ensure that another Cruft's Cat Show would take place. In September, 1894 they announced that 'several leading Cat fanciers have asked Mr Cruft to continue holding his great London Cat Shows, which were so auspiciously commenced last March, but as the first fixture lost considerably over £100, Mr Cruft does not feel at all inclined to go on with any further exhibitions of cats, unless those who benefit by them are disposed to lend a helping hand'. The fact that the chief beneficiary of the cat and dog shows was intended to be Charles Cruft himself was being diplomatically ignored, though it was recognised that 'Mr Cruft does not for one moment wish to hide the fact, that so far as he is personally concerned these Cat Shows must be a purely commercial transaction. He has not the slightest interest in Cats, but is willing to place his knowledge and energy at the disposal of those friends of Poor Puss who may desire it, provided he is not left to do all the work, and then find himself out of pocket at the finish'. Exhibitors were encouraged to rally round by the suggestion that, during the early days of his dog shows, 'Mr Cruft had to face losses, but exhibitors soon saw that it was to their interests to support such undertakings'.

Here's an odd thing, especially after Mrs Cruft's claim that they had shared their home with a cat. What possible help to Cruft's Cat Show could *Fur and Feather's* assertion that its promoter had 'not the slightest interest in cats' have intended to be. Nevertheless it seems that subscribers were forthcoming for, in March 1895 Cruft tried again and once more *Fur and Feather* were predictably unrestrained in their enthusiasm.

> 'No better place than the St Stephen's Hall, the entrance to which is opposite Westminster Abbey, for the purposes of such an exhibition, could be found in any part of the country, the prize list is by far the most liberal, and the schedule the most extensive ever known, the judges are all thoroughly competent authorities, every possible precaution that can be desired will be taken to ensure the safety and comfort of the Cats, and, lastly, Mr Charles Cruft's lengthy experience will assure both exhibitors and the public receiving every possible courtesy and attention at the hands of the director who has well earned himself the soubriquet of the "Prince of Showmen" '.

A Miss Harper was moved to give public support to the venture though perhaps her motives in doing so were no more altruistic than were those of Cruft himself.

> 'My friends among the intending exhibitors at Cruft's Show, are pleased with the care to be paid, in order to avoid infection, by new woodwork, etc., for the pens, and, of course, the necessary precaution will be also taken with regard to the zinc wires, if new, to have them well scalded, as the omission of this duty has been fatal in its effects to kittens in previous shows. Everyone knows the habit of licking the wires of the cage that kittens indulge in, and it is to be feared that many of the deaths after they have returned from shows are to be attributed to this cause'.

Having done her best to let Charles Cruft know what she and her friends expected the good lady then took the opportunity of letting the judges know what she expected of them.

> 'My Silver Emperor will make his debut at the Great International Show. It was at first thought unadvisable to send him, as he had commenced to shed his coat, but as this is likely to be the case with many other long-haired Cats, we shall not, on his account, prevent him from making his bow to the public on March 13th, and trust his other excellent points will fully atone for this passing defect'.

Sadly Silver Emperor was not among the winners.

After the show *Fur and Feather* was once more lavish in its praise but among the bouquets were one or two brickbats. The hall's decorations were praised but exhibitors were said to have 'groaned at the absence of the velvet curtains and the little tea tables'. The entry, smaller than in the previous year, was blamed on the trying time of year, which in some ways was better than that chosen by Cruft for his dog show. But even without a big entry a number of judges struggled to complete their assignments. It seems that Cruft had tried to economise by reducing the size of his judging panel. He also tried to economise by replacing the previous year's splendid catalogue with a very ordinary and much cheaper affair. Cruft seems not to have had his heart in the event. Was his absence of interest in cats the reason for his apparent lack of enthusiasm for his cat show? Against such a background it is, perhaps, hardly surprising that there was little or no mention of public enthusiasm for the event. If the writing was already on the wall *Fur and Feather* steadfastly refused to recognise the fact or, at least, to admit it to their readers. In March of 1896 they reported that the show had been postponed from its usual March date owing to the pressure of Charles Cruft's other business commitments. In fact Charles Cruft had already decided that he would run no more cat shows. He had tried twice and on both occasions had been faced with unwelcome and unaccustomed failure. Cruft was far too good a businessman to pursue lost causes. He was certainly not going to try again, henceforth all his energies would be directed towards dog shows.

For the first ninety-nine years of its life Crufts Dog Show was held in London, indeed it was, for some years, London's only major all-breed championship dog show. As a result of its move to the National Exhibition Centre at Birmingham London is now without a major championship dog show. With a single exception all Crufts shows have also been held in February, a month when travel can be difficult and when London is not at its best. Charles Cruft also chose to run his cat show in March. Why did he choose such a potentially inhospitable time of year for these events?

In 1936 he told a reporter that he had 'selected the date for his annual

Charles Cruft in 1931.

show at the Royal Agricultural Hall with a good deal of discrimination, as, by the second week in February, gundogs are released from their duties and can take part in the competition of the show ring if their owners desire'. The explanation sounds very convincing, as Cruft undoubtedly intended that it should, though it does not explain why February was chosen as the date for his terrier shows and March as the date for his cat shows. Neither gundogs nor their handlers were deeply involved in either of these enterprises.

It is true that working gundogs would be free from other duties after 1 February, they would be in fit and hard condition, too fit and hard perhaps for today's show ring tastes. Their owners might be returning to their London houses and keepers would have time to send or take the dogs to Cruft's. Even so the early Cruft's Shows were not well patronised by gundogs. Furthermore February was much too early for Cruft's to expect support for classes for working terriers and hounds which were still fully occupied in the field. What just might have been true for gundogs did not hold good for the majority of sporting breeds which Cruft hoped to attract to his show.

There must be some other explanation for Cruft's choice of the February date. It might well be that the best terms he could negotiate with the Agricultural Hall made a February date necessary. It is also possible that Cruft's preference for late winter dates might also have been the product of a purely personal interest which he chose not to discuss. Late winter dates would allow him to do all the major work for the shows during the winter months and leave the summer comparatively free for other interests. Charles Cruft enjoyed sailing. It was his interest in sailing which had brought him into contact and friendship with Lord Alfred Paget who, though lacking any interest in dogs, had been among those who gave their names and influence in support of Cruft's first terrier show. Might not Charles Cruft have chosen a February date so that he could be free to sail during the summer months?

Much of the success of Cruft's Show was based on Charles Cruft's ability to attract and manipulate publicity but to suggest that the entire success of the show depended on publicity would be unjust. With the aid of a small, loyal and dedicated staff Charles Cruft was able to offer to visitors an unmatched canine exhibition. He also offered to his exhibitors services which were, in many ways, far better than, even with the aid of twentieth-century technology, any show of comparable size, including Crufts itself, can nowadays achieve. Though Cruft also insisted on some arrangements which would not be to the liking of modern exhibitors and which they might not readily accept.

The regulations in force for what, with typical lack of modesty and regard for the truth, he advertised as his Twelfth Great Dog Show on 12, 13 and 14 February 1896 might surprise modern exhibitors. Entries closed on 27 January, just fifteen days before the show opened. With all the aids provided by the wonders of twentieth-century technology exhibitors are now accustomed to entries closing six or seven weeks before the show. Of such is progress made. Another advantage which Cruft offered his exhibitors was that entries received more than eighteen days prior to the show could be cancelled not less than eight days before the show and seventy-five per cent of the entry fee refunded.

The entry fee in 1896 was 10s (50p), but exhibitors putting in two or more dogs in the same class could have this reduced by a half for the second and subsequent dogs. Dogs had to arrive at the show between noon on 11 February and 9.30 am on 12 February, and Charles Cruft not only arranged for special trains to bring dogs and exhibitors to the show but even had specially designed carriages to carry dogs in comfort and safety. Having arrived at the show dogs were expected to remain there until the show closed at 10 pm on the final day. However these stringent conditions could be avoided by exhibitors who, on payment of £1.00 deposit, were allowed to take their dogs home at 10 pm each evening, providing they were returned by 10 am the following morning when part of their deposit would be retained. Exhibitors who wished to take their dogs home early on the last day could do so at 4 pm on payment of 5s (25p) and at 7 pm on payment of 2s 6d (12½p). Otherwise dogs were expected to remain within the show for all the three days. Of course they were not confined, unattended to their benches throughout this period. They were exercised by attendants provided by the show, before 9 am or after 5.30 pm on each day and would be 'fed and attended to free of expense to the Exhibitor', though on payment of 2s 6d (12½p) an exhibitor might purchase a special keeper's pass so that he or his kennel man might have the privilege of caring for the dogs themselves.

In those days the Kennel Club's authority was not fully established and so Charles Cruft had to exercise whatever discipline he regarded as necessary. He did so easily enough because awards and prize money were not handed over until after the show had closed and so could be withheld from any fractious exhibitor. Dogs which were not benched according to Cruft's stipulations, were removed from the show without authority or which were returned late could expect to forfeit any prizes they might win. Even in the payment of prize money Charles Cruft held all the aces. Prize money varied from class to class depending largely on the generosity of the breed's own supporters. Most often it was £2.00 for a win, £1.00 for second and 10s (50p) for third, though unless more than three dogs were entered only one prize was offered. Charles Cruft expected his judges to decide whether this should be a first, second or third prize. Those who exercised what Cruft regarded as undue generosity might well find the extra sum being deducted from their already meagre judging fee.

Charles Cruft as seen by Mac.

The service to exhibitors and the public was provided by a very hard-working staff of which Charles was himself doubtless the most hard-working. Indeed it is said that, during the period of intense activity between close of entries and the show itself Charles fortified himself with innumerable cups of tea and, in order not to waste unnecessary time on the frequent journeys which such a copious liquid intake might produce, had, behind a discreet screen in his office, a bucket filled with sawdust.

His wife, Emma, acted as his Treasurer and his Secretary, from 1925 until his death, was Miss Hardingham. Her assistant was Teresa. The staff at his home at 12, Highbury Grove, London N5 consisted of Kit, his cook, Gillow, his chauffeur, two maids, Sophie and Beatie, and Barlow, his gardener. Doubtless, too, his country home at Windmill Farm, Coulsdon Common, Surrey also had its staff. Charles Cruft lived very comfortably on the proceeds of his show.

Charles Cruft ran every Cruft's Show until 1938, forty-five shows, excluding the earlier terrier shows, in all. On the way he was to break every record and most of the rules in the book. He and his shows became famous throughout the world. When he ran the first Cruft's Show he was thirty-nine years old. He was eighty-six years old when he ran his last show.

He became unwell soon afterwards but quickly rallied. On 12 September, however, *The Times* published the simple notice that 'On Sept 10, 1938 Charles Cruft passed peacefully away, aged 86. Funeral on Wednesday next at Highgate Cemetery, London at 1.30pm from 12, Highbury Grove, N5.'. *Our Dogs'* announcement contained slightly more information and said that 'at 5.30 a.m. on Saturday, September 10, Mr Charles Cruft, world famous as the promoter of the biggest dog shows on earth, passed peacefully away at his home, 12, Highbury Grove, London, N.5, from heart failure.'.

The news stunned the dog show world and on 16 September *Our Dogs*, under the heading of 'The Man Who Made Dog Shows', devoted its Editorial to this remarkable man's remarkable career.

> 'The death of Charles Cruft takes from the world's dogdom its most famous name. To most people it was the name of a show, but to those whose duty it was to record the history of canine affairs, it was the name of the man who made dog shows. As long ago as 1886, when dog shows were few, obscure and largely disreputable, Charles Cruft foresaw that these events had tremendous possibilities if correctly handled. How right he was is shown by the huge entries which his own and other events now attract, and by the high place dog shows hold in the sporting and social life of this and other countries.
>
> Of Cruft as a man very little is known, for he was never very talkative about his private affairs. Of Cruft as a showman we know almost everything, for although not a seeker after publicity for himself, he used every means to keep his show before the public. It is this knowledge of the value of publicity in any form, allied with his own shrewdness, business ability and willingness to work that placed his show and his name high above any others in the dog show firmament. He was never content for his show to stay at one level; for him there was always something better, and when the show's entries began to approach 10,000, he set this tremendous total as his ambition. He reached it with his 50th show in 1936, and thereby broke all world records.
>
> Energy, determination, and an intimate knowledge of dog fanciers and their needs were the forces in Charles Cruft which thrust his shows to such heights, and he well earned such descriptions as the 'Canine Barnum' and 'The World's Greatest Dog Show Impresario'. Applied to anyone else these would be ridiculous exaggerations, but they fitted Cruft perfectly, for he had the grand manner of the early

showmen. There has been no one like him, and there never will be. He stood alone, and his influence will be felt for ever.'.

When, following Charles Cruft's death, and the Second World War the show again took place, this time under the Kennel Club's management, Mrs Cruft published her own, brief, assessment of her husband's career.*

* *Mrs Charles Cruft's Famous Dog Book*

'With the revival of Cruft's International Dog Show at Olympia in October 1948, another bit of English life slipped back into the picture of peace, for Cruft's is recognised as the most famous dog show in the world. Everybody knew Cruft's in pre-war years, for it may be said that it was one of the events of the year, ranking with Ascot, Epsom and the Boat Race in popularity.

The dominant personality of my late husband, Charles Cruft, was missed, for he built this show up from his first Great Terrier Show in 1886 held at the Royal Aquarium, on the site of the Central Hall, Westminster.

He was a born showman, and in the same class as the great Barnum, for, like Barnum, to Charles it was always the Show that mattered.

It became Cruft's Dog Show in 1891 and the advertisements claimed that it consisted of "the largest number and the finest collection of dogs ever brought together. Every breed represented. Dogs from all parts of the world".

Held at the Royal Agricultural Hall, Islington, there were nearly 2,500 entries and 2,000 dogs, with 473 classes and 20 judges who carried out their work in the 12 judging rings. From then on until 1939, with the exception of the years 1918–1920, the First World War, the Islington venue became internationally famous.

After the 1914–1918 war, the show became a two-day event and visitors came from all over the world. In 1925 the most numerous entry was provided by Alsatians and there was a total of 8188 entries of all breeds. In 1937 the Coronation show with 9949 entries and 4352 dogs was held.

The 52nd and last exhibition Mr Cruft arranged was in 1938, and before the next show came around he died. The following year I organised the show myself, then came the Second World War which stopped the exhibition from 1940 until the great first post-war Cruft's Show took place at Olympia on October 14th and 15th, 1948, under the auspices of the Kennel Club to whom I handed over the reins for their permanent and very excellent organisation.

The 1948 Cruft's Show was a sensational success with a record number of nearly 50,000 visitors, who began queuing up outside Olympia long before the official opening hours with queues reaching alarming proportions.

It was with great pleasure that I attended to present the cups to the principal winners, and I was greatly impressed by the organisation and the arrangements, particularly the preservation, in spite of the unavoidable change in venue, of the familiar and traditional atmosphere of this great international show.

Fashions in dogs change with the passing of years, popular breeds are in the main determined by the standard set by Cruft's, for everybody who admires beautiful dogs has seen nothing in the dog world until a visit has been paid to this great show where the cream of dogdom is exhibited, and it is my advice to all who may read this book to try their best to attend this show at least once, for until you have been to Cruft's you haven't seen what a thoroughbred dog should look like'.

In 1952, the centenary of Charles Cruft's birth, which went largely unmarked by the Show he had created, Leo Wilson writing in *Our Dogs* recalled that:

'only a handful of us doggy folk followed his remains to their resting place. . . . The plain truth is that although Charles Cruft might be respected for his skill in running the greatest dog show on earth he was not particularly beloved. There were those who respected his judgement in all matters appertaining to dog shows, and there were others who envied him the living he wrested out of Cruft's Show, but he was not a man who endeared himself to the majority of showgoers, and the main reason for that was probably because it was felt that everything he did was with an eye to business.

It might be said that dogdom would be better off if more people had an eye to business when running dog shows, and indeed that viewpoint is not without foundation, but many of the things Charles Cruft did in the way of business – though little in themselves – tended to irritate.

For instance, it was the custom before the war at a two-day show where a dog had to be brought back on the second day even though not required for competition to charge a deposit of £1 as the dog removed on the first day and this was refunded when the dog was brought back on the second day.

Charles Cruft used to take a deposit of a guinea and return a pound only.

Most people resented it however and felt that Charles was 'catching them for a shilling'.

Again, free passes and catalogues were as scarce as hen's teeth at Cruft's and even the Press had to pay for any over the minimum requirements. Consequently it became a point of honour with many show regulars that they wangle their way into Cruft's without paying, and there was a constant warfare between Cruft and the regulars on the one hand to extract the last possible shilling, and on the other to avoid spending a halfpenny more than was necessary.

In the old days of Cruft's at the Agricultural Hall in Islington, there used to be a little teashop just round the corner where the 'boys waited on show days sipping cups of coffee or tea whilst others went inside on one pass to collect a number of other passes for their friends. These passes were the rare stand passes which had not to be given up. Most of the Cruft's passes could only be used just once – and there were no pass-out checks!

With all his faults and failings, however, Charles Cruft had one outstanding virtue: he made Cruft's pay and pay handsomely. So much so indeed that he lived comfortably off the proceeds of this one show per year and managed to leave his widow a very tidy sum at his death. . . . Again Charles Cruft had a real flair for picking judges. He did not always have the best judges – some of our very best never judged at Cruft's because they could not see eye to eye with the great Charles on the subject of remuneration – but he specialised in the unusual and had an uncanny knack of sensing when a judge was likely to draw an entry. . . .

Although he was master of publicity he sometimes fell foul of the newspapers. One very important paper had a rule which was kept to the day of his death to the effect that the name of Cruft was never to be mentioned, and this paper, when forced to print news and pictures always referred to it as 'a dog show in Islington' which must have amused the old boy more than somewhat.

His great asset was his ability to get good publicity points for his show as entries from Royalty at a time when the Royal House was but little interested in dog shows. It was said of Cruft that it was he who made dog shows respectable and this largely refers to his being able to attract patronage from notabilities.'

Born in 1852 Charles Alfred Cruft was one of four children. He first married in 1878 to Charlotte Hutchinson, the daughter of an Islington carpenter, and the marriage produced four children, Charles Francis, Louise, Cecil Arthur and Clara Helen Grace. Charles again married, this time to Emma Isabel Hartshorn in 1894. There were no children of this second marriage.

Charles Alfred Cruft's will had been drawn up and signed on 21 January 1938, less than eight months before his death. The total effects were valued at £30476. 9s. 3d, which, after a number of bequests, were left to his widow and to his daughter Clara Posse, known to the family as Birdie, who received £2000. Two grandchildren, Charles Cruft, who was present at the 1990 Crufts Show, and Betty Cruft each received £500, as did two nephews, Kenneth and John Hartshorn. A third grandchild, Ruth, who sent flowers but did not attend her grandfather's funeral, received nothing. No less than eight nieces, Kate Pope, Violet Cleve, Clare Elizabeth Avenell, Doris and Maud Keele, Minnie Evemy, Hessie and Nessie Hartshorn, each received £50, as did Frank Hartshorn, a grand-nephew. Joan Cruft, Charles' cousin and Kate Hempstead, the maid who had been with the family for more than thirty years also received £50 but only on condition that she was still employed by Charles Cruft and was not under notice of dismissal at the time of his death. Lieutenant Arthur Cruft RN, a cousin, received £100 (was this as a result of Charles' affection for Arthur or for his naval occupation?) but, Charles' wife and daughter apart, the major bequest went to his secretary, Miss E. Hardingham who had worked for Charles Cruft since 1925, had helped to organise so many shows and who was to remain faithful to the show after Charles' death and even when ownership had passed into the hands of the Kennel Club. Miss Hardingham received £500.

There is no mention of any children, other than Birdie, being present at the funeral, sending floral tributes or being remembered in Charles' will.

Emma Isabel Cruft, Charles' widow, died on 5 September 1950. She was then living at 84a Aberdeen Park, London N5. She left £47,376 2s 9d, the two major beneficiaries in her will being her brother, Dr Ernest Hartshorn, his wife, Gertrude Annie, receiving £250, and Kate Hempstead, the maid who had served the family during its halcyon days at Highbury Grove. Both received £2000 but Kate also had Mrs Cruft's bedroom furniture, bedding and linen. Frank Hartshorn, Ernest's son, received £1000 plus all the royalties from Mr Charles Cruft's book which wouldn't, in fact, be published for almost another two years. Perhaps Frank Hartshorn was the man responsible for its eventual public appearance. Grace Berther, Mrs Cruft's sister, received £1000 as did Birdie – who the will identifies as Mrs Cruft's step-daughter. Birdie apart, no children of the first marriage nor any of Charles' grandchildren were remembered in Mrs Cruft's will.

By 1923 the Cruft's Committee included Charles Francis, Cecil Arthur Cruft, his two sons, and Dr Ernest Hartshorn, his brother-in-law. F. C. Posse, who had married Birdie in 1902, appeared briefly on the Committee in 1914. The Secretary was Mr Charles Cruft, Mrs Cruft at the time was the unofficial Treasurer but, from time to time, also served on the Committee.

Emma assisted her husband from the year of their marriage, Charles junior had been helping his father from about 1909 and Cecil appeared in the scene in the early 1920s. Birdie's husband served on the Committee and Emma's brother was a Cruft's committee member from at least 1909 and remained so until at least 1932.

Cruft's was a real family business!

2. The Development of Dog Shows

*I*f it can fairly be suggested that a dog show is a gathering of people who share a common interest in dogs and who meet in order to compare one dog with another then it is surely reasonable to suggest that dog shows must have been taking place almost ever since, more than 12,000 years ago, the relationship between dog and man was first established. In those distant days man would be most interested in finding the best dogs for hunting, herding, guarding or for the pot. Only when civilisation had progressed to the point at which keeping body and soul together did not occupy man's entire attention could he permit himself the luxury of an interest in the appearance of his dogs, though appearance and function must always have been closely related. The Babylonian, Chinese, Egyptian, Inca and Sumarian civilisations, and many more, produced dogs which were appreciated for their appearance as well as for the work they might do and the companionship they might offer. Owning a good dog was a source of pride and owners would gather together to compare and discuss their favourites. By deciding which was best and then by breeding from the best they could further improve the qualities they regarded as desirable.

Although these informal events must have been taking place for very many years there appear to be no references to formal dog shows held prior to about 1775 when John Warde, one of the peripatetic huntsmen who did so much to popularise foxhunting, was hunting a pack of hounds from his home at Squerries, near Westerham in Kent. During the summer he held hound shows both as a way of retaining contact outside the hunting season, with those who shared his passion for foxhunting and also as means to show off the qualities of his hounds, especially, perhaps, of the current year's puppies. Hound shows just such as these continue to form an important part of the summer activities of most hunts and are invariably delightful and enjoyable occasions.

Warde's hound shows would have been attended by Masters of other packs and one of these was Thomas Coke whose Holkham Sheep Shearings were so influential in popularising the agricultural methods being developed during the latter half of the eighteenth century. Coke's Sheep Shearings led directly to the formation of the agricultural societies whose shows, many of which still provide classes for dogs in addition to those for agricultural livestock, remain such an enjoyable feature of our own summer calender of events. An early entrant to this field of activity, though possibly not the first, was the Agricultural Society of Durham which was holding shows which included classes for dogs from about 1783.

However, alongside this essentially bucolic interest in dogs, there was, during the eighteenth century, an equally important growth of urban interest. People were moving from the countryside to live in towns and to work in the newly developing industries and were reluctant to forgo all contact with animals and, not surprisingly, they turned to dogs to help repair their loss. It has been estimated that every second town household might contain a dog. Nowadays only about one in four do so.

Even that most urban of men, Dr Samuel Johnson, took an interest in the appearance of dogs. During a visit to Ashbourne in 1777 Dr Johnson was introduced to a Bulldog for which the animal's owner, his old friend, Dr John Taylor, had the sort of strong and uncritical regard which must surely be regarded as an early example of 'kennel blindness', a condition which has, since those days, sometimes seemed to have reached epidemic proportions. Boswell records that 'Taylor, who praised every-thing of his own to excess, in short, whose geese were all swans, as the proverb says, expatiated on the excellence of his bull-dog which, he told us, was perfectly well shaped. Johnson, after examining the animal attentively, thus repressed the vain-glory of our host:– "No, Sir, he is not well shaped; for there is not the quick transition from the thickness of the fore part, to the tenuity – the thin part – behind, which a bull-dog ought to have".' Those who blame what they regard as the exaggerations of the modern Bulldog on the demands of dog shows or the baneful influence of the Kennel Club might care to reflect on Samuel Johnson's critical comments made over two hundred years ago.

Johnson, usually a determined and unrepentant philistine of all matters visual whose interests often reflected what was going on around him, demonstrates appreciation, not influenced by function, of the appearance of the Bulldog. He did so at a time when the popularity of baiting sports was declining though they would remain legal for another sixty years. He also provides a critique which would not be entirely out of place in a modern dog magazine.

It was not long before the enjoyment of the companionship which dogs provided and pride in their appearance, as well as in their other accomplishments, began to lead to a changed attitude towards dogs. The brutal, old, gladiatorial sports, the source of great cruelty, though stoutly defended by church and state alike, continued to lose popular appeal. Breeds which were originally bred for pastoral or sporting use came to be appreciated, by town dwellers, for other than utilitarian or sporting reasons and an interest in breeds which offered no more than companionship and beauty began to develop. Formerly such an interest had been confined almost exclusively to the aristocracy but now toy and exotic breeds were to be found even in the most humble homes. As the popularity of these breeds spread it was inevitable that their owners should gather together to share their enthusiasm and enjoyment and to seek to extend their knowledge.

One such meeting was advertised in the February, 1834 issue of the *Sporting Magazine*, 'The show, of 9lb spaniels for a silver cream jug will take place at Charlie Aistrop's, the Elephant and Castle, on Wednesday'. The advert, included along with other items of interest to the 'Canine Fancy', was flanked by a challenge from 'Thomas Williams of Liverpool, (who) will match a dog, of 18½ lbs weight, against the Birmingham dog, of the same weight, for £10, £20 or £50. His money is ready at the Newmarket Tavern, Maddox-street, Liverpool'. Below this announcement was a report of an 'Extraordinary birth! at which a bitch belonging to Mr C. R. Peck of Ware, Herts, (partly Newfoundland) produced last week, at one litter, and by one dog the extraordinary number of seventeen puppies. Three were still-born, eight she has since smothered by overlaying them, three have been drowned, and three are now alive; she was two days in her trouble. When she was about two years old she had fourteen puppies by one dog. She is now about four years old, and has never had puppies but twice'. Thus did a popular periodical from the early part of the nineteenth century reflect the growing and varied urban interest in dogs. Eleven years earlier the same magazine had published a very different report about Charlie Aistrop's activities.

> 'The Westminster Pit was crowded on Tuesday evening, Jan 18, with all the dog fanciers in the metropolis, to witness a battle between the celebrated dog Boney and a black novice called Gas . . . The stakes were forty sovereigns, and everything was arranged to the satisfaction of the amateurs. The pit was lighted with an elegant chandelier and a profusion of waxlights. The dogs were brought to scratch at eight o'clock in excellent condition, and were seconded by their respective masters. Boney was the favourite at 3 to 1, and so continued till within ten minutes of the termination of the contest – a confidence arising solely from his known bottom; for to the impartial spectator Gas took the lead throughout. The battle lasted an hour and fifty minutes, when Boney was carried out insensible. He was immediately bled and put in a warm bath. There were nearly 300 persons present'.

Charlie Aistrop was the owner of the notorious Westminster Pit who only took to an easier life as a publican after his wife had been killed while feeding the Pit's bear. Aistrop was an unusual character who, as a young boy, had turned his back on a well-to-do family in order to indulge his passion for dogs among the denizens of London's underworld. Many of London's public houses were run by retired or failed pugilists. Josh Hudson had the Half Moon Tavern, Tom Belcher the Castle Tavern, Holborn where he was succeeded by Tom Spring. Jack Randall, the Nonpareil, was at the Hole in the Wall, Chancery Lane, where his successor was the lad from Preston, Bob Gregson. Tom Cribb kept the Union Arms, Panton Street, Tom Shelton the Black Bull, Smithfield. Ben Burns kept the Sun, Windmill Street and Big Bill Eales the Prince of Mecklenburgh Arms, Manchester Square. These, and others, had their dog pits and most also provided facilities for the dog fancy to gather together to indulge in more innocent pleasures. It was in these public houses that the urban dog show had its true origins.

We need only turn to Henry Mayhew's *London Labour and the London Poor*, first published in 1851, for a detailed description of what an evening spent in one of these doggy pubs might have been like.

> 'I arrived at about eight o'clock . . . The front of the long bar was already crowded with men of every grade of society, all smoking, drinking, and talking about dogs. Many of them had brought with them their "fancy" animals, so that a kind of "canine exhibition" was going on; some carried under their arm small bull-dogs, whose flat pink noses rubbed against my arm as I passed; others had Skye-terriers, curled up, like balls of hair, and sleeping like children, as they were nursed by their owners. The only animals that seemed awake, and under continual excitement, were the little brown English terriers, who, despite the neat black leather collars by which they were held, struggled to get loose, as they smelt the rats in the room above, and were impatient to begin the fray.
>
> . . . Sleeping on an old hall-chair lay an enormous white bulldog, "a great beauty", as I was informed, with a head as round and smooth as a clenched boxing-glove, and seemingly too large for the body. Its forehead appeared to protrude in a manner significant of water on the brain, and almost overhung the short nose, through which the animal breathed heavily. When this dog, which was the admiration of all beholders, rose up, its legs were as bowed as a tailor's, leaving a peculiar pear-shaped opening between them, which, I was informed, was one of its points of beauty. It was a white dog, with a sore look, from its being peculiarly pink round the eyes, nose and indeed at all edges of its body.
>
> On the other side of the fire-place was a white bull-terrier dog, with a black patch over the eye, which gave him rather a discoverable look. This animal was watching the movements of the customers in front, and occasionally, when the entrance-door was swung back, would give a growl of inquiry as to what the fresh-comer wanted. The proprietor was kind enough to inform me, as he patted this animal's ribs, which showed like the hoops on a butter-firkin, that he considered

there had been a "little of the greyhound in some of his back generations".

About the walls there were hung clusters of black leather collars adorned with brass rings and clasps, and pre-eminent was a silver dog-collar, which, from the conversation of those about me, I learnt was to be the prize in a rat-match to be "killed for" in a fortnight's time.

As the visitors poured in, they, at the request of the proprietor "not to block up the bar", took their seats in the parlour, and, accompanied by a waiter, who kept shouting, "give your orders, gentlemen," I entered the room.

I found that, like the bar, no pains had been taken to render the room attractive to the customers, for, with the exception of the sporting pictures hung, against dingy paper, it was devoid of all adornment. Over the fire-place were square glazed boxes, in which were stuffed forms of dogs famous in their day. Pre-eminent among the prints was that representing the "Wonder Tiny, five pounds and a half in weight, as he appeared killing two hundred rats. . . . Tiny had been a great favourite with the proprietor, and used to wear a lady's bracelet as a collar".'

The 'Wonder Tiny' who was such a great favourite of the proprietor was, in fact, the Old English Terrier which had achieved fame by killing two hundred rats in fifty-four minutes. Tiny belonged to Jemmy Shaw, a retired pugilist of no particular note, who, until 1852, was landlord of the Blue Anchor, Bunhill Row, St Lukes. In 1853 he took over the Queen's Head, Windmill Street, Haymarket following the death of its landlord, Jem Burns, another pugilist, whose defeats at the hands of White Headed Bob and the fearsome Ned Neale had earned him fame of a sort. After his retirement from the ring, in 1825, Jem Burns had run shows for Bulldogs of which he was a well known breeder. Mayhew's description can, therefore, be identified as of an evening spent with Jemmy Shaw at the Blue Anchor. Another dog show, which took place in 1855 when Shaw had become mine host at the Queen's Head, is the subject of a painting which now hangs in the Kennel Club Smoke Room, where it serves as a reminder of one of Cruft's humble progenitors.

It would be wrong, however, to allow Mayhew's fascination with low life to obscure the fact that even he recognised that the long bar at the Blue Anchor was 'crowded with men of every grade of society'. It is true that it would still be some years before showing dogs would be regarded as a ladylike occupation but it was not so disreputable as to deter respectable members of society from becoming involved. In 1851 the *Illustrated London News* turned its attention to one of these increasingly popular events, this time held in a public house in Denmark Street, St Giles. The report stressed that '. . . Many a young male scion of a noble house has not only been in its precincts, but has fairly and boldly placed his noble person on a bench in the veritable crib of Charlie Aistrop', before going on to describe the dingy surroundings and the dogs in some detail.

'At this place a club is held, by one of the rules of which, each member is expected (in fact, we believe, compelled) when he attends, to bring a dog for show or sale, as he thinks proper; thus ensuring a good show night, which is on a Tuesday evening; and here may be seen the most beautiful specimens of spaniel, Italian greyhound, and, of late years, of the Isle of Skye terrier.

The show dogs, or Fancy Pets, as they are termed, are solely valued for beauty of their respective sort. The King Charles, that has now for many years stood as prime pet with ladies, ranks in estimation as he more or less exhibits the following perfection:– Smallness of size, symmetry as to proportions, richness of colour, and length of ears. The black-and-tan are the most admired – the depth of colour in the black, and richness of the tan, constituting beauty of each colour. The absence of white greatly enhances the value of these colours; thus, as a nominal price, we will say that a fairish-coloured black-and-tan dog, with white on his feet, white in front of his neck (alias a frill to his shirt), and a little white on his nose, is worth five guineas; take away the white paws, he is worth ten; with no white in his neck and chest, £20; with no white at all, £40. We merely mention a supposed price, to show how certain perfections raise it where fancied but not intrinsic merit is the standard by which price is measured. Spaniels are often to be seen at spaniels shows for which £150 would not be taken, and those not the property of gentlemen or men of large means either. There is one dog, called Prince, the property of a person called Jeffries; for this animal (of course having been esteemed quality in perfection) we believe £250 has been offered and refused. The price these dogs are valued at is no doubt perfectly ridiculous; for, as to use as spaniel for sporting purposes, the King Charles is good for nothing; the Blenheim, though often not exceeding him in size, is; he, in fact, where covers are not too strong for him, is a merry little fellow, who will rattle game up in good style.

Italian greyhounds are chiefly valued for perfection in symmetry and colour, they are dogs of undoubtedly less intellect than other breeds; but, though it is not generally supposed to be the case, their speed is sufficient to enable a brace of good ones, on a level and smooth down, to catch a hare, if they get a favourable start. They may, however, in a general way, be held as quite useless.

To what is held as beauty in the Isle of Skye terrier we are quite a stranger, never having taken the trouble to enquire; who brought such shapeless little monsters into vogue, we know not; they have been a rich harvest, however, to the dog-stealers, for any turnspit-legged, long backed little mongrel they could lay their hands upon, from not being thought worth being kept out of danger, they did, and he was sold as an Isle of Skye of the purest breed; but, supposing he was so, it would speak but little in his favour, for they are by no means good dogs for destroying vermin, which is the leading merit of the terrier, but few of the Isle of Skyes have any idea of the thing. We never saw one yet of a beautiful or rich colour, and their symmetry is, in point of beauty of proportion, on a par with that of the crocodile or alligator; however, any one wishing to learn what merit and recommendations they have, may see some of the choicest specimens at Aistrop's'.

Urban and rural dog shows continued to thrive during the first half of the nineteenth century but, before they could develop into something other than events of purely local interest and significance a further ingredient was necessary. That ingredient was to be provided by the advent of the railways which enabled 'The Fancy' to travel greater distances to dog shows.

Prior to the advent of the railways a prize fight at Moulsey Hurst might entice thousands of people to make what they regarded as the long and arduous ten mile journey from London. Crawley Down, another popular venue, over twenty miles away was too far for most Londoners. To travel further for a day's enjoyment would have been out of the question. The dog show did not yet exist which could exert even a fraction of the appeal of a good fight.

However, by 1840 the railway system made it possible to travel in relative comfort and at unprecedented speed from London to Lancaster, Leeds and York in the North, to Swindon in the West and down to Southampton on the South coast. By 1855 there were very few major towns not served by the new railways, which enabled foxhunters and their mounts to travel from London to the shires for a day's hunting and for sporting dogs to be transported to distant moors. It was inevitable that the railways would soon be used to travel to dog shows.

Perhaps the first of the shows which recognised the importance of railway travel was an event which has come, quite wrongly, to be widely regarded as the first dog show. This was an event held as part of a well established poultry show which took place at the Corn Market, Newcastle-upon-Tyne on 28 and 29 June 1859. The show was not a financial success. It made a loss of £15.00 to be carried by its three organisers. However such corporate acceptance of financial responsibility did not prevent one of the three from later claiming to be the sole originator and promoter of the event.

'To Mr W. R. Pape', said *Our Dogs* in 1908, in a report which relied entirely on evidence provided by Pape himself, who was by then the only surviving member of the partnership, 'belongs the honour of conceiving and carrying to a successful issue the first dog show. . . . Mr Pape saw earlier than any other breeder that uniformity of type in the different varieties of dog could only be brought about by competitive shows – in other words, in order to arrive at a common understanding of the points required it was necessary that breeders should have opportunities to compare their dogs, and that the only means of doing this was, as Mr Pape saw clearly, by providing prizes for competition and appointing men to judge who knew what was required, and whose decisions would be respected'.

Though there has seldom been a more lucid explanation of the purpose of dog shows the report does Mr Pape more honour than he deserves. A more accurate account appeared in the *Newcastle Courant* for Friday, 1 July, 1859:

'The new feature of the addition of Sporting Dogs to the show of Poultry was a great attraction, and tended in no slight degree to the success of the meeting, the arrangements were admirably carried out; litters, with proper divisions, round three sides of a spacious building were set apart from the dogs, which were chained and sufficiently protected by barriers from any chance of injuring or alarming the visitors, and in this section the prizes given, two valuable guns, from the manufacture of Mr Pape, gunmaker, of this town, were probably a sufficient inducement to produce twenty-three entries for Pointers and thirty-seven for Setters, many being from different parts of the kingdom. . . . It may be remarked as creditable to the breeders of Sporting Dogs of this district, that the palm for the best Setter was carried off by William Jobling, of Morpeth, that for Pointers being gained by Richard Brailsford, Knowsley, Lancashire'.

The show consisted of just two competitive classes, both barred to bitches, and was supported by an exhibition of puppies and, doubtless, other dogs, some of which would have been available for sale. The judges for Pointers were J. H. Walsh, Thomas Robson and Joseph Jobling. Walsh was then Editor of *The Field* and a journalist whose *nom de plume* of Stonehenge was already very well known. He had previously explored in print the idea of just such a show and it may well have been his writing which had provided the idea which Messrs Shorthose, Reid and Pape brought to fruition. Thomas Robson, was a member of a dynastic, sporting Northumbrian family which, over many years, provided the Masters for a number of the local packs of foxhounds and which was closely involved in the development of the Border Terrier. The third was Joseph Jobling of Morpeth, whose Setter had been acclaimed the best at the show. The judges for Setters were, once more, J. H. Walsh, Frances Foulger, gamekeeper to His Grace the Duke of Northumberland and Richard Brailsford, whose Pointer had won its section of the show. Brailsford was then gamekeeper to Lord Derby and will become more familiar a little later in this account. Though Messrs Pape, Reid and Shorthose had not run the first dog show they had done something which was to prove to have almost as much importance. The show had attracted exhibitors from Manchester, Huddersfield, Lancaster, Penrith and at least one judge had come from London. It had been demonstrated that, with the aid of railway travel, a dog show could attract national support.

In August yet another development was to take place when the Cleveland Agricultural Society, having satisfied themselves that the classes for hunters, which had been included in their 1857 show were well supported, finally capitulated to the persuasion of one of their members and tried a few classes for hounds. Their persuasive member was Thomas Parrington, a Yorkshire farmer who hunted with the Sinnington and was its Master from 1876 until 1884. Did his idea stem from a knowledge of the shows which John Warde had been running some years previously? The first show, held at Yarm, was not well supported but within a very few years over sixty packs were represented at the event. From its original venue the show moved to Redcar, Malton, Beverley and York, all under the direction of Thomas Parrington. The success of the venture led, in 1877, to the show's final move to Peterborough and there it remains, having become established as the world's most important show for working hounds.

In November, 1859 Richard Brailsford took matters a further, important, step forward, by running a show in Birmingham. In 1892 *The British Fancier* published an appreciation of his efforts:

'Mr Richard Brailsford was an old man in the early part of the "sixties" and to him is ascribed the initiation of the great national Show at Birmingham. He was an enthusiast in dogs, especially pointers and setters, and well known throughout the country not only as a scientific breeder, but as a splendid handler of dogs. He came mostly to the front while in the employment of the Earl of Derby, and for more than fifty years – that is going back to the commencement of this century – was noted as one of the most celebrated of dogmen. About the years 1863 and 1864 Mr Brailsford looked after Lord Derby's pointers, and a draft of seventeen were sent to Tattersall's to be disposed of under the hammer. This sale realised the goodly sum of 397 guineas, or rather more than an average of £30. All ages were included in the lot sent, so it will be seen Mr Brailsford's name was well to the fore as a breaker and handler. He also lived with Lord Chesterfield. After many years trying to arrange public competitions for dogs, he was successful. He persevered, and at last succeeded in getting up the National Show of Sporting Dogs at Birmingham, which, in a few years afterwards, proved one of the greatest attractions to the sporting public of the three kingdoms. In the year 1864 Mr Brailsford was presented with a medal by W. Moult Esq., in consideration of his valuable service in floating the great show at Birmingham. He then (1864) retired from the "fancy", and carried on the business of a vermin trap manufacturer, and from his known abilities and great experience in using them, Mr Brailsford had a long list of high-class patrons as customers'.

The first Birmingham show took place at Bretherton's Repository, in the Cheapside district, but beyond that all that is known of the event was that the classification provided for 'Pointers (large size), dogs; ditto bitches; small size Pointers (no dogs entered but some bitches); Pointer puppies; English Setters, dogs; ditto bitches; Setter puppies, Retrievers, Clumber Spaniels, Cockers, or other Spaniel breeds'. The show was, perhaps, the first to offer such a wide classification, was independent of any other event and attracted exhibitors from far and wide.

During 1860 dog shows, both urban and rural, continued to be held much as they had been for some years past. Charles Lane records one such held in White Ladies Road, Bristol in November or December of that year but it was in Birmingham that the major changes were taking place. On 3 and 4 December, 1860 the First Exhibition of Sporting and other Dogs was held at the Midland Counties Repository, Cheapside, Birmingham. The show attracted 267 entries, which because each dog could only be entered in one class meant 267 dogs, far more than anything which had, as far as we know, been previously achieved. The success of this show resulted, in part at least, from the generous classification which Richard Brailsford had put before his potential exhibitors. There were a number of classes for Hounds judged by Mr C. Wickeder, thus further developing John Warde's earlier initiative. Inevitably, after Brailsford's experience the previous year in Newcastle, there were also classes for Gundogs. Pointers were judged by Messrs Moore, W. Lort and H. B. Leigh, Setters by Major Irving and Mr W. Brooks. Then, taking a leaf out of the shows which Charlie Aistrop and his friends had been running, there were classes for what Brailsford described as Toy Dogs. These included such very un-Toylike breeds as Mastiffs, Newfoundlands, Dalmatians, Bull-dogs, Sheep-dogs, Black-and-Tan Terriers, White and other English Terriers, Scotch Terriers and Foreign Non-Sporting Dogs.

The show attracted far greater notice from the general press than could nowadays be expected. On 12 December *The Illustrated London News* published a full and well informed report of the event.

'Every domesticated creature in the range of nature, from the bull to the canary, has been made the subject, individually or collectively of a show, but until 1859 dogs seemed quite left out of the question. In August of that year the long-talked of hound show became a reality at

Redcar and then Birmingham furnished the very promising germ of one more universal in its character. The same idea was tried at Newcastle; and now Birmingham brings the original idea pretty near to ripeness, in only its second essay. To Messrs Burdett and Cartwright, who worked ceaselessly at their labour of love, the praise is especially due; and Messrs Brailsford, a celebrated family of gamekeepers, who were engaged during the last three weeks to superintend the arrangements and the arrival and departure of the candidates, lent most important aid. Unfortunately the Society, the Birmingham Dog Show Society, which was formed in 1859 for the first show under the Presidency of the Viscount Curzon, thought it most prudent not to sever themselves from the cattle show, and hence, instead of getting Bingley Hall, they had to be content with the very limited gallery accommodation which Bretherton's Repository could furnish. It would have been well, too if the dogs could have been arranged on raised platforms, instead of lying on a level with the floor, as the space between them was not more than sufficient to accommodate one crinoline, the dogs were polite to the last degree; and, though they occasionally had a battle royal among themselves, we only heard a rumour of one man having been bitten. Still, with all these dis-advantages of space and difficulty of sight, it was a grand success, great was the disappointment that it did not continue open for another day or two; and, as for some weeks back Pointers and Spaniels have pretty nearly a holiday time of it, it is a pity that the usual notice, "BY SPECIAL REQUEST", did not adorn the dead walls, as it was, about 7800 spectators attended, and brought nearly £500 to the funds'.

The general arrangements appear to have suffered from the inexperience and lack of confidence of the organisers, which is, perhaps, hardly surprising since none of those involved had experience of more than one or two shows and none could have any experience of shows of such a size. The public were, nevertheless, attracted to the event, and in far greater numbers than the account suggests. In 1861 17035 people paid £792.11.0 to view the dogs, in 1862 the gate rose to 29137 and the income it produced to £1302.17.10, in 1863 21561 people paid £1114.15.0 and in 1864 the number rose to 23629, largely because 2636 Birmingham schoolchildren had been given free admittance to the event, the gate produced £3324.6.0. It is apparent that, within a very few years of the first show to attract a national entry dog shows provided a popular source of interest and entertainment. Nor was this interest neglected by the national press which produced accurate and well informed reports which contrast sharply with what tends to appear today.

'While exactly a hundred Pointers and forty-three Setters were entered', out of a grand total of 267 entries, 'other parts of the list presented a very meagre aspect. The two Pugs never put in an appearance at all; and the Blenheims, King Charles's and Italian Greyhounds only mustered two entries apiece.' But then it must be remembered that these breeds were probably already quite content with the sort of shows they had enjoyed for some years. They would need evidence to show that supporting the new ventures would be to their advantage. 'Great things were predicted of Lord Bagot's Bloodhounds, but Mr Jenning's winner, of the Feversham, Wombwell and Rothschild blood, flung them completely into the shade, and sat up, a very king among dogs, lazily blinking over his victory. The Foxhounds were a mere name, both in quality and number, and, considering how many kennels there are within an hour's ride of Birmingham, it is rather strange that a ten guinea cup and three other prizes should not have aroused the masters and huntsmen into action'.

The Illustrated News' appraisal of the arrangements, exhibits and judges of the second Birmingham Show repeats regrets about the lack of support from the local packs of hounds.

'Warwickshire held its own with Lord Curzon's Watchman, and Cheshire with Fatima, and, as these were the only two kennels that sent, nobody was disappointed. The Netton Harriers were alone in their glory, without a prize, and so were the Wiltshire Beagles, whether justly or not is another question. Other hounds there were none, as the journey was too far for the Durham men, and Colonel Ingle's Deerhound was a grand winner in a class which was quite unworthy of him; and his fair companion, Brimstone, had the same honour. Momentum, the sire of some good winners, and the elegant necked Malibran, did no discredit to the world of the leash'.

Momentum and Malibran were coursing Greyhounds which like many other hounds might have been expected to be otherwise engaged during the winter. It is hardly surprising that a show which took place at the height of the hunting season would fail to attract entries from working hounds and especially when they were already well served by their own summer shows.

The report then went on critically to examine the gundogs and their judges.

'Pointers of large size were bravely headed by a liver and white dog belonging to the Hon. H. W. Powys, well worthy of his Edge heraldry, and with only one fault – viz., that he was five years old. A capital lemon and white of Mr Smallwood, who was, if we mistake it not, second last year, came fifth this, and the whole class was highly

Dog shows attracted their full share of Victorian sentiment.

commended. Such sweeping eulogism of forty-four saves a great deal of trouble, but we should have thought that a little more sifting might have reasonably reduced some from the H.C. into the C. ranks. In judging the opposite sex, the Rhadamanthuses, Messrs Moore, Leigh and Lort, were equally sweeping in their condemnation; and, although their opinion was pretty generally endorsed, it seems to us that they might have found second. Mr Comberach's winner was very modestly entered in the catalogue with no pedigree and at £30; and we believe that she changed hands. The sales, however, were disappointing and £150 was the sum total. Considering the season and that sporting dogs were the great staple, we can hardly wonder at such a result.

In the Pointer dogs of small size, Mr Henry Gilbert, of Kensington, came to the fore again with the well-known lemon and white. His champion, Bob, is the son of Nell, with which he won here last year, and a great beauty he is too. The Earls of Derby and Lichfield were second and third in this class, in which Mr Samuel Ashworth showed a clever Sancho and Rob, although neither was commended, the same three owners were the first three again in a very strong companion class; but this time Mr Gilbert found the Earl of Lichfield in front of him. Mr Gilbert considered this his Venus better than her brother, and her expressive head and beautifully turned outline make her pretty nearly perfection. The Setters were not wonderful in any way; the stamp of the old English Setter which we remember twenty or thirty years ago seems to have very much departed; but the blood-red Irish Setter was the very model of his kind. The Retrievers also boasted of two grand specimens; but many of the Clumbers were out of condition'.

So much then for the gundogs, which were obviously a very mixed bag and with an equally mixed bag of judges. Nor was the reporter in any mood to spare other breeds.

'The Boarhounds hardly carried out our ideas of Wouvermans, and with the exception of one cream with a black muzzle, the Mastiffs fell below the regular John Bull Type. The Newfoundlands were clever, but wanted size; in fact we saw nothing there to the eye beyond twenty-six inches; and in spite of their true St John beauty we longed for one or two of that thirty-two inch stamp which Mr Goater of Hammersmith, was so proud of breeding. Teddy, from Rugby, was a clever little Foxdog. The winning Italian Greyhound seemed very nice, so far as we could see it, but, like the spotted dogs, it curled itself round its cage and refused to show itself to the public. It would be an immense advantage if Toy Dogs could be seen out of their cages but most probably their owners would never consent to such exposure, and the owners of such valuable little sires may well be chary of having them stroked all day, or, perchance, transferred in a capacious inner pocket. Considering how well the Leicestershire and Warwickshire Sheepdogs muster at Sparkenhoe Club each September, we did expect to see their class better filled; but England has only a moderate champion; and a wiry-haired Scotch lass, with a face intelligent enough to know a Southdown from a Leicester, and all the crossbreed ewes and wethers into the bargain, walked off with the £2 to Hurley, Warwickshire'.

So Sheepdogs, too, already had their own shows one of which took place at the Sparkenhoe Club each September. But for how many Septembers had the show been taking place and for how long would the ability to work sheep be an important consideration in assessing sheepdogs?

The Illustrated London News' reporter then turned his attention to some of the more exotic breeds represented at the show.

'Neither the Cuban Mastiff, nor the St Bernard, was a very favourable type, and as for the poor white Esquimaux, it was by the merest chance we saw him at all in his window retreat. . . . The prize Black and Tan Terrier and her brother from Liverpool, were extremely good of their kind. The Toy Spaniels, however, were below mediocrity; and the Scotch Terriers were so inferior that no one could be selected as really unimpeachable specimens of its kind. The dog which obtained the prize in this class was very beautiful, and showed all the characteristics of the Skye Terrier except colour, which was pure white; but its competitors were deficient in shape, in tail carriage, in length of leg and in texture of coat, that there could be no comparison between them. The Bulldogs were equally defective – the white bitch which obtained the prize being, on the whole, the best, but still very inferior in all points but tail, to one of her competitors, which was deficient in this respect, having a very screw tail, hardly two inches long'.

The reporter then tried a modest prophecy, 'The success of the experiment is assured', he said, 'It has won a name already and when it has flitted from the Repository, and taken up its local habitation at Bingley Hall, in a more genial season of the year, it will be quite as much a Birmingham institution as the great Cattle and Poultry Show, the Town Hall organ, or John Bright himself'.

The show did move to the Bingley Hall and was to remain there until 1971 when, for a few years it went to the Stoneleigh National Agricultural Centre before, in 1989 moving to Perry Park in the heart of Birmingham. The Great Cattle and Poultry Show, the Town Hall organ and John Bright's opposition to the Corn Laws are no longer great talking points in Birmingham but the National Dog Show continues to go from strength to strength.

It was in 1861 that dog shows, of the type pioneered in Birmingham really began to take off. Birmingham held its second show in December, this time in Tennant Street, off Broad Street, and attracted 535 entries. During the early part of the year, and with a fine disregard for what had gone before, the 'First' Exhibition of Sporting and other Dogs was held at the Belle Vue Zoological Gardens, Manchester and in July Northern exhibitors again assembled at the North of England Exhibition of Sporting and other Dogs held at the Royal Agricultural Hall, Leeds. The panel of nine judges included, as well as Lord Neville, Sir W. Cooke Bart, Captain Harrison, and Messrs Lort, Smith, Solly and Leacroft, the very same Thomas Parrington, whose efforts had brought the Cleveland Hound Show into existence. At this show Bloodhounds, Greyhounds, Pointers, Setters and Harriers in the Sporting division received strongest support while among the best supported non-sporting breeds were Mastiffs, Newfoundlands, Dalmatians, Black-and-Tan and English Terriers and Scotch Terriers, which at that time included Yorkshire Terriers, doubtless to the chagrin of their partisan Yorkshire supporters.

This Leeds show is perhaps particularly significant for two reasons. It appears to have been the first major dog show which was organised as an independent event rather than as an offshoot of another organisation already catering for other forms of livestock and perhaps more significantly was held at the New Agricultural Hall in Islington, London, though it was still called the Northern Exhibition of Sporting and other Dogs. Over a five day period from 24 to 28 June it attracted no fewer than 803 entries. Having tasted a major dog show it would not be long before London would have its own event but for the meanwhile all the major developments continued to be in the North and the Midlands.

In the space of three years entries had increased from 59 to 830 and the pattern which future shows would follow was beginning to emerge. There was already a move away from the sporting breeds towards those whose only future would be as companions or in the show ring. For the gladiatorial breeds and for those which had already foregone contact with their sporting past dog shows offered a new and legitimate outlet for the enthusiasm of their supporters. Though for some breeds dog shows had arrived too late to keep them in existence. Early arrangements tended to reflect the lack of any central authority and gave rise to such anomalies as the classification of terriers, which were still working regularly with hounds, among the non-sporting breeds where they found themselves alongside Mastiffs, Dalmatians, Bulldogs and the imported Newfoundlands, Italian Greyhounds and Maltese Terriers all of which were very capable of providing good entries.

The growing popularity of foreign breeds was already apparent, the trend has continued to the extent that some of the native breeds to be seen at this show no longer exist. Gone are the Black-and-Tan Terriers, the White Terriers and, perhaps for the best, the Small Size Bulldogs, while the breeds which filled the Extra Class, the equivalent of the modern 'Any Variety Not Separately Classified', already included such exotic creatures as Egyptian dogs, Chinese dogs, Chow-Chows and Boar Hounds all of which have since increased their popularity though under different names. At the third Birmingham Show in 1862 St Bernards and Esquimaux dogs made their show ring debut. Fox Terriers, a very British breed which would eventually become the most popular show dog, had to wait until, in March 1863, London embarked on its own show at Cremorne in Chelsea, before they could make their debut as a separate variety.

At this show a first attempt was also made to resolve the confusion which surrounded the Scotch terrier classes by dividing them into White Scotch, Fawn Scotch and Blue Scotch Terriers. At Cremorne, too, Scotch Collies, French Poodles, Wolfhounds and Australian dogs made their appearance in the ring. Then, in May 1863, the First Great International Dog Show, held at the Agricultural Hall, Islington attracted no less than 1678 entries which, since a number of the entries were in brace and team classes consisting of more than one dog, meant that there were probably more than two thousand dogs in the hall.

Inevitably still more exotic breeds made their appearance in the ring, including Monster dogs, Greek, Manilla and Sicilian dogs and even Brazilian dogs. In 1864 the second show, again held at the Agricultural Hall, Islington, was the first to introduce 'Champion Classes', though in the absence of any agreed and enforceable definition of what precisely entitled a dog to the title of champion these classes tended to do little more than contribute to a state of confusion and uncertainty which many exhibitors were already beginning to find intolerable. Later in the year the Second International Show at the Agricultural Hall provided evidence of the increasing popularity and established respectability of dog shows when H.R.H. the Prince of Wales, later to become King Edward VII, was among the winning owners in the Harrier classes. More and bigger shows were held each year and more and more breeds were given separate classification. Entries well in excess of one thousand became commonplace and it seemed as though the pattern for the future was set.

In 1866 the name of Mr John Douglas, then employed by His Grace the Duke of Newcastle, appeared as one of the judges at the Sixth Manchester Dog Show. He judged again at Manchester in each of the following four years before, in 1871, spreading his wings to become a show manager in Edinburgh and Dublin. This duel career continued and in 1873 he judged in Glasgow, ran a show in Edinburgh, and took charge of the Kennel Club's first show before rounding off a busy year by judging yet again at the Manchester show. During the next few years John Douglas managed several shows each year as well as continuing his career as a judge. He managed shows in Brighton, Bristol, Dublin,

CATALOGUE AND AWARDS

Corrected K.C

OF THE

THIRD ANNUAL

GREAT SHOW

OF

TOY DOGS,

TO BE HELD

UNDER THE REVISED RULES OF THE KENNEL CLUB,

IN

ST. STEPHEN'S HALL,

WESTMINSTER,

MONDAY, TUESDAY, AND WEDNESDAY,

DECEMBER 5, 6, & 7, 1887.

President.

SIR WILLIAM HEATHCOTE, BART.

Patrons.

GENERAL LORD ALFRED PAGET.
SIR HUMPHREY DE TRAFFORD, BART.
MAJOR-GENERAL RAINES, C.B.
COLONEL G. NOEL MONEY, C.B.

CAPTAIN MOLESWORTH, R.N.
CAPTAIN COLLIS.
C. I. HENSLEY, ESQ.
C. E. CRESWELL, ESQ.
T. H. BOLTON, ESQ.

Committee.

BERRIE, J. W., ESQ., President Toy Spaniel, Pug, Bulldog, Bull Terrier, and Poodle Clubs.

COLLIS, CAPTAIN.
CHATTERTON, F. M., ESQ.
CRUFT, CHARLES, MR.
FOSTER, M. A., MRS.
FORDER, MRS.

GRAVES, K., MRS.
HOLDSWORTH, MISS.
JENKINS, MRS.
SHEFFIELD, W., ESQ.
SPENCER, RUSSEL, ESQ.

Judges.

J. FOSTER, ESQ., PUGS.
MONS. VANDER SNICKT, FOREIGN.

H. W. ALDERSON, ESQ., YORKSHIRES.
CAPTAIN HUGH COLLIS, SPANIELS.

J. W. BERRIE, ESQ., OTHER VARIETIES.

Veterinary Surgeon.

MR. A. J. SEWELL, M.R.C.V.S.

Secretary.

MR. CHARLES CRUFT, 325, Holloway Road, London, N.,
And during the Show, St. Stephen's Hall

CATALOGUE

SHOW OF
SPORTING DOGS
AT
"OLYMPIA,"
KENSINGTON,
APRIL 26, 27, 28, & 29,
1887.

MANAGER—CHAS. CRUFT.
SECRETARY—
HARRY ETHERINGTON,
152, FLEET ST., E.C.

SHOW OF SPORTING DOGS.

(Left) Prior to 1891 Charles Cruft learned his trade as the manager of shows of all sorts. The supporters who would help him to launch his all breeds show were already with him in 1887 for his third Toy Dog show. (Right) The yachts on the catalogue cover of Charles Cruft's 1887 Show of Sporting Dogs offers a clue to his main recreational interest.

Edinburgh, Hull, London and Manchester and firmly established himself as a first-class, highly professional show manager. The extent of his experience helped to underline the problems emerging as a result of the absence of an organisation with the authority to enforce a set of agreed and clearly understood rules as well as to help shape the future of dog shows and of pedigree dogs.

In spite of, or perhaps even because of the prevalence of aristocratic patronage, rules, where they existed at all, were frequently ignored. The size to which shows had so rapidly grown completely outstripped the authority which individual novice organisations could hope to wield. Chaos was never very far away. Charles Henry Lane describes some of the problems.

'It was formerly not uncommon in some breeds, where the dogs were much alike, for a good specimen to be shown, say, on Tuesday, taken out that night, of course a substitute brought in on Wednesday morning, shown again somewhere else on the Wednesday, and on some occasions, where dates and distances permitted, at two or more shows during the week, either no name or pedigree being given, or a different name at each show, and, the same owner having a number of dogs of the same colour "the changes were rung" to suit the circumstances of the case!

In those days, too, it was not safe to claim a dog at a show unless you had some positive means of identification, or you were more than likely to find a very inferior animal in its place at the end of the show.

Lending and borrowing were everyday occurrences, and if an exhibitor found a dog entered (as the questions of age, colour, name and even sex, were treated in the most free-and-easy manner!) was not very "fit" or in good form when the show came off, he would substitute another of his own (or somebody else's) instead.

The Kennel Club put an end to all these anomalies, or, at any rate, made them difficult and dangerous, and we do not see so many of the dyed chests, feet, etc., as used to be prevalent; in fact, the doggy atmosphere is clearer and purer, and while, at that time, a person known to have a personal, "peculiar and particular" (like Mr Weller's knowledge of London was said to be) knowledge of dogs was straightaway looked upon as rather a shady customer, to whom it was desirable to give a wide berth, and classed amongst what our friends in the North call "Pigeon-fleers"; now, the highest in the land, from Their Majesties the King and his charming and universally popular Consort, I think would not be ashamed to be called Doggy People, and as for the nobility, I could mention even the names of all distinguished people, including Her late Majesty Queen Victoria, other members of the Royal Family, British and foreign Princesses, Countesses, etc., whose dogs I have had the pleasure of judging or seeing at some of the shows'.

The Kennel Club, which had been formed in 1873, achieved all that Charles Lane suggested and more, but it was not formed with the intention, no matter how laudable, of making dog shows fit for the Royal Family. Indeed the Kennel Club was not even originally conceived as a means by which dogdom might be governed. In June 1870 G. H. Nutt had run a show, called the First Grand Exhibition of Sporting and other Dogs at the Crystal Palace in London. 'First' shows seem to have continued to be held for a number of years after showing dogs had become a widespread and popular activity. Nutt's effort attracted an entry of 895 and was repeated in 1871 and 1872, under the management of the ubiquitous John Douglas. This first Crystal Palace Show had been inspired by Mr S. E. Shirley and Mr J. H. Murchison, assisted by an influential committee, but because it was not a financial success a number of the committee declined to serve after the first year. The remainder pressed ahead.

Succeeding shows, though coming closer to solvency, underlined the need for a well thought out set of rules which would govern competition and conduct at future shows. These rules were drawn up by Shirley and a committee of twelve at a meeting which took place in April, 1873. As a result of this meeting the Kennel Club came into being. The twelve included four who had been on the original Crystal Palace Committee. Mr S. Lang, who kept a large kennel of Setters, Mr J. H. Whitehouse of Pointer fame, Mr J. C. Macdona and Mr J. H. Dawes as well as Mr S. Lang, who had judged at all three of the Crystal Palace Shows as well as elsewhere. The Kennel Club's own first show took place in June, 1873, as an extension of the well established Crystal Palace series, and it was to John Douglas that the Kennel Club turned to guide them through their inaugural event at which their newly minted rules were given their first practical test.

For a number of years the Kennel Club ran two shows a year, one at the Crystal Palace, though in 1877 they had a brief flirtation with the Agricultural Hall, Islington, and one at the Alexandra Palace, Muswell Hill, London. Such was the enthusiasm of the new organisation that, in 1878, just five years after their inaugural meeting and the subsequent inaugural show, John Douglas found himself in charge of a December show, called the Kennel Club's Twelfth Annual Exhibition of Sporting and other Dogs, at the Alexandra Palace. It attracted 1058 entries but more importantly was, as a result of the Kennel Club's carefully worded rules, free from many of the problems which beset many shows. John Douglas was quick to recognise the merits of these rules and to use them at other shows of which he was the manager and it was not long before other shows too were seeking Kennel Club permission to make use of their rules. It was from this that the Kennel Club's influence and authority began to emerge.

By 1886, when Charles Cruft was to embark on the series of terrier shows which would grow into Cruft's Show, the Kennel Club were licensing fifty-four shows a year, almost double the number in existence only three years previously. In 1887 the Kennel Club, at a show held at Barn Elms, attracted no less than 2012 entries, a number which was regarded as truly prodigious. Dog shows had grown from their twin rural and urban roots to become a major recreational activity which interested people of all ages, from all walks of life and from all over the country. They had developed a format which was now governed by a set of widely accepted rules and a group of people whose expertise could be relied upon. They provided a focal point for all those who were interested in dogs, were appreciative of quality and who enjoyed competition. They satisfied a need which had begun to emerge when interest in dogs had ceased to be purely utilitarian and which had developed as more and more people came to appreciate the companionship, security, pride and interest which ownership of a good dog could offer.

3.   The Great Terrier Shows

By 1886 Charles Cruft's reputation as a show manager was well established, his apprenticeship had been served, and served well, at shows throughout Britain, as well as on the continent. He had seen how dog shows were arranged in different countries and had further widened his experience at shows for different animals. He had realised what their strengths were and had thought about what was needed to make them better. His position and influence at Spratt's had enabled him to build up an unrivalled organisation capable of supplying the equipment and staff needed to run even the biggest show and he had, during his years as a salesman, built up a network of influential contacts amongst whom were people ready to assist him to make the next step in an already formidably successful career.

One of Spratt's best customers, certainly one they would not have been anxious to displease in any way, was the Duchess of Newcastle. Her Grace was an enthusiastic exhibitor of a number of breeds including, of course, the Clumber Spaniels which had originated on the Clumber Park estate. The Duchess's kennel housed several other gundog breeds as well as Borzois, said to have been the best collection in any kennel outside Russia, Deerhounds and Whippets but its main claim to fame would eventually be based on the Smooth and Wire Haired Fox Terriers which were added to the kennel in 1893, at that time among the most popular breeds in the country. Her Grace was one of the fifty ladies who helped to form the Ladies' Branch of the Kennel Club in 1897 and was its first Chairman, though she resigned the position soon afterwards. Doubtless her interest in Fox Terriers had been kindled before 1893 when she made her debut as an exhibitor with Cackler of Notts but whether her interest was sufficiently developed prior to 1886 for her, as has been said to have been the case, to suggest that Charles Cruft might try his hand at running a London show to cater exclusively for terriers seems doubtful. Certainly Her Grace was not among those whose support for the events, and its immediate successors, was acknowledged by Cruft.

Support also came from Sir Humphrey de Trafford whose home at Trafford Park provided palatial kenneling for a number of breeds. Originally Sir Humphrey's interests had been confined to working gundogs and to coursing Greyhounds which provided their owner with

an interest when he was not playing polo or hunting. Like the Reverend
Jack Russell before him Sir Humphrey, while a student at Oxford, had
bought a Fox Terrier which introduced him to an activity which was to
captivate him for the rest of his life. Sir Humphrey made a modest debut
in the show ring at the Oxford Terrier Show in 1882 and became a
member of the Kennel Club two years later. Within a few years he had
extended his kennel to include a number of breeds, Pointers, Setters,
Retrievers and Spaniels among them. He also owned Dandie Dinmonts,
Old English Sheepdogs and Greyhounds but it was the kennel's Fox
Terriers which attracted the most early notice. General Lord Alfred
Paget, whose links with Charles Cruft appear to derive from their mutual
interest in yachting rather than from any great interest in dogs, also gave
the project his support and agreed to act as one of the show's first
patrons. Though these would soon be replaced by Sir Humphrey whose
connection with dogs and enthusiasm for dog shows was already well
established. It seems possible that Sir Humphrey's contribution to the
early development of Cruft's has been undervalued.

During its thirteen year history the Kennel Club's influence and
authority had grown considerably. In 1885 the Committee had taken
determined action against a number of abuses which had been brought
to their attention, and which prior to the Kennel Club's existence would
have gone unpunished, if not unnoticed. One case involved the
fraudulent purchase of a Fox Terrier at the Brighton Show, another the
sale of a dog with false papers but increasingly the Kennel Club's work
arose out of a need to attend to some of the irregularities which had
become commonplace at shows. Charges arising out of unregistered dogs
being exhibited, others exhibited with a false date of birth, under false
names or in classes for which they were unqualified were heard but
perhaps the most significant were the cases which dealt with attempts to
gain unfair advantage at shows. They had considered the case of a poodle
whose colour had been enhanced by the use of dye and of a Wire Haired
Fox Terrier shown with alum in its coat. Both were matters which would
again raise their heads over one hundred years later.

The climate in which Cruft made his debut as an independent show
promoter was one in which many of the old abuses were being firmly
tackled and, as a result, dog shows were becoming more attractive to
people in all walks of life. It was a climate in which the popularity of dog
shows could increase rapidly but it was also one which would place
restraints which an enterprising showman such as Cruft would sometimes find irksome.

The First Great Terrier Show took place on 10, 11 and 12 March 1886
at the Royal Aquarium Westminster, a venue much used for all sorts of
displays, entertainments and exhibitions and enjoying a prominent site,
opposite Westminster Abbey, now occupied by the Methodist Central

Hall. The show received enthusiastic support from the public and mixed reception from the press, in Charles Cruft's exacting terms, came uncomfortably close to being a failure. Even so it says a great deal for Cruft's abilities as a publicist that he managed to interest the press in what was, in fact, a comparatively modest venture. The entry of 534 terriers was very creditable but fell a very long way short of the 1701 entries from all breeds which were attracted to what the Kennel Club, with just as much disregard for accuracy as Cruft himself might have shown, chose to advertise as its 26th show, held at the Crystal Palace over four days in January.

Those to whom the catalogue ascribes responsibility for the event were the five Patrons, General Lord Alfred Paget, Major General Raines, CB., C. I. Hensley Esq., C. G. Cresswell, Esq., T. H. Bolton, Esq., and the General Manager D. De Pinna, Esq. With the exception of Cruft's veterinary surgeon none of the other principals at his first terrier show were members of the Kennel Club or, apparently, had previously demonstrated much interest in dog shows. Alfred Sewell, Cruft's veterinary surgeon, would, in 1905 be appointed as Honorary Veterinary Expert to the Kennel Club and would write two, very well received books on matters canine.

The Times commented on the 'new and spacious building over the swimming tank, where there is ample light' and was delighted that 'the arrangements for the show are excellent, and as there is plenty of room between the benches it bids fair to be highly successful'. *The Illustrated London News* devoted an entire page to the event:

> 'The Royal Aquarium, Westminster which has on many occasions been the scene of dog shows of various kinds – of collies, bull-dogs, toy-dogs, and pugs, last week made a new departure when the first exhibition of terriers was opened to the public for three days. This show presented the best features to which visitors of older exhibitions of a similar description are accustomed. The entries were over five hundred and fifty in number, and the animals, divided into fifty-seven classes, were a creditable collection. All arrangements, including those for benching and feeding, were excellent; ample space was provided in the judging rings; the wide avenues between the rows of benches allowed visitors to move about and examine the dogs with freedom and comfort; and the ventilation and lighting were good.
>
> The general arrangements, in the hands of Mr C. Cruft, left nothing to be desired, except that at one period of the afternoon, owing to the influx of visitors the stock of catalogues was temporarily exhausted'.

Nowadays daily newspapers often seem unaware of the existence of any of the three thousand or so dog shows which the Kennel Club licenses each year. Crufts is the only one which attracts their attention and they are, apparently, unimpressed by the fact that interest in dogs is such that about one quarter of the population share their home with one. In 1886 things were very different. Even Cruft's modest debut among terriers did not escape their notice. It is, perhaps, doubtful whether a show's success was entirely dependent upon the amount of space available between benches, necessary if crinolined ladies were to view the dogs in comfort, but it was certainly high on Cruft's priorities that both the public and exhibitors should be provided with conditions which they found comfortable.

The Kennel Club was somewhat less sanguine about the new venture. In March, just a few days after the show had taken place, the *Gazette* gave it a cautious welcome:

> 'The Show although held under the Kennel Club Rules, appears to be a speculation on the part of the authorities of the Aquarium, there being no committee, but simply managers and a Vet (Mr A. J. Sewell, who examined every dog previous to its entrance)'. Though the *Gazette* failed to mention it they could not have been unaware of the fact that A. J.Sewell was already a leading figure in the Kennel Club and it seems most unlikely that they did not know of Charles Cruft's part in the venture. 'The catalogues (which were all sold out by 2 pm on the first day) show a great amount of amateurish get up (if we may use the expression). In several instances the numbers miss ten, and in one instance a hundred figures. There is also an absence of rules and regulations therein which, to the novice exhibitor, is confusing. We saw one good gentleman take a dog off his bench, upon which we expostulated with him, but were met with the remark that "when a dog is for sale in the catalogue anyone may take him off to have a look at him". Upon telling this gentleman that he would most likely get turned out if seen by anyone in authority, he quickly replaced the "tyke". The show itself was good both as regards quantity (there being 538 entries) and quality, and the attendance, we may say, was enormous. The judging gave general satisfaction. One peculiar feature we must draw attention to, and that is, that Mr Alfred George both judged and exhibited, but, of course, not in the same classes'.

The enormous number of visitors attracted to this first London terrier show must have pleased Charles Cruft because his primary interest in running these events was in the profit they yielded. They were indeed speculative ventures as the *Kennel Gazette* had suggested. Even at this first show Cruft had made use of some tricks to attract attention which he would continue to rely on. He would continue to make use of aristocratic patronage and would keep the Kennel Club at arm's length by continuing to ensure that senior Kennel Club members were deeply involved in his shows. He would also continue to take a rather cavalier attitude to the rules to which the Kennel Club rightly attached such importance. Facts fed to the press would enable them to write interesting stories about his shows but they would not always be facts based on the unsullied truth. What the *Gazette* had seen as a sign of amateurism in the catalogue, the fact that a few numbers between the last dog in one class and the first in the next were missing, meant that Charles Cruft could arrive at a final figure which made the entry look far bigger than it actually was. This was a trick he would continue to use, because, in spite of being well known, the press were prepared to enter into the conspiracy. Contrast the *Illustrated London News* report that there were 550 entries in 57 classes at the show with the fact that the catalogue showed 539 entries in 41 classes, divided between 14 breeds, three of which were divided into two varieties.

Cruft had engaged Mr R. W. Remington as Superintendant, he acted as Manager and Mr A. J. Sewell was his veterinary surgeon. There were five judges, Mr L. P. C. Astley, Mr A. George, Mr T. Hodges, Mr J. Pratt and Mr James Taylor. Astley was one of the most popular judges of whom it was claimed that 'on an average, he judged dogs, somewhere or other, about four days a week throughout the year'. A chemist by profession his enthusiasm for dogs led him into a career as a judge and as a journalist. He was an exhibitor of Fox Terriers, Scottish Terriers, Rough Collies and Schipperkes and also kept Pile Game Bantams, Gold-pencilled Hamburghs and other varieties of exotic poultry as well as Show and Flying Homing Pigeons, all of which he showed and won well with. He was also in demand as a judge of cats which he also showed with some success. Astley had a reputation for making his decisions in the ring quickly but was well liked by exhibitors who seldom disputed his decisions.

James Pratt, whose passion was for Skye Terriers some of which had found their way into Queen Victoria's ownership, was a familiar and extraordinary figure around his Paddington home. He was invariably surrounded by a pack of Skye Terriers and dressed in what he believed to be the appropriate Scottish regalia, topped by a century-old bonnet which had formerly belonged to the big game hunter Gordon Cumming. Pratt was not the last judge or exhibitor to make use of unusual apparel in an effort to make himself noticeable.

Alfred Astley judged the five classes provided for both Smooth and Wire Haired Fox Terriers. In Smooths he found his winner in J. R. Whittle's Brookhouse Nick, while in Wires he was unable to decide between Maxwell and Cassell's Jack's Yarn and Sir Humphrey de Trafford's Barton Wonder. Sir Humphrey was doubtless consoled by winning both puppy classes and being placed first and second with his bitches. Dandie Dinmonts, with four classes, provided another win for Sir

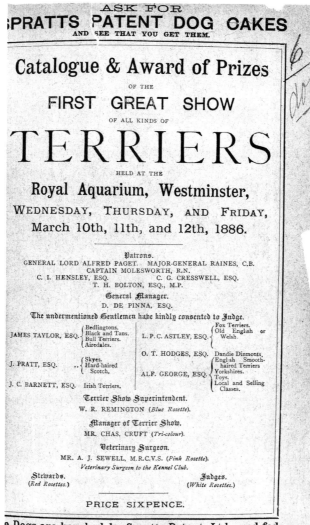

ASK FOR

SPRATTS PATENT DOG CAKES

AND SEE THAT YOU GET THEM.

Catalogue & Award of Prizes

OF THE

FIRST GREAT SHOW

OF ALL KINDS OF

TERRIERS

HELD AT THE

Royal Aquarium, Westminster,

WEDNESDAY, THURSDAY, AND FRIDAY,

March 10th, 11th, and 12th, 1886.

Patrons.
GENERAL LORD ALFRED PAGET.   MAJOR-GENERAL RAINES, C.B.
CAPTAIN MOLESWORTH, R.N.
C. I. HENSLEY, ESQ.   C. G. CRESSWELL, ESQ.
T. H. BOLTON, ESQ., M.P.

General Manager.
D. DE PINNA, ESQ.

The undermentioned Gentlemen have kindly consented to Judge.

JAMES TAYLOR, ESQ.	Bedlingtons. Black and Tans. Bull Terriers. Airedales.	L. P. C. ASTLEY, ESQ.	Fox Terriers. Old English or Welsh.
J. PRATT, ESQ.	Skyes. Hard-haired Scotch.	O. T. HODGES, ESQ. ALF. GEORGE, ESQ.	Dandie Dinmonts. English Smooth-haired Terriers Yorkshires. Toys. Local and Selling Classes.
J. C. BARNETT, ESQ.	Irish Terriers.		

Terrier Show Superintendent.
W. R. REMINGTON (Blue Rosette).

Manager of Terrier Show.
MR. CHAS. CRUFT (Tri-colour).

Veterinary Surgeon.
MR. A. J. SEWELL, M.R.C.V.S. (Pink Rosette).
Veterinary Surgeon to the Kennel Club.

| Stewards. (Red Rosettes.) | Judges. (White Rosettes.) |

PRICE SIXPENCE.

e Dogs are benched by Spratts Patent, Ltd., and fed
on their Meat Fibrine Dog Cakes.

Charles Cruft always regarded his first terrier show, held in 1886, as the first Cruft's Show.

Humphrey, this time with Jennie Deans under O. T. Hodges. Four classes were provided for Black and Tan Terriers, a breed which has since disappeared from the scene, they were judged by J. Taylor who also judged Bedlingtons, Bull Terriers, split between large and small terriers, and Airedales. Skye Terriers, split between Prick and Drop Eared dogs were judged by James Pratt. Hard-haired Scotch Terriers, Bedlington Terriers and Irish Terriers, had three classes each, while Airedales and Toy Terriers each had two, the latter being split between Rough and Smooth coated dogs. The rest, Welsh or Black and Tan Wire-haired Terriers,

English Smooth-haired and Yorkshire Terriers, had one class each.

The *Kennel Gazette*, in spite of having received a general impression that the quality of the dogs was good, felt it necessary to point out that the prominent feature of Black and Tan Terriers was the want of condition of the dogs, the criticism was even extended to include some of the winners. Yorkshire Terriers too were said to be disappointing because 'north country exhibitors did not patronise the classes and, consequently, they were unworthy of notice'. What the *Gazette* meant was that Mrs M. A. Foster, whose Yorkshire Terriers were generally regarded as the cream of the breed, had not entered the show but had chosen to remain, with her dogs, in her Huddersfield home. She could hardly have been expected to make such a journey in March in order to compete in one class at a show which was very much an unknown quantity but whatever doubts she and other exhibitors may have had the show was an undoubted success and all the omens suggested that it would go on to even greater success.

In the following year the show moved to St Stephen's Hall, Westminster and offered a much larger and improved classification. There were 75 classes and 30 special prizes which attracted about 500 dogs, too many for the spacious layout to be maintained and there were complaints that ladies wearing crinolines had difficulty in moving between the benches, though the spacing of benches was very generous compared with modern standards. The London and North Western Railway was persuaded to make special arrangements to convey dogs to the show, a service which Cruft would continue and considerably extend in later years and which was to ensure that his shows would receive the support of exhibitors from all over Britain. Mrs Foster took the train from Huddersfield and won first in the Yorkshire Terrier class with Lady Bective and second with the appropriately named Daisy II. The new venture was also graced by the arrival on the scene of a President in the form of Sir Humphrey de Trafford.

The show was run under a new set of Kennel Club Rules which had come into force at the beginning of 1887 and included a requirement that 'total blindness shall absolutely disqualify; partial blindness shall have great weight against a dog. Should a dog appear to be deaf or lame it shall be disqualified, unless the owner can satisfy the judge that such defects are temporary'. How a judge was expected to identify partially blind dogs or what arguments would be regarded as acceptable proofs that deafness or lameness were temporary were not explained.

In 1888, for reasons which are no longer apparent, though probably not unconnected with his desire to increase his profit, Cruft ran two terrier shows, one on 20, 21 and 22 March and the second on 14, 15 and 16 November. At the March show Clydesdale Terriers, a soft coated version of the Skye Terrier which must have been a nightmare to groom and which are now extinct, made their Cruft's debut. At this show there was an embarrassing mix-up with some of the dogs which had been sent to the show by rail to be cared for and shown by Spratt's representatives. Some of these dogs had the wrong labels attached to them and, as a consequence, some dogs which were not at the show were credited with having won prizes and owners were alarmed, when they collected their dogs from the railway station after the show had ended, to find strange dogs emerging from their boxes. It was not the sort of thing anyone would have expected from the super efficient Charles Cruft and it was not repeated.

The November show attracted no less than 1134 entries from about 700 dogs in 164 classes. The increase was partly due to a general preference among both exhibitors and spectators for the November rather than the March date but also, perhaps largely, due to the fact that the Fox Terrier Club, the Collie Club and the Toy Dog Club all decided to use the event as their club show and was also helped because classes for Pugs, Schipperkes, Toy Terriers as well as for any other variety, won by an Otterhound from the Kendal pack, were also available. The show also offered classes for Black-and-tan Terriers, the old English breed which now survive only in the form of Welsh Terriers, and for White English Terriers, a breed which is now extinct. Already Cruft was developing a method of attracting attention by providing classes for minority breeds, especially foreign ones, which would attract public interest far out of proportion with their numbers.

> The *Kennel Gazette* was not noticeably more favourably inclined towards 'the fifth show of the series inaugurated by Mr Charles Cruft', than they had been towards the first. They reported that it 'was held in St Stephen's Hall . . . and was a very successful one, although the unfortunate absence of the popular founder, together with some changes in the usual procedure, led to confusion, which provoked much grumbling. There were many and loud complaints about the catalogue, which gave but a single number to each dog. This arrangement has much in its favour, but as some dogs were entered in six, eight, ten, twelve, and even more classes, the array of prize tablets was simply bewildering in many cases. This probably accounts for a statement in some of the dailies that the arrangement of the catalogue was about the worst ever seen. Mr Kear made an efficient manager, and although the absence of the "master's eye" was noticeable on the first day, things were all in good trim by closing time. The show was thoroughly disinfected with "Microbene", the latest candidate for favour, Spratt's Patent had their usual display of collars, &c., and Hippacea was well in evidence. The quality throughout was excellent, the classes for Skyes, Dandies, and Scotch Terriers being far above average'.

It was one of the hallmarks of Cruft's Shows that he would continue to provide publicity for the commercial firms which gave him their support.

In 1890 the Fox Terrier Club again supported Cruft's Terrier Show. Smooths provided about 270 entries and Wires about 200. The Collie Club and the Toy Dog Club also returned for their Club shows and Cruft added another 56 classes to bring the number up to 220 thereby attracting about 1500 entries, all but treble the entry attracted to his first terrier show just five years previously. The show had not only succeeded in attracting exhibitors but was already a firm favourite with the public. A visit to Cruft's was already becoming an annual event for many Londoners. The success of the show, Charles Cruft's handling of its affairs and, doubtless, the telling advocacy of its influential supporters, were instrumental in persuading the Kennel Club to a warmer view of the event and it became a show at which points towards the title of champion could be won. It was, however, at this show that Charles Cruft revealed a tendency to follow somewhat too closely along the path trod by Phineas Barnum by mounting an exhibition of 'stuffed dogs, or dogs made of Wood, China, etc'.

The first of Cruft's terrier shows, just five years earlier, had attracted 534 entries at a time when the Kennel Club's own show could expect over 1700 entries, admittedly from a far greater range of breeds. By 1890 Cruft, by the astute use of publicity and by adding a few more breeds to his schedule, had increased the number of entries at his show to over 1500. The Kennel Club's show, held at the Agricultural Hall, Islington, in that year attracted just 1221 entries, and this in spite of the fact that it was one of the first to be designated as one of very few at which two points might be won towards the title of champion. The comparison provides a measure of the way in which Cruft's venture rapidly established a popular appeal.

4.   *The First Decade*

*B*y 1891 Charles Cruft had run six terrier shows and had established such a personal reputation that they were already popularly known as 'Cruft's Shows' although Cruft himself had continued to use what he must have regarded as the grander title of 'The Great Terrier Shows' but cannot have failed to appreciate the marketable significance of the way in which his unusual name was becoming well known. During the series of terrier shows he not only added to his already considerable experience but also demonstrated his ability in the most convincing way possible as step-by-step he improved each successive event. By the end of the series he had introduced a few breeds which, even at a time when classification remained somewhat uncertain, could not possibly be regarded as terriers. The next steps were obvious. Cruft's Show had to become a show open to all breeds and the necessary change of name would have to incorporate what had already become the most famous name in dogdom, that of the show's organiser Charles Cruft.

The 1891 show opened on Wednesday, 11 February, and continued through Thursday and Friday. It was held at the Agricultural Hall, Islington, which Charles Cruft had astutely and confidently leased for several years on the understanding that the authorities would not allow any other dog shows to be held there. He thus expressed his confidence in the future of his new venture and, at the same time, made sure that any competitors, which might arise or which already existed, and these included the Kennel Club's own show, could not make use of the very best venue which London had to offer.

The show was noticed by *The Field*, though not with the sort of uncritical attention which Cruft sought. Not only was the report rather dismissive of the quality of some of the dogs but it even got Cruft's name slightly wrong.

> 'Some six or seven years ago Mr C. Crufts (*sic*) held a show of terriers at the Westminster Aquarium, and arranged such a liberal classification that in due course the entries reached such a total that could be called nothing less than extraordinary. Indeed, so successful were these terrier shows, that this year their promoter added dogs of other kinds, with the result that during the present week a huge assemblage of canines has taken place at the Agricultural Hall, Islington, no fewer

The quality of Cruft's earliest prize cards was high. Cruft went to the top canine artists, in this case Arthur Wardle, and allowed them a free rein to produce an excellent design. The absence of a printed date on the card demonstrates Cruft's concern for economy.

than 2437 entries being received. Of course there were not that number of dogs, because very many of them were entered in more than one class, and several local divisions assisted to swell the total, as did the team competitions and the breeder's prizes. But it was a great show nevertheless. The awards of the prizes continued throughout the Wednesday, and the show closed on the Friday evening. Taken throughout, the collection of dogs was fairly high-class, the non-sporting divisions being by far the best, whilst pointers, setters, and other varieties of the more important sporting groups were not nearly equal to what is seen at Birmingham and at some of our Kennel Club shows. The management was, of course, admirably superintended by Mr Crufts (*sic*), who certainly is to be congratulated in making the largest show of dogs ever brought together by the private enterprise of a single individual, and it quite received that warm patronage from the public its expensive arrangements deserved'.

The show included classes for thirty-five breeds, with many divided into several varieties, plus what were referred to as 'Foreign Dogs'. Hounds were represented by Bloodhounds, Bassetts, split between Smooth and Rough coated dogs, Dachshunds, Deerhounds, Greyhounds, Whippets and Borzois or Russian Wolf Hounds, Gundogs by Pointers, split between dogs over 55lb and under 55lb, Setters, split between English, Gordon, Irish and Field; Retrievers, split between Flat Coated and Curly Coated, and Spaniels, split between Field or Black, Liver or Sussex, Clumbers and Cockers. Terriers comprised of Dandie Dinmonts, Scotch Terriers, Skyes, both Prick and drop eared, Clydesdales, Bedlingtons, Wire-haired Fox Terriers, Welsh Terriers, Smooth Fox Terriers, Airedales, Old English White Terriers, and Black and Tan Terriers, split between dogs over 23 lb and dogs over 16 lb. Among the non-sporting breeds were St Bernards, Mastiffs, Great Danes, Newfoundlands, split between Black and other than Black, Collies, both Rough and Smooth, Old English Sheepdogs, Bulldogs, over 40 lb and under 45 lb, Italian Greyhounds, Poodles, Pomeranians, Dalmatians, Yorkshire Terriers, Pugs, Schipperkes and Toy Spaniels, with separate classes for King Charles, Blenheims, Rubies and Prince Charles.

The Field's review of this inaugural show was restricted because

'with so many large shows now being held, and that of the Kennel Club and Manchester near at hand, we shall do here no more than give a comparatively brief notice of the chief features of the present exhibition, especially as most of the chief winners have recently been noticed in these columns . . . Bloodhounds did not muster in any great force . . . There was a large collection of St Bernards but including a vast quantity of rubbish . . . Great Danes mustered in force . . . Deerhounds were somewhat better . . . Newfoundlands were numerous and of good quality . . . Of the Landseer's similar remarks apply . . . All good, speedy Greyhounds should now be in training, and there were few present on Wednesday in the show ring . . . There were a lot of Retrievers but still the same old faces . . . The best Irish Setters were Major Jameson's . . . Among Pointers were several excellent specimens . . . but the competition was not very keen . . . Just as is always the case now, Collies mustered in great force but there is the same story, the same old faces . . . The Dalmatian Club supported their pets strongly, and a good show was made of this variety of spotted dog, but Mr H. Droessen won the majority of the prizes because his dogs were the best . . . There is just now an attempt to boost the Whippet, a cross-bred dog used either for racing or rabbit coursing. Classes were provided for them and the winners Mr H. Vickers' Zuber and Herndell are graceful animals, miniature Greyhounds, in fact, but without the delicacy or fragility of the pure Italian strain'.

In spite of having their Club Show the following week Fox Terrier exhibitors remained loyal to Charles Cruft and provided about 200 entries among which were said to be some promising youngsters, including Francis Redmond's Devonian who was:

'beaten in bone and terrier-character. Irish Terriers looked rather meagre after the great collection at Liverpool . . . Welsh terriers contained most of the same faces that have so recently appeared at other shows . . . Scotch Terriers included most of the recent winners, though the classes were well filled . . . Skye Terriers were comparatively small classes, and but fair in the matter of merit . . . but Mr Leatham had a very nice lot of Dandie Dinmonts on this his first appearance in the judging ring . . . Mr Weaver won in challenge dogs with Darkie Deans, and Mr C. H. Lane (who was judging in another part of the show) in bitches with Little Beauty . . . Although the Bedlington Terrier Club sent their challenge cups for competition, and various medals too, this variety of north country terrier was not fully represented, and the classes would have been very bad indeed had not Mr Allcock brought to town several of his cracks . . . There was nothing particularly smart in the way of old English Terriers; but of Bull Terriers the collection was quite tip-top . . . Black and Tan Terriers were generally poor . . . White English Terriers were quite as numerous as they are usually found nowadays . . . The Toy Spaniels were benched and caged in a room by themselves, not far removed from the madding crowd . . . Yorkshire Terriers proved, as usual, little short of a monopoly for Mrs Foster . . . There were some half a dozen Italian Greyhounds entered, but not any of them really tip-top . . . The Maltese dogs appear to be going out of fashion, and high class specimens are nowadays extremely rare . . . The variety class, under 7lb, included mostly cross-bred terriers of little merit in any way'.

Schipperkes, regarded as a breed whose rapidly increasing numbers marked it as one for the future, also remained loyal but although the entry was regarded as 'first rate' comment was made about the number of soft coats and long backs while *The Field* thought that the 'little black dogs looked quaint and odd, especially so as they were benched in one of the darkest parts of the building', the darkest corner, apparently being reserved for Bulldogs. The entry in Dalmatians was bigger than any previous show had attracted, while in the Foreign Dog classes Esquimaux dogs, a Samoyede sledge dog shown by the Prince of Wales, a Huska bred by Mr Taunton and the King of Norway, a Dingo, also shown by Mr Taunton, several Chow Chows and two dogs described simply as 'Chinese'. 'Mrs Waner's Ah Te won a second prize in the Chinese group, a handsome animal, which is more than can be said of Mr Bosley's Chinese, of an ugly yellow colour, with little coat, and a cherry-coloured nose'. Poodles must have presented an interesting spectacle because not only were classes split between colours but special classes were also provided for corded coats. Mr Sanquinette's Cup for the Best Poodle in all Classes was won by Champion Achilles who also sired the first and second prize winners in the puppy class.

King Haakon of Norway, breeder of the Huska, was married to Maud, a daughter of the Prince of Wales, later to become King Edward VII and sister of the future King George V. Perhaps his involvement in dogs was a product of his connections with the British Royal Family. Certainly a great deal of public attention was focused on the dogs shown by the Royal Family. These were 'benched in a roomy kennel, apart from the exhibits of the populace, the latter were able to view them to their heart's content'. The Prince of Wales won with Perla 'an interesting specimen of the Samoyede sledge dog, pure white and not altogether like a collie in appearance, but smaller and even prettier'. He had also won every prize in the class for Rough Bassets, which *The Field* described as 'pretty little hounds, and they nearly approach our English rough-haired beagle than any other of the foreign importations Miniature otter hounds almost in appearance, and very likely to give good sport in hare hunting'. In the classes for the Pomeranian or Spitz dogs, said *The Field*, 'Her Majesty was again an exhibitor, sending three pretty little creatures, a fawn or sable and white in colour, quite diminutive, not more than about 7lb weight each, and extremely nice dogs, though of a colour not often shown here. This being the case, a special class was provided for them, and Fluffy and Gena each won first prizes, Nino being very highly commended'. The Queen had taken a fourth prize with a Rough Collie, the royally named Darnley II. Charles Lane, who judged the Royal Pomeranians was forthright in his criticism of the Queen's dogs. Gena, he said, 'wants more length of muzzle', and was equal first with Fluffy of which he had nothing critical to say, while Fluffy's litter brother Nino was said to be 'the better of the two, but very shy and a bad shower' which meant he got no better than reserve. Also among the winners was 'Huska – another good Esquimaux, bred by Mr Taunton and the King of Norway'.

How Charles Cruft had managed to attract the enthusiastic support of the Royal Family, including Queen Victoria, her son the Prince of Wales and her granddaughter's husband, King Haakon, remains a mystery. The Royal Family's association with dogs was not new, indeed the Prince of Wales was the Kennel Club's Patron, but this was their first venture into the competitive world of dog shows.

Apart from the fact that the 1891 show was the first organised by Charles Cruft which was open to all breeds and the first to carry his name a number of things indicate the way things were likely to develop. He had faced and withstood competition from other, already well established, shows. He had retained the loyalty of those who had supported his terrier shows and had sought new support by classifying breeds which other shows ignored. He had received Royal support and had used this to offer the public a rare opportunity to see the Royal dogs. He was not only building on his past experience but was also making innovations which would attract the public in the future. These included a number of very Victorian classes for stuffed dogs, tried out first at his final terrier show, and which was eventually to become an art exhibition as part of Cruft's Show which now exists both in the form of individual stands at the show and separate exhibitions in galleries throughout London during Cruft's week.

Victorian sentimentality allowed stuffed dogs to be regarded very differently from what today's tastes would allow but views of what was happening just a couple of miles down the road from Cruft's inaugural show may have changed very little. As spectators and exhibitors left the Agricultural Hall in Islington on the last day of the 1891 show PC Ernest Thompson discovered the mutilated corpse Frances Coles, a Whitechapel prostitute. It was assumed, probably wrongly, that she was Jack the Ripper's ninth victim. The incident gives some idea of the sort of London into which Charles Cruft launched his show.

There is a slightly closer connection between Jack the Ripper and Crufts than is provided by the unfortunate Frances Coles. In October, 1888 Sir Charles Warren, the Police Commissioner, was impressed by a letter which appeared in *The Times* and which extolled the value of Bloodhounds in tracking malcreants. He thereupon opened negotiations to buy a pair of adult Bloodhounds, Barnaby and Burgho, from Edwin Brough, a breeder and exhibitor from Wyngate near Scarborough. Trials were run in Regents Park, in one of which Sir Charles himself acted the part of the fugitive, and the dogs were used, unsuccessfully, in an attempt to track a burglar through the busy, cobbled Whitechapel streets. Eventually, however, negotiations foundered and the two dogs returned to their north country kennels to continue their careers in the show ring.

Typically Cruft made good use of his inaugural success and of the attention devoted to it when the time came to advertise the 1892 show. He slightly and advantageously misquoted *The Times* 'It is certainly the

CRUFT'S ROYAL AGRICULTURAL HALL, LONDON,

DOG FEBRUARY 10, 11, 12, 1892.

IF YOU HAVE NOT RECEIVED
A SCHEDULE,
WRITE FOR ONE AT ONCE.
ENTRIES NOW TAKEN.

SHOW,

£2,000 IN PRIZES, INCLUDING 200 SPECIAL PRIZES.

PRESS OPINIONS.

TIMES.—It is certainly the largest show ever held in this country.

DAILY CHRONICLE.—Surpasses any previous canine exhibition, both in number and quality, and reflects the greatest credit upon **Mr. C. Cruft.**

DAILY NEWS.—Mr. Cruft is certainly to be congratulated on having scored a record........Taken all round the show is a sound one.

STANDARD.—Surpasses any previous canine exhibition.

DAILY TELEGRAPH.—A dog show of unprecedented dimensions.

MORNING ADVERTISER.—In short, the gigantic entry must be regarded as a tribute not only to the personal popularity of the promoter, but to a desire on the part of exhibitors to support to the utmost of their ability a series of free and independent shows in London..........one of the largest and best ever held.

Cruft makes clever use of press comments on his first show in order to promote the second.

largest show ever held in this country'; *The Daily Chronicle* 'Surpasses any previous canine exhibition, both in number and quality, and reflects the greatest credit upon Mr C. Cruft'; the *Daily News* 'Mr Cruft is certainly to be congratulated on having scored a record . . . Taken all round the show is a sound one'; the *Standard* 'Surpasses any previous canine exhibition'; the *Daily Telegraph* 'A dog show of unprecedented dimensions'; and the *Morning Advertiser* 'In short, the gigantic entry must be regarded as a tribute not only to the personal popularity of the promoter, but admire on the part of exhibitors the desire to support to the utmost of their ability a series of free and independent shows in London . . . one of the largest and best ever held'. The show was grandly, if somewhat inaccurately, advertised as Cruft's Eighth Great Show of Dogs and Exhibition of Sporting Appliances. There was £2000 in prizes on offer including 200 specials. For this show Cruft had added a crown, presumably on the basis of the Royal patronage his show had received in the previous year, to the emblem of a St Bernard's head enclosed in an inscribed dog collar. Nearly one hundred years later the emblem is still in use.

By this time Cruft had made arrangements with the Great Northern Railway to 'convey Dogs, &c., for exhibition at this Show from Inverness, Perth, Dundee, Glasgow, Edinburgh, Newcastle, York, Hull, Leeds, Halifax, Bradford, Wakefield, Liverpool, Lynn, Manchester, Huddersfield, Sheffield, Barnsley, Derby, Rotherham, Nottingham, Leicester, Lincoln, Grimsby, Boston, Spalding, Wisbech, Peterborough, Cambridge and other towns on and in connection with their system to King's Cross'. For its part the Midland Railway was also running trains with through vans from the towns on its system and promised that 'arrangements will be made for the return of the traffic at the close of the Show, in through vans, from St Pancras'.

For some reason Spratt's Patent Limited felt it necessary to ensure that there were no doubts about who was responsible for the event. In a letter to the *British Fancier* Spratt's company secretary, William Holder, said 'as there seems to be a little misapprehension in the minds of some people as to our relationship with this show, we wish to reiterate that we have no connection with the undertaking whatever further than supplying our representative Mr Cruft with the benches and fittings, food and staff, just as we should any other show organiser or society. The venture is entirely Mr Cruft's own, and he alone is personally responsible'. It was not a statement which was designed to help Cruft. Already the Kennel Club were feeling uneasy about shows run by individuals for private profit and it would not be long before Cruft surrounded himself with a carefully selected Committee who would carry out his wishes while representing his cause in the halls of power.

The press was once more impressed and acknowledged that:

> 'in many respects it eclipsed any of his former efforts, and although the total entry of 3025 is swelled considerably by duplicates and omissions, it is still a prodigious collection, and on the whole quite an average in point of merit. The arrangements were much on a par with last year, and although defective here and there in detail, were as a whole satisfactory. Considering the heavy calendar which many of the judges had to get through, and the complications of the specials, the awards were concluded in excellent time, and catalogues with full awards on sale on the second day of the show'.

It must have added considerably to the interest of spectators to be able to go round the show on the second and third days with a catalogue which gave all the awards won on the first day.

Once more Her Majesty the Queen was an exhibitor and again was among the prize winners, this time in open competition with some of the country's top Pomeranian breeders. H.R.H. the Grand Duke Nicholas and Prince Oldenbourg had sent over from Russia a team of Borzois but could not beat Mr Muir's Koratai. Baron Von Gingins from Hessia had sent over a team of Wire-haired Griffins. 'Poodles were acclaimed as the finest collection ever congregated, and Dachshunds were only saved from utter mediocrity by Mr Vale's contingent, who carried all before them'. But as well as catering for the Fancy Cruft provided a few superlatives for the public to admire. 'The "Biggest Dog in the World" was on exhibition', Mr Willson's Thibet (Tibet) Sheep Dog, as was the smallest adult dog in the world, Mrs Foster's 2½lb Yorkshire Terrier Bradford Ned. The Lord Mayor and Lady Mayoress of London arrived in fine style having been brought from the Mansion House 'in a brougham drawn by a magnificent pair of bays'. However Lord Mayor Evans appears to have been disappointed that 'there was not an honest bred English Foxhound in the show to look at'.

The *Kennel Gazette* again refused to be impressed. The Bloodhounds, judged by Frederick Gresham, were won by Hodson's Rollick, a promising young hound, very shy in the ring, 'short of leather, wanting at least an inch more length in ears and for his size he should also be longer in head; he wants more wrinkle and a better peak'. In Irish Wolfhounds the Open Class winner Myshall, stood alone, in Mastiffs 'with the exception of the winners' were described by Norman Higgs, the judge, as 'a very bad lot' while Foreign Dogs, judged by Charles Lane, seemed most remarkable for the absence of the best known exhibitors and the unusually small classes. No entries were received in the Pointer and Flat Coated Retriever challenge classes and the only entry in the Challenge Class for Sussex Spaniels was absent. In Blenheims Prince Karl, 'a nice dog, rather too large and light in nose' had a walk over. However Dalmatians again gave the show their enthusiastic support, producing thirty-nine exhibits and Borzois had 'an excellence and number of the exhibits were simply astounding, and the judge's task was a very trying one'. Dandie Dinmonts too 'turned out well, with a nice lot of Mustards intermixed'.

In October, 1892 Cruft sought the Kennel Club's permission to run his shows under their rules, he was, in effect, acknowledging the advantage which might be had by submitting to the Kennel Club's growing authority. However, when the K.C. Committee came to examine the terms under which Cruft intended to operate they took exception to a clause which laid down 'that Mr Chas. Cruft be empowered and instructed to act as he thinks best in the interests of the Show and all matters relating thereto'. The Kennel Club would have none of it and insisted that the Cruft's Committee must be 'solely responsible for the conduct of their Show and cannot delegate their powers to anyone'. Cruft, of course, meekly but doubtless with his tongue firmly in his cheek accepted the condition but his Committee remained nothing more than a device for rubber stamping whatever he chose to do.

The 1893 show was, predictably, once more hailed as 'the largest gathering of canines ever assembled in this or any other country. When we say that this show reached upwards of 3000 entries, or 2000 dogs, its colossal character will at once be seen. Although the largest show numerically ever organised, it is not the best in point of merit, though, of course, a good average one'. Problems were experienced because Spratt's had an impossibly limited time in which to erect the benches and, as a consequence, the start of judging was delayed, and was not completed until the second day and then only by using substitute judges, but 'when the machinery had been set in full motion, everything went fairly well'. Though Schipperke exhibitors, perhaps accustomed to a better service from their Club Secretary were said to have shown 'a considerable amount of wrath . . . (because) . . . exhibits were not benched until after three o'clock, and only then by the owners themselves'. Even worse was an incident which took place among the Borzois. Apparently:

'Mr E. Block, who brought the team of Borzois from Russia, was not well satisfied with his visit, and he promptly returned home at the close of the show, at which he had not found a customer for a single specimen, in fact, we believe he only disposed of one during his visit. The worst part of the business was that some of the younger hounds fell ill with distemper, but the report that one died on its bench at Cruft's, we understand was incorrect. That they were forbidden entrance to the show is a fact, and that they afterwards found their way on to their benches is equally true, but they were removed after the first day, it is hoped before they had done mischief. It will be to his own interests if Mr Cruft makes better provision at his next show for discarded dogs than he did on this occasion. . . . We hear the Kennel Club are investigating the case of Mr Block's distempered Borzois, being benched and competing at Cruft's after disqualification by Mr Sewell. It is, of course, a serious breach of exhibition law, which, when properly brought home, the offender should be fittingly punished, although as the owner is a foreigner, every leniency will, no doubt, be shown him.'

The explanation which Cruft offered to the Kennel Club was a lame one. It revealed that he 'supposed that the dogs had been taken into the building by the exhibitors, although he had specially appointed a man to remove dogs rejected by the veterinary inspector, that he had no hospital prepared, but that his instructions were that the dogs must be tied up against the wall'. He said that about forty dogs had been rejected by the veterinary inspector and that only the Russian dogs had evaded inspection before they reached their benches. The Kennel Club placed the blame firmly on Cruft's management of the show and his failure to provide a place to which diseased dogs could be taken, but, having expressed their view took no further specific action. They did, however, revise the rules not only to make better provisions necessary but also to make the Show Executive responsible for enforcement of the rules at the show.

It seems very likely that Charles Cruft had himself over-ruled his veterinary surgeon's opinion and had allowed the diseased dogs entry to the show. He may well not have anticipated any punitive action by the Kennel Club whose authority was by no means fully established and who were, in any case, seeking to persuade him to relax his monopoly of the Agricultural Hall to enable them to continue to hold their show in the building. Nevertheless it seems that Cruft came very close to being disowned by the Kennel Club but they eventually agreed to overlook the matter on the assurance that 'Charles the First' would not offend again in future.

Kennel Club shows had been held at the Agricultural Hall since 1888 but, unless Cruft could be persuaded to relax his monopoly of the building, the 1893 KC Show would have to be in a new venue. They apparently failed to persuade Cruft to relax his hold over the Agricultural Hall because in 1893 the Kennel Club returned to the Crystal Palace, a venue they had not used since 1887.

Reservations about the overall quality of the dogs were underlined by the fact that 'champions were conspicuous by their absence' in Bloodhounds, there was 'a most deplorable falling off' in Great Danes, St Bernards were 'a large lot, but the quality was not up to the mark', the entry in Borzois was 'not equal to that at Liverpool', Beagles too failed to attract any champions and Irish Setters could not be said to be 'extraordinary in quality'. Even so a number of breeds produced numerically strong, good quality entries, Fox Terriers alone producing four hundred dogs and more than double that number of entries. Once more the Royal Family gave Cruft their loyal support:

> 'Her Majesty sent a very large contingent of dogs from the Royal Kennels at Windsor Home Park, and was very successful, winning many prizes with her beautiful Pomeranians, one or two of them descendants of the Royal dog Marco. . . . But the Queen did not stop here, Her Majesty's favourites appropriating several specials, and the prize for best team of Pomeranians. . . . H.R.H. The Prince of Wales was also a very large exhibitor, and if not so successful as his Royal mother, yet won several prizes with his well-known wire-haired Basset Hounds'.

The gate was disappointing and, in spite of Cruft's efforts, the show closed without any exciting incident having happened', though the prospect of a walking match between Dockleaf and King Orry, two Bulldogs whose owners were proud of their dogs' athletic abilities certainly caused great excitement among many exhibitors. Cruft was by no means disheartened and expressed his confidence by extending his monopolistic lease on the Agricultural Hall for a further seven years and even expressing an intention to run two shows, in spring and autumn, each year.

Although there had been some praise for the 1893 show the overall tenor was not only much more critical than in previous years but Cruft had come very close to losing the Kennel Club's support, without which his enterprise would have been at an end. In the following year the *British Fancier* found it necessary to assure exhibitors that the show would be held under Kennel Club rules but, at the same time, to remind them that it was not a championship show, a fact which makes the extraordinary entries, albeit often slightly exaggerated by 'imaginative accountancy', all the more remarkable. Cruft was not the man to make the same mistakes twice and at the close of the 1894 show it was generally pronounced 'the best conducted of the series'. He seems to have concentrated his energies on running a show which would be above any criticism rather than, as in previous years, embarking on yet more innovations. Though Cruft did, of course, ensure that the show was bigger than ever.

By the time the 1895 show came along a new canine paper, *Our Dogs*, had appeared on the scene. It was the product of the joint enthusiasm of Theo Marples, a friend of Cruft's for many years, and Sir Humphrey de Trafford who by now had become President of Cruft's Show. If Cruft thought that he might be able to rely on uncritical comments from his friends he was quickly disabused. *Our Dogs'* initial remarks about the 1895 show accepted that 'the show in point of both numbers and quality exceeds any of its predecessors. An entry, deducting the art section, leaves it at the respectable total of 2849, but this, it must be borne in mind, is an inflated entry, inasmuch as every brace counts two, and the individual dog in every team is given a number which, with the auction class, goes to swell the whole to the figures above'. What Cruft had also been in the habit of doing, and public exposure would not prevent him from continuing, was in addition to counting entries in the art section, so that a stuffed dog or a painting was added to the grand total, and counting brace and teams and dogs sent for sale in a way which further helped his purpose, was to leave strategic gaps between the number which ended one class and that which began the next. By this means the last number in the catalogue would be appreciably higher than even his other manipulations could achieve. If the public were going to be attracted to the biggest dog show in the world then Cruft, one way or another, would give them what they wanted.

But *Our Dogs* weren't finished with their friend. They went on to record 'that every year exhibitors cry aloud at the many little items of indifference, not to say injustice, shown towards them, as alleged, by the management, they seem to forget their grievances and to yield to the invitation of the wily promoter and the flash schedule of prizes, which the "British Barnum" offers. The catalogue is a monument of commercial enterprise, and in point of fact inconveniently cumbrous in its crowded pages of advertisements, which are so intermixed with the show matter as to render its perusal a matter of much inconvenience. The show was, speaking generally, well organised, although, as usual, it suffered from the little drawbacks over which the management has no control. For instance, the very slow rate at which some of the judges performed their duties quite upset some of the arrangements. The ladies had a sore time of it, and the judges a worse in the darkness of the corner set apart for the judging of the Pomeranians and some of the Toys. The awards of the foreign judges were watched with great interest. Mr A. Latz created some little amusement by his measurement of the Borzois by the aid of a tape, a proceeding as illusive as it is ludicrous, unless it were possible to work out by arithmetic all the exact proportions of the dog's anatomy, which is necessary to arrive at excellencies and defects mathematically. . . . Mons. F. de Medeleer's awards were as unaccountable as they were unexpected, which will be seen when we state that the distinguished Belgian Schipperke breeder withheld the first prize for want of merit in, perhaps, the best class of Skips ever seen in England, whilst the Belgian champion from Blackpool was despatched without a card. . . . The judging was so protracted as to run into the second day before it was finally concluded.'

If anything the criticism directed at the 1896 show was even sharper. There was ready acknowledgement of Cruft's ability to attract large numbers of entries but large numbers were not matched by quality and Cruft's very obvious intention to make the show profitable remained a matter for comment even though his management of the show was, by now, giving rise to fewer criticisms.

'Although its proportions exceed those of any other show there is manifest the same mediocrity as has characterised most, if not all, its predecessors. As an honest exposition of the talent and status of dogdom, the Kennel Club's fixture stands in contrast to Cruft's, and must take precedence. Still, Mr Cruft has a happy knack of getting entries, and a show of dogs alone which reaches upwards of 3000, with the supplementary exhibition of pictures and other appurtenances, is certainly a huge affair. The catalogue is a marvel of commercial enterprise in its way, and the most comprehensive and complete dog show catalogue ever published. To the ordinary reader its page after page of advertisements, mixed up with the particulars of exhibits is an obnoxious arrangement although it will no doubt be a pleasant item to its author. Look where one will, at the premium list arrangement, at the catalogue, or at the management, the one thing seems to have been the guiding theme, viz., money – making it pay; and it is to the credit of its prime promoter that whilst many shows do not pay, Mr Cruft's undertaking comes out on the right side'.

Typically Cruft made selective use of *Our Dogs* scathing comments about his catalogue by advertising it as 'a marvel of commercial enterprise'. It had already been said that if Cruft received a guinea he would never return more than a pound but whilst his desire for profit may well have been rather too obvious for Victorian susceptibilities a number of his practices seem now to be perfectly acceptable and may simply have appeared before their time. For example exhibitors who wanted to compete for any of the hundreds of special prizes to which his advertisements devoted such attention, though many were not provided by Cruft at all but by individuals or by breed clubs, had to become subscribers to the show. Subscribers having the obligation to pay a subscription without, as members would have, any right to influence the management of the enterprise. Each year Cruft collected a large number of subscriptions from people anxious to compete for special prizes which he hadn't provided.

Far worse than the rather dubious nature of the commercial aspects was that, since only subscribers could win specials, in a class in which a subscriber with a very mediocre dog was beaten by good dogs belonging to non-subscribers it would be the mediocre dog which would win the special. The system turned the whole purpose of dog shows on its head but it is one which is now adopted by a number of societies. So too in all sorts of publications are advertisements mixed up with editorial material, indeed we would be hard put to it to find any periodical which doesn't employ precisely such an arrangement, inconvenient and obnoxious to readers though it remains.

One of the new trophies which Cruft's had on offer was a massive silver cup especially made by the Silversmith's Company and donated by Jaeger whose managing director Mr J. Taafe J.P. had insisted that a model of S. J. Stephen's Fox Terrier Stipendiary stand atop the trophy. The trophy was intended 'for the best conditioned dog, surely an odd qualification which, without collateral conditions, will allow of the worst dog in the show winning it!'. In fact the trophy, in this initial year at least, had precisely the opposite of its intended effect. Visitors 'were surprised to see the wretched condition in which a number of dogs were sent to the show, and which were, of course, properly consigned to the hospital by the able veterinary surgeon, who discharges the huge task of examining this large collection of dogs. How exhibitors can be so unmindful of their own or their dog's reputations, to say nothing of their callousness to their neighbours' dogs, in sending dogs to a show in such a state, . . . we cannot imagine'.

For its first six years of existence Cruft's had been uncritically welcomed by the popular press but had received a very mixed reception from the specialist press whose reporters were better able to see beyond and behind the gloss with which Cruft covered the entire event. It still remained very much on the cards that, in spite of Cruft's sometimes rather dubious efforts, the show was not producing the sort of return he wanted and it was, perhaps, for this reason, as well as the born showman's love of novelty, which led Cruft into paying greater attention to the subsidiary exhibitions of 'sporting appliances' and art works and to the wide range of trade stands which could be viewed at the show. He also sought out novel or neglected breeds and provided them with the sort of classification they could expect at no other show. It didn't matter to him that the classes were badly filled because the prize money to be won, and which had been widely advertised, was automatically reduced when numbers fell below a profitable level.

The important thing, in Cruft's eyes, was to be able to lay claim to providing far more classes than any other show, to be able to give the public a view of unusual breeds of dog, as well as of subsidiary exhibitions sometimes only tenuously connected with dogs, and as far as quality was concerned he was content to let the public's tendency to assume that the biggest was also the best answer all his critics. He was simply not interested in the dogs except as a means to an end. If poultry or cats or any other form of livestock could have yielded the same returns his name would now be associated with some animal other than dogs.

The need to allay concern raised by the way in which the show had allowed its own veterinary inspection to be circumvented in order to allow diseased Russian dogs into the show resulted, at Cruft's suggestion, in this aspect being given some prominence in the specialist press.

> 'No dog show in the kingdom is submitted to a more efficient and able veterinary examination than Cruft's, and the executive are to be highly complimented upon the splendid staff of inspectors, holding high positions in the profession, which are annually engaged to pass the exhibits at this great canine gathering. . . . We understand that out of the large number of dogs entered, only seven were rejected by the veterinary surgeons, which is an exceptionally clean bill of health for so large a show'.

Fear of frightening potential exhibitors rather than fear of the Kennel Club may well have motivated Cruft but it is to his credit that henceforth the conduct of the veterinary inspection was exemplary.

In 1897 the Kennel Club gave permission for its rules to be used at fifty-one shows of which twenty were regarded as Championship Shows. Of these only seventeen were all breed shows and these included Derby, Liverpool, Leicester, Manchester, Dublin, Royal Aquarium (Pet Dog Show), Armagh, Limerick, Strabane, Darlington, Nottingham, Birkenhead, Edinburgh (Scottish Kennel Club), Crystal Palace (Kennel Club), Belfast and Birmingham and, for the first time, Cruft's Show.

The entry for the 1897 show had once more increased, this time to 3072, needless to say:

> 'the largest ever obtained in connection with any show; but whilst numerically the show was an undoubted success, disappointment as to the all-round excellence of many of the classes was expressed by many critics present. Not that this matters one iota to the great Charles, who is much too conservative in his ideas to mourn the lack of quality so long as quantity is well represented, and that, in this particular, he gained his heart's desire, was shown by the mammoth entry. Sentiment in connection with Cruft's would be laughed at, for we all know the keenness of the British Barnum; but we cannot but express our regret at the meagre support accorded the venture by class exhibitors. There is plenty to be won at the show, if *kudos* is the aim of the breeder, whilst as regards "pots and pans" the specials are valuable and varied enough to please the most mercenary. It is, however, notorious how competition for the most coveted awards is so hedged round with restrictions that to become qualified to enter the lists with an idea of annexing specials, one is mulcted to a considerable tune. If, however, exhibitors *will* enter under such conditions, they have, in the words of Chevalier, "only themselves to blame". However, we all know what Cruft's is, and this year was no exception to what is now looked on as the general thing. It is, of the kind, a rattling good fixture, but, thank goodness, there is not another of the same kidney.'

One of the problems which even experienced exhibitors laboured under at this time, and goodness knows what occasional spectators made of the process, was the absence of any clear definition as to precisely what constituted a champion. The Kennel Club had itself not attempted to define the qualifications required of a champion until 1877, when three first prizes were all that was necessary. This was subsequently tightened to 'four first prizes at Shows registered in the Stud Book, one of the four first prizes being in a Champion Class'. This remained in force until 1885 when the number of wins required was increased to seven, three of which had to have been won in a champion class (one of the three being at one of the Kennel Club's own shows of which there were two each year, both held in London). A dog had to have not less than four wins before it could compete in a champion class. Even so the misleading term 'champion prize', of which a dog had to win three before it could claim the title of champion, remained in force until 1901 when the present term, Challenge Certificate, came into use.

The inability of Cruft's to attract an entry of quality dogs which, we might presume, would be owned by 'class exhibitors' perhaps lay in the absence of champion classes. Wins at Cruft's would assist a dog to qualify for competition in champion classes but, for those already qualified, would offer no other attractions. In 1897 the absence of quality was apparent in a number of breeds. St Bernards 'a very big section, relieved from mediocrity by the presence of Lord Hatherton'.

Prior to the 1897 show there had been some problems raised by the representatives of the London County Council who felt that the benching had, bearing in mind the vast numbers of visitors attracted to the show, been too closely spaced for either safety or comfort. As a result Spratts, at the eleventh hour, were obliged to dismantle, move and re-erect large sections of benching. Neither exhibitors nor visitors were aware of the trouble which had attended the efforts to make the show ready for them. Nor would they have been aware that the Prince of Wales' success in winning a first prize with Perla and van Willigen's Joop, who was second in the same class, would be followed by an official complaint. Perla was registered and shown as a Lapland Sledge Dog, Joop was shown as an Esquimaux dog. The basis of the complaint was that both were 'in every respect identical with all the dogs in the Elkhound class'.

For some unfathomable reason 1898 was a year in which shows failed to attract what they had come to regard as their customary entries.

> 'Even the wand of the "British Barnum" has this year failed to avert a contraction in the entry of this great fixture. Matters looked so serious for Cruft's Show at the time entries should have closed that an extension became necessary, and piteous appeals had to be made through a portion of the press to save the reputation, if not the fate, of the show. Even with the assistance of a "valuable paper", "valuable journal", etc., etc., and other efforts, the entry refused to rise to last year's level by some 200 entries, which is a little show in itself. The public is slow to learn, but in time, tire of the system of throwing sprats (no reference to the great Bermondsey firm, be it understood) to catch mackerels, which Cruft's Show has perfected'. With very few exceptions it seems that 1898 shows had suffered much the same fate, though since other shows did not exist primarily, indeed solely, with the intention of producing a profit a drop in entries was of less consequence to them than it must have been to Charles Cruft. It was noted that this need to attract entries resulted in a marked reduction in 'the indifference, and even rudeness in some cases', shown by 'leading

officials' which 'is certainly a move in the direction of arresting the waning popularity of this London Show'.

It was conceded that some changes had been made to Cruft's rather too profit-conscious regulations, though he had not yet steeled himself to dispense with the mercenary conditions which were hedged around the specials and which

> 'diverted so many from the leading winners to very highly commended, and even to commended dogs, quite contrary to the wish and intention of the donors, simply because exhibitors had not thought fit to subscribe one guinea a year to Cruft's Show'.

The organisation of the show proceeded along what was coming to be regarded as Cruft's well oiled lines. Only one judge, Charles Lane who was a member of the Cruft's Committee, rather spoiled the picture, by being very slow in completing his task and 'was judging black Pugs by gaslight up to a quarter of an hour before the show closed, viz., 9.45 p.m. Having started at 10 a.m. our Bristol friend nearly judged the clock round'. Earlier in the day Lane had had the by no means inconsiderable task of judging Maltese and Pomeranians, little wonder with such a schedule that he went on well into the night.

If Charles Lane's tardy judging caused some annoyance to Pug exhibitors their annoyance was perhaps balanced by the delight of the Cruft's President Sir Humphrey de Trafford at having, for the third successive year won the Jaeger 60 guineas cup for the best conditioned dog, possibly the nearest thing which Cruft's then had to a best in show award. Nor could Sir Humphrey have been less than delighted that his team of Irish Setters won second in the team competition, and his Irish Setter won the Sporting Bowl for the best sporting dog.

The last show of the 1800s might perhaps give some indication of the progress which Charles Cruft had made since 1891. Matters did not begin in an auspicious way but with probably the most damning attack yet by his friend Theo Marples and his President, Sir Humphrey de Trafford.

> 'A huge classification is promulgated in connection with this fixture, and exhibitors are informed in big type that there will be "no amalgamation" (although there may be cancellation), but judges are empowered to award one prize only where there are but three entries, which may be a first or may be a third. No show executive can boast of such an array of specials, but few of the more important ones can ever be won at all, and before any given by Cruft's committee can be won exhibitors must become subscribers to the show of at least one guinea, besides their entrance fees. For the convenience of subscribers a form is craftily – we mean Cruftily – inserted in the schedule authorising their

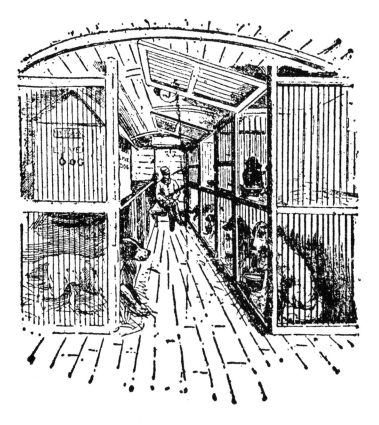

Charles Cruft even de-signed a special railway carriage for carrying dogs to his and other shows.

bankers to pay Cruft's the subscription which only needs filling up once when it will run for years indefinitely without any more trouble to the subscriber, and Cruft's Show will simply draw their guineas annually. But these are not all the advantages on tap at Cruft's. There is the Welcome Club, where more guineas are "welcomed" into Cruft's Show exchequer. Although exhibitors year after year realise that "all is not gold that glitters" in connection with the attractive premium lists of some dog show promoters, and in time tire of "dropping the substance for the shadow", somehow or other this great showman seems to be able for the time being to soothe their susceptibilities by some novelty, some new attraction, in his invitation to exhibitor's flies to "walk into his parlour", and into which he succeeds in alluring them. He has now got his show in full working order to "step inside, the performance is just going to begin". "The British Barnum" has lost one of his outside performers, and is this year relying on the little man with the big drum, who gives an occasional blow on his own trumpet, to play to the people inside, and again hopes to have a crowded house'.

Our Dogs' references to Cruft's use of 'another drummer' was a thinly veiled reference to the fact that Cruft had used another canine journal to promote his show and had done so by a public exchange of mutually laudatory letters.

Nor did matters improve but continued with a dispute between Charles Cruft and the South of England Black-and-Tan Terrier Club, a newly formed club which sought, unsuccessfully as it has since transpired, to try to revive the failing fortunes of this old British breed. The Club had written to Cruft to ask him to provide classes for the breed. These classes would be supported by the Club by the donation of specials providing that a judge from their club list was appointed. It was the sort of request which shows nowadays are invariably delighted to receive and ready to accede to. The reply from Charles Cruft, however, pointed out that 'for years I have been asking the Black-and-Tan Club to do something for us, but they have always turned a deaf ear to us. . . . I am asked to make certain classes and you will nominate the judge. I thank you for your most liberal and generous offer; but, as I have neither the power nor the inclination, I beg to decline. We have done without the Club for so long, we shall have to continue for this year. I am certain my committee would not allow you to dictate to them who they should elect to judge upon any conditions whatever'.

Whether Cruft had deliberately confused the request from this newly formed Southern Club with the older national organisation which had, apparently, spurned his overtures we cannot know, nor can we know whether his unjustified umbrage at being dictated to was calculated or the result of misreading the Club's perfectly reasonable proposal. We might, however, note that Cruft's displeasure was kindled by the refusal to support his show rather than what might have been seen as a failure to give the breed much needed support. Doubtless, however, Cruft said neither more nor less than the truth when he expressed certainty that his committee would not accept the Club's suggestion. His committee did precisely what he told them.

The first decade of Cruft's ended with a detailed assessment of the way in which the Show's rules acted unfairly against unsuspecting novice exhibitors.

> 'No other show in England, we believe, issues a premium list upon the same lines, in which many of the prizes and specials offered are so misleading. In fact, we are rather surprised that the Kennel Club will sanction Cruft's schedule, issued in its present form'. Attention was drawn to the small print of Cruft's rules which, contrary to the impression given by publicity and by various statements in the catalogue, stipulated that 'in all Open Classes if there are not more than two entries, a Prize Medal will be given for the prize; if more than two entries but under five, the First Prize will be £2; if there are five entries, a Second Prize of £1 will be given; and if there are seven entries, there will be a Third Prize of 10s'.

The value of Cruft's medals, which were bought cheaply by the gross was well known to seasoned exhibitors. Criticism which at first had understood the need to run the show as a sound commercial venture had subsequently sharpened into suggestions of a rather grasping and short sighted attitude and was now sharpened even further to the point at which it came very close to an allegation of sharp practice. In many respects the press were prepared to go along with Cruft's imaginative use of supposed facts. They were happy to advertise the 1900 show as the 16th Cruft's Show, knowing full well that it was only the 10th. They were content to accept that the Cruft's committee, so impressive on paper, was nothing more than a device for rubber stamping Cruft's own decisions and to offer a buffer against any Kennel Club criticism.

The committee consisted of Sir Humphrey F. de Trafford, Bart., who was still the President, C. Macdona, M.P., Chairman, Walter Glynn, vice-Chairman, Captain J. G. W. James and Messrs G. Ballard, J. S. Cowell, Jesse Fabian, Alfred George, H. Haylock, W. N. Higgs, Charles Lane, John Powers, G. W. Wharton, Harold Wood and Moses Woolland. At that time Sir Humphrey, Walter Glynn, a shipping magnate, and Harold Wood, a breeder and exhibitor of Scottish Terriers, were all influential members of the Kennel Club's Committee. Charles Lane was a well known exhibitor as well as a powerful journalist, John Powers was an exhibitor of Collies who was instrumental in ensuring that the breed gave its support to Cruft's inaugural efforts, Moses Woolland, an architect and successful businessman, bred and showed Spaniels.

After a couple of years in which the entry had not been as large as he would wish Cruft needed a big entry for his 1900 show, it was numbers not quality which attracted the public. In fact he was able to announce that the show had received 2203 dogs, large enough to attract the public though not nearly as large as he had laid claim to in the past. However even this number had been produced by manipulating the way in which the catalogue was numbered with even more vigour than he customarily employed.

But, serious though the accusations of chicanery might be, the worst criticism which had consistently been levelled against the show was its failure to attract top class entries. Let us take a close look at what was said about the quality represented at the 1900 show. The entry in St Bernards was described as numerically good but 'with few notable exceptions, the quality was inferior', Mastiffs were said to have 'showed no improvement over other shows held during the last few years'. Only one pack, the Dumfriesshire was represented among a very small entry of Otterhounds, in Dachshunds quality was said to have been 'conspicuous by its absence', Newfoundlands were won by an elderly dog still able to compete in the lower classes, quality seems not to have been high throughout the show.

Nor was everyone fooled by Cruft's method of inflating the apparent entry in order to create the sort of press story which might attract public attention. One exhibitor sat down to investigate the catalogue with some care.

'Sir, – Much comment has gone forth during the past week on the "enormous" number of dogs at Cruft's Show. Anybody turning to the end of the catalogue, on page 336, would naturally suppose that there were 2,203 dogs entered. On counting through the catalogue it will be found that the true number is 1,572. The method of arriving at the large number given is delightfully simple, and is simply to skip out numbers here and there, until in the end 631 dogs have been added to the actual number. The following table speaks for itself, and shows "how it is done":–

Number of dogs, as per catalogue	Actual number properly counted
99	79
300	251
500	417
700	566
1000	780
1400	1088
1600	1224
1801	1357
2203	1572

How long will the Kennel Club countenance this style of conducting a show?'

It seems that Charles Cruft, while establishing a show which was, when measured by the tests used by an unrepentant show and businessman, a success but that, by the end of the century he had failed to produce a show which commanded universal respect among exhibitors or which could be regarded as a top class exhibition of good quality dogs.

5. Into a New Reign

*T*he 1901 Cruft's Show took place under the cloud of Queen Victoria's death and of a refusal by Theo Marples, by then one of the country's leading judges, to officiate at the show which he had so consistently criticised. Cruft responded by not inviting Marples to the Press Luncheon. Theo Marples had to buy his own lunch. By the time the 1902 show came round, however, the rift had been healed and invitations were forthcoming and accepted.

It was, however, the weather rather than the relationship between Charles Cruft and Theo Marples which produced the lowest temperatures.

> 'The present Cruft's show will be memorable for one thing, and that is the extreme coldness of the weather. It was simply perishing in the great Agricultural Hall, and even northern exhibitors, who are supposed to be more inured to the cold than the Cockney, complained. We felt for the ladies, who must have felt the pinch'.

Nowadays when even tented shows held in October are heated it is difficult to appreciate that the Agricultural Hall, with its vast space and glass roof, was totally unheated. February, 1901 may have been unusually cold but it could never be expected to be tropical.

However the dispute between Cruft and Marples did not prevent recognition of Cruft's efforts to improve his show. He was commended for not whitewashing the barriers which surrounded each ring and which had, in the past, marked the clothing of the ladies and gentlemen who leaned on them.

Of the quality of the breeds on display there was, as usual, little praise. St Bernards were described as 'goodish', Great Danes as 'a fairly good group', Deerhounds were 'very strong' but in Collies there was 'much dissatisfaction'. The Rev. Hans F. Hamilton 'did feel keenly the defeat of his dog, Tartan, who was never in such form, and Lady Craven was under the impression that her dog had not even been looked at.' Collies had been judged by Mr A. J. Webster from Ayr.

Temperature apart it seems that the 1901 Cruft's Show was remarkable because in Greyhounds, Mr F. H. Bottomley's, Helen Macgregor, swept all before her to win three firsts and the championship while the same owner, in 'Whippets or Miniature Greyhounds was equally lucky, capturing nine firsts and Lady Grosvenor's 25-guineas cup outright'. Emphasis was placed on the word outright because 'when a special is won at Cruft's outright we think it deserves emphasising'.

During 1901, and to come into force on 1 January 1902 the Kennel Club had outlawed the sweepstake system, whereby prize money was adjusted according to the number of entries in the class, at shows where championship points were on offer. As a result of this change Cruft was obliged to amend what many exhibitors had come to regard as one of the worst aspects of his show, indeed it is entirely possible that the change in the Kennel Club rules was made in order to achieve just this effect because few, if any, other championship shows used the sweepstake system.

In 1902 entries for Cruft's closed on 27 January, the show took place, just sixteen days later, from 12 to 14 February. This short interval between close of entries and the show itself was not an unusual one but Cruft had more than a usual number of entries to deal with. Receiving, processing and producing a catalogue, especially one which contained a mass of advertisements and other material, for a show with nearly 3000 entries in the space of little more than two weeks must have demanded a very efficient office organisation. The show itself was commended for being well run, and, in spite of arctic weather conditions, attracted even more spectators than usual as well as an increased number of doggy folk.

Facilities for railway travel to Cruft's had consisted of special carriages attached to regular trains but in 1903 Cruft had managed to persuade the railway companies to introduce reduced fares for Cruft's exhibitors and visitors. This was regarded as a significant breakthrough because 'if these cheap bookings were timed to suit exhibitors there would be a very much accelerated traffic in this direction, and dog shows would also benefit by increased entries, since many exhibitors would themselves go with their dogs, who now send them, and would no doubt enter more dogs as a result'. More and more innovations which were introduced by Cruft were the sort which would assist all exhibitors and other shows. His motives may not have been altruistic but the benefits of many of his innovations were felt well beyond his own show.

Whether it was cheaper railway travel, the 35 classes which Cruft had added to the schedule or even more imaginative counting of entries which resulted in an increased entry, to 3129, for Cruft's, 1903 is difficult to say but Cruft was not slow to ensure that the press were aware that 'this certainly exceeds the total entry of any other show ever held in the world'. He also provided the press with a proposed order of judging, a plan of where each breed would be benched and, within a few days of entries closing, details of the entry in each breed. In addition the press were also able to publish a list of what were described as 'the more notable exhibitors' which included Lady Dunleath, The Countess of Rosslyn, Lady Holland, Princess Montglyon, assorted other titled ladies, the Right Hon. Lord Redesdale, Sir Claud Alexander and various gentlemen of military or civil rank. Was Cruft trying to demonstrate that, with his principal Royal supporter now dead and others absent, the show remained attractive to 'quality exhibitors'?

Certainly he pulled out all the stops for his 1903 show and was rewarded, not just by a record entry, but by spring-like weather which also produced a record gate.

> 'On entering the show itself, if there was no other indication of success it was to be seen in the countenance of the "British Barnum", whose features had a very "carriage paid" look about them. But the fact of the entry being a record had already been heralded throughout the length and breadth of the land. This was enough to put Mr Cruft on good terms with himself, and when it is recorded that the gate was on all fours with the entry, there can be little wonder at him being all smiles. In fact we never remember seeing the great showman in a happier mood, and Mr Cruft can be a very acme of courtesy when he likes'.

Nor were the press any less impressed by the arrangements for the show than they were with Cruft's unaccustomed geniality. 'The arrangements in connection with the show were all that could be desired. Everything has been so well thought out in connection with this show, and all details so perfected, that only the most stupid can go wrong or suffer inconvenience.' Furthermore it seems too that the quality of dogs attracted to Cruft's had also begun to improve and in a number of breeds the quality of the entry received favourable comment.

The 1904 show 'voted the best which the astute Mr Charles Cruft has had the pleasure of engineering' continued the trend. The worst the press could find to say was that the hall was not clean and there were not enough catalogues or stewards. Hardly the sort of criticisms with which Cruft had had to contend in the past. In 1904 the Kennel Club had licensed 386 shows and thirty-eight had been held under Kennel Club rules. Of these twenty-seven were ranked as Championship Shows, though only sixteen of these were all breed shows, perhaps only now was Cruft's beginning to reap the benefit of being among this exclusive band.

The Liverpool Championship Show which had traditionally preceded Cruft's and with which the quality of dogs attracted to Cruft's had often been unfavourably compared had come to an end in 1904 and so, in 1905, Cruft's had the privilege and undoubted advantage of opening 'the season in connection with the more classical fixtures, but it is a very hard show to follow – in fact, it stands with only one rival, viz., the Kennel Club's Show.' Because of its new position as the opening championship show of the season Cruft's found itself as the first show at which the Kennel Club's remodelled rules could be subjected to a practical test.

The decision to amend the rules had largely been forced on the Kennel Club by a member of the Committee, Edgar Farman, who was also Editor of *The Dog Owners' Annual* in which he had described the existing rules as 'a complicated mass of disordered sentences, framed with no system, full of repetition and complexity' and this of a set of rules which, when they had first appeared had been welcomed largely because they were so superior to anything which had gone before. The criticism, though perhaps justified, provides a measure of the way in which the Kennel Club's existence had not only improved matters in the world of pedigree dogs but how it had also increased expectations.

Since the 1904 show Sir Humphrey de Trafford had relinquished his position as Cruft's President, having retired from the Kennel Club Committee four years previously. He was replaced as Cruft's President by His Grace The Duke of Beaufort whose previous connections with the world of dog shows had not been apparent.

'Mr Charles Cruft must have shaken hands with himself when he closed his books with the record entry of 3854, which exceeded last year's total, also a record, by about 300 nominations. The show . . . was not only a colossal one, but we never remember seeing the Agricultural Hall so well attended. Everything that an ingenious mind and long experience of the showman's art seems to have been thought out by the "British Barnum", even to an addition of sixpence to the entrance fee to meet the increased toll levied by the Kennel Club under its new rules for the privilege of holding a show under its auspices. It is the larger shows that will feel this new tariff most, and, of course, none more than Cruft's, which will be mulcted in the sum of about £20. To meet this Mr Cruft has contrived to collect into his coffers 3,854 sixpences, or a little short of £100! That is true cruftonian finance, and worthy of a Goschen, a Harcourt, or Ritchie! "it's an ill wind that blows nobody good", and Mr Cruft will no doubt feel that this increased KC impost has been a "blessing in disguise".

We never remember seeing a more orderly or better managed show, less friction and less grumbling at the judging, although there was some dissatisfaction, and in one or two cases the awards were certainly such as could not well be sustained. The quality was above the average seen at Cruft's Show and the bill of health almost a clean one, we understand. . . . Mr Cruft himself was more genial than we have ever seen him, at the show – and well he might be. He was here, there, and everywhere, being ably assisted by his son and heir, Charles the Second, and will never be dead while his son lives. Mrs Cruft has invariably assisted her intrepid husband in his managerial duties, but has, we regret to learn, been indisposed, but still bravely put in an appearance at the show. Mr Cruft himself was a bit off colour, but the big entry and the big gate proved excellent healing medicine'.

In 1906 Cruft's began to feel the benefit of Liverpool's demise in the form of an entry of much improved quality but even so it still fell well below that to be seen at either the Crystal Palace, where the Kennel Club held its shows, and Manchester, then embarking on developments which would eventually lead to proud, though not unjustified, claims to being 'The Northern Classic'. There had been shows in Manchester almost from 1860 but the Manchester Society didn't come into being until, and as a direct result of, a show to celebrate the Queen's Golden Jubilee in 1887, the present Manchester Show Society being founded in the following year.

'Invariably the show attracts a good entry and a large attendance of the public, and as a commercial speculation must be a good thing for the promoter, who, if rumour speaks truly, annually nets a handsome profit from the enterprise. What that profit is in actuality may only be guessed at, since no figures are ever issued to the dog-loving public, but it may be taken for granted that out of 22 shows which have now been held the promoter has amassed a snug fortune.

No one, we are sure, begrudges him of it, but one would expect so successful a showman to extend a little more consideration towards his patrons in many ways. Grumblings are both loud and deep at the unnecessary "wait" on the first morning of the show before early arrivals from the provinces can enter the show. It is neither conducive to the health, well-being, nor temper of either owners or exhibits to be kept hanging about an hour or two in the cold raw morning air before the dogs can be taken in the hall to their benches. If, however, Mr Cruft is anxious that you should not be in the hall too soon he takes pretty good care that you shall make up for it by staying as late as possible at night, and if you happen to live far away, and wish to get home on the evening of the last day of the show, you will have to pay 5s (25p) or 2s 6d (12½p) for the privilege, a condition which we make bold to say should not be imposed, but which many pay rather than spend another night, and, incidentally, an hotel bill in town.

Then, again, most of the principal special prizes – at all events those worth winning – are confined to subscribers to Cruft's Show, which means a guinea per annum for the privilege of competing for special prizes which at shows promoted by canine associations are open to everybody, subscribers or not.

The show, big as it is, is not actually of such leviathan proportions as would appear on the surface. The catalogue contains classes numbered up to 592, but there are not actually 592 classes by a long way, and although the entry has been stated to be 3,888, it does not pan out to that number by some hundreds.'

Year after year the same criticisms had been made and, year after year, Cruft had chosen to ignore them. The show was a speculative enterprise intended to produce profit for Charles Cruft. There have been other shows run for private profit but none have survived for long and few others, if any, have received the Kennel Club's even reluctant blessing. Cruft may well have liked dogs, it would have been extraordinarily churlish not to since it was dogs that turned him into a rich man but he didn't share his exhibitors' interests or enthusiasms. He wasn't interested in dogs except in so far as they could be used to increase the profit which his show generated. Nor was he, during these early years, interested in satisfying the customers unless satisfaction resulted in an increased profit. Exhibitors, as far as Cruft was concerned, could grumble as much as they liked and the press could annually repeat their catalogue of criticism but unless, by responding to this dissatisfaction, he could increase the profit his show produced he was unlikely to change anything. Which is not to say that Cruft was resistant to change, indeed the history of Cruft's is a tale of change and innovation. He was, however, resistant to changes which did not increase profit.

In 1906 he sought to increase the show's public appeal by a display of 'commendable patriotism in having his bevy of keepers dressed in sailor uniform, the kennel "Jack Tars" being also drilled to their duties by a show general, which formed a novel feature of the show'. Whether this inappropriate nautical flavour was a product of Cruft's own interest in sailing, the ready availability of nautical uniforms or was conceived as a means to appeal to their Majesties. Queen Alexandra, who as Princess of Wales had been a regular exhibitor, having re-established Royal patronage of the show by entering a team of Borzois and Toy dogs, though the death of her father, King Christian IX of Denmark, plunged the court into mourning and resulted in the Royal entries being withdrawn. However Cruft wasn't going to let a little matter of Royal mourning prevent him from letting the press know of the renewed and very welcome Royal support.

It was in 1906 that a new trophy made its strangely unheralded appearance and embarked on a short and almost unnoticed career. In the past there had been trophies for the best terrier, best retriever, best sporting breed, best pet dog (pet being used to describe dogs, other than toys, which had no sporting purpose), best toy dog and best conditioned dog but none which could, even remotely be regarded as an award for the best dog in the show. What now might seem to be a logical and obvious extension of deciding which was best in the various groups of dogs represented at this and other shows is something which appears to have been regarded as having no importance. However, in 1906, what was described as a 'syndicate of judges, including Mr F. Gresham, Mr Elias Bishop, Mr E. B. Joachim, Mr H. Hewlock, Mr H. Sawtrell, Mr J. Edkins, Mr F. C. Hignett, Mr L. P. C. Astley and Mr W. H. Reeves' selected 'from a rare muster in the ring when competition for the antique silver cup for the best champion in the show was reached. . . . the Collie, Wishaw Leader, proved to be the winner, the Retriever, High Legh Blarney, being reserve'. The competition still didn't refer to the Best in Show winner, and still would not do so for a number of years, but it might not be unreasonable to regard the Collie, Ch Wishaw Leader as, in all but name, the first Cruft's Best in Show winner.

One of the advantages which Cruft's show enjoyed as a result of the disappearance of the Liverpool Show was that, as the first major show of the new season, a number of puppies would make their show debut. Additional interest would be generated among breeders and exhibitors by seeing how the winning dogs of the previous year had developed during the winter and how they would fare against the newcomers. This, in itself, made the show especially exciting, even for seasoned old exhibitors, and doubtless also added to the excitement felt by casual spectators. The show retained this particular source of excitement until the Kennel Club, faced with a need to reduce the show's size, was obliged, in 1965, to restrict the number of dogs entered at Cruft's. As a result Manchester, as the show after Cruft's and the first major championship show of the new season open to all competitors, inherited this particular mantle.

Although the quality of the dogs, in 1906, was said to have been good all round quality seems to have been very varied. Bloodhounds were said to be 'select, but call for little comment', St Bernards were 'a grand collection' with added excitement being provided by the debut of Nobility, a son of Ch. Tannhauser. Great Danes were more remarkable for quantity than quality, while Newfoundlands were said to be 'more select than numerous', though a new Landseer, King Nep, made a successful debut. Mastiffs were poor in both numbers and quality, as they had been for some years and in Deerhounds 'honours were aisy'.

1907 seems to have begun with a distinct lack of enthusiasm among exhibitors. The Rotherham show, just four days before the show was due to take place, had received only five entries in twenty-five classes. Bolton was in an even worse plight with five entries in 215 classes. Cruft's too did not come up to its usual numbers, even after these had been subjected to the usual manipulations. 3473 entries must have been a disappointment. Disappointment was allayed by the fact that Queen Alexandra had again entered a number of dogs. So also did the Countesses of Aberdeen, of Cairns, of Gosford, of Chesterfield and the Baroness von Boesalager whose support was astutely used by Cruft to even further boost his show's prestige.

The top entry in 1907 was made by the two Fox Terrier breeds with 302 entries, the various Retrievers produced 252 entries, Bulldogs 276 and Pomeranians 165.

Mrs Vale Nichols' Pomeranian, Ch. The Sable Mite, was Best Champion and won the Cruft's Pet Dog Bowl in 1907.

That year new grumbles surfaced. Spectators, by now accustomed to the sort of facilities provided at other shows, especially the Kennel Club Shows at the Crystal Palace, were critical of the absence of ringside seating. Judges, who at Cruft's were older than at most other shows, also found the absence of seating and the imposition of heavy work loads, burdens which they were becoming less prepared to accept as a necessary part of the alleged privilege of judging for Charles Cruft.

During the show Cruft was himself taken ill and his place was briefly taken by his son, Cecil, but 'the excitement of the event and the great responsibility of it made him forget his gout, the pain from which he seems to have postponed until the show is over, when he will doubtless count up his gain. This is a fine thing for gout.'

During the show itself secretaries from St Albans and Darlington were busily touting for entries for their shows and after it Burton-on-Trent and Wakefield admitted to having received no entries for their 66 class show, Kings Lynn were finding that £250 in prizes and numerous specials were not exerting any great attractions for exhibitors. St Albans, however, were the only ones who openly placed the blame on competition from Cruft's. They had 225 classes, 75 specials and some of the best judges but had received fewer than 50 entries. They simply couldn't compete with Charles Cruft's extravaganza. It would appear that, even in 1907, some shows were beginning to feel the adverse effects of a congested show calendar.

For the second year there was a competition for Best Champion all breeds in the show, it was judged by Theo Marples and Chris Houlker who awarded the prize to Mrs Vale Nicolas' Pomeranian Ch. The Sable Mite. Unfortunately, like so many of Cruft's other special prizes, and certainly those which might be regarded as having some real significance, the prize was open only to competition by Cruft's subscribers and so unless those who were prepared to part with a guinea each year were also those who owned the best dogs we cannot say with certainty that the award represents the judges' free choice for the best dog in the show or even of the best champion. Indeed there were years when the best champion was beaten in other classes which were not confined to subscribers. Nevertheless it was certainly a step towards a competition to find the best dog in the show.

In 1909 Charles Cruft decided, after a show at which entries had been, by his standards, disappointing, to celebrate the Show's Silver Jubilee. That it was only eighteen years after the first Cruft's Show was neither here nor there. By including his Terrier Shows he could get to twenty-three years and that was close enough to a Silver Jubilee for his purposes. In any case should anyone point to the discrepancy he could cite the precedent set by the Kennel Club themselves who, within five years of their foundation in 1873, were advertising their twelfth annual

Theo Marples was both a critic and friend of Charles Cruft. He was also a regular member of the panel of judges which decided the destination of the show's many special prizes and trophies.

show. It seems that the standard of numeracy was not high among dog show promoters and, in Cruft's case at least, tended to be used to improve the show's attraction.

Even so the entry was, once more, down. One reason for the drop was undoubtedly Cruft's refusal to use the entry forms which the Kennel Club had recently made standard for all shows held under their rules. If he had expected the Kennel Club to display their customary tolerant attitude towards him he was disappointed and he had to withdraw his forms and make use of the Kennel Club's.

In Britain it had become customary, as it still is, to bench dogs according to their breed. On the continent dogs were usually benched according to their ownership. Cruft's early experience had been on the continent and he must have realised that such a system, while inconvenient for spectators and exhibitors alike, would be very much easier for the show management. The degree of inconvenience to spectators and exhibitors and the advantage to the show's management being increased as the size of the show increased. In 1909, once more displaying his true priorities, he dispensed with the usual British benching arrangement and adopted the continental system. The result was chaos. Cruft was strongly advised not to repeat the experiment.

One of the talking points of the show was a proposal then being considered by the Kennel Club which would mean that 'no sporting dogs should be allowed to qualify fully as champions on the show bench until they had competed at field trials, and had been awarded a prize or at least a certificate of merit'. It had already become apparent that a number of sporting breeds were beginning to develop two distinct types, the one to be found in the field and the other in the show ring. This alarmed many of their supporters and especially those who were interested in both activities. The Kennel Club's proposal must, however, have alarmed show promoters who, if it was accepted, could expect far fewer champions at their shows. Eventually the proposal was adopted in a slightly diluted form in that it was applied only to gundogs, other sporting breeds such as hounds and terriers having no restriction imposed on them, though some breeds would continue to persuade the Kennel Club to include them. To what extent the restriction has achieved its intended effect is debatable but there can be no doubt but that its intentions were laudable.

Uncharacteristically Cruft refused to accept the dogs entered by Lord and Lady Decies, which arrived at the show without the labels issued by Cruft's. 'The executive of Cruft's Show', a somewhat tongue in cheek report said, 'are noted for the rigid manner in which the rules of the show are interpreted'. The incident was perhaps given less notice than it might otherwise have been because Queen Alexandra was once more among the Borzoi exhibitors though was not among the winners. A visit to the St Bernard and Collie rings by 'the notorious young lady' Miss Violet Charlesworth also set tongues wagging. Sadly the lady's notoriety did not rest on any activities as a militant suffragette or even as a courtesan but quite simply on a propensity, which would nowadays be unremarkable, if not unexceptional, for wearing masculine clothing. Miss Charlesworth might even be regarded as the forerunner of a fashion which, according to Croxton Smith, Patrick Chalmers would later claim made men and women at dog shows virtually indistinguishable.

Chalmers mentioned his difficulty to a stranger standing by him at the ringside.

'That young person over there, for instance', he said, 'boy or girl?'

'Oh, she's a girl,' said the stranger. 'I happen to know; she's my daughter.'

'Sorry; I didn't know you were her father.'

'I'm not; I'm her mother.'

Mrs Borman's Borzoi, Ch. Ramsden Rajah, won Cruft's Hound Bowl in 1909.

Thus far in the extraordinary career of Cruft's its founder had claimed to have achieved entries of 3888 twice, once in 1906 and again in 1908. Both were a huge increase over the 536 entries attracted to his first terrier show and the 2437 attracted to the first Cruft's Show in 1891. Perhaps it was inevitable, therefore, that from 1908 he would face a period when entries were less easily come by. In spite of an increased number of classes the 1909 show had 325 fewer entries than in the previous year and in 1910 another 86 entries were lost, again against an increased classification. Cruft, however, must have taken some consolation from the fact that a number of other shows, including the Scottish Kennel Club's and the Kennel Club's were also finding it difficult to retain their former popularity among exhibitors. In 1910 Cruft had scheduled classes for 47 breeds, plus classes for foreign dogs. Fox Terriers, Smooth and Wire, and Spaniels each with 298 entries achieved the highest numbers, though Fox Terriers appeared to be losing popularity while Toy Spaniels were gaining it. Behind them were Pomeranians, whose 203 entries was an increase over previous years, no other breeds got more than 200 entries though seven – Airedales, Bulldogs, Retrievers, Scottish Terriers, Toy Spaniels, West Highland White Terriers and St Bernards, whose entry was double that of 1909 – all managed over a hundred. At the other end of the scale the combined classes for Skye and Cairn Terriers had a mere five entries, Maltese had seven, Mastiffs eight and Otterhounds had ten. Was this the start of the gradual slide in the popularity of British breeds?

Once more, however, Cruft managed, by luck or good management, to produce an event which detracted interest from his falling entries. Queen Alexandra had signalled her intention of visiting the show and 'naturally, the great Charles was highly elated at this gracious Royal recognition of his efforts to maintain for the City of London a show of dogs which has become international in its character, and in magnitude and importance only second to the Kennel Club's great show itself.' Although the visit seems to have been arranged on the spur of the moment it was not an event of which Cruft was without previous experience. Though Cruft's had not previously been honoured by a visit from Their Majesties it had been 'his pleasant duty to make arrangements for the reception of Her Majesty (then T.R.H. the Prince and Princess of Wales) at a dog show held at Laycock's Dairy Yard, in Liverpool Road, N., nearly forty years ago. About ten years later, at the York Dog Show, Mr Cruft was again called upon to prepare for the reception of Their Royal Highnesses.' Cruft knew precisely how to deal with this welcome and exciting turn of events. A Royal box, surmounted by the Royal Arms, was hastily prepared, and:

> 'furnished in luxuriousness which would, we should say, almost vie with the Royal box at Ascot. The tapestry was recherche, the suite of furniture being gilt, upholstered in pale blue silk – the Queen's favourite colour. A slope was arranged for the march past of the prize winners, who were appropriately marshalled to the point of inspection by the show stewards, attired as "Jack Tars". Nearby trade stands were decked in flags. After viewing the larger dogs paraded before her the Queen visited the smaller dogs on their benches and is said to have taken especial interest in the Pekingese and the West Highland White Terriers.

However the great Charles' elation must have been tempered by what was described as a 'boycott' by Pomeranian exhibitors. It seems that the Secretary of the Pomeranian Club had written to Cruft to ask if, in deference to the delicacy of both these small dogs and his lady members and with regard to an exceptionally cold winter and the Agricultural

Hall's nonexistent heating, Cruft might agree to Pomeranians leaving the show at 8 pm rather than 10 pm as was customary. Cruft's reply was predictable and so a number of lady members of the Pomeranian Club, though not the Club itself, decided to organise a boycott. The result was an increase of nineteen in the Pomeranian entry!

Cruft must have faced 1911 with some trepidation because he had lost his position as the first major championship show of the year to the Birmingham National Dog Show, held in January about three weeks prior to Cruft's. He had also to combat the growing reluctance of exhibitors to support three day shows, a format to which only Cruft's and the Kennel Club Shows continued to cling. Even so the entry was up by 205 on the previous year, the weather was fine and mild and the gate enormous. As far as the dogs were concerned the talking point was the first appearance, at Cruft's, of Sealyham Terriers, with a very creditable fifty-six entries, and 'which appear to be thoroughly "catching on". They

Mrs Mayor's Bulldog, Ch. Silent Duchess, won Cruft's Non-Sporting Bowl in 1909.

seem to be a hard-bitten terrier, so far as appearance goes, with the type getting more and more fixed. Mr J. H. Howell M.F.H., judged, and paid attention, of course, to their underground proclivities.' Concern was expressed at the poor entries and standard of Mastiffs and Welsh Terriers but gossip centred around the appearance of 'at least one out-and-out Pomeranian – attempting to personate the breed' in the Shetland Sheepdog classes, of some misdemeanour in the Rough Collie classes which called for Kennel Club investigation and of the theft of the gold collar from round Mrs Knowles' Pug's neck. Bulldogs made the top entry of 220, followed by Wire Fox Terriers with 216, and Pomeranians with 200. Clydesdale Terriers had 5 entries and were soon to follow the Old English White Terrier into oblivion.

A small innovation introduced by Cruft was to supply his patrons with 'very pretty badges of a golden hue'. It is a tradition which the Kennel Club maintains, if in somewhat modified form.

In 1912 Cruft achieved what he liked best, another record entry and one which, at 3950 must have been tantalisingly close to 4000 to tempt him to inflate it just a little more. Quality was said to be noticeably below that present at the Kennel Club's show. 'The not very elaborate judges' badges this year were a cardboard representation of the shamrock, the meaning of which perplexed most people. The most feasible solution of this tribute to the Emerald Isle was the incident of the great effort which is being put forth by Parliament this year to pass a Home Rule Bill for Ireland'. Was Cruft allowing his private opinions to obtrude on the show or was another explanation the real one?

Of the dogs, Otterhounds with a single entry for Mr S. W. Varndell, Master of the Crowhurst Otterhounds, had the lowest entry but the talking point of the whole show was 'the exhibition by Col the Hon. le Poer Trench of a quartet of yellow Russian Retrievers, bred by the Colonel, and whose ancestors were originally imported from Russia in Asia in 1858 by Lord Tweedsmouth (then Mr Marjoribanks), and which were until comparatively recently kept and bred exclusively in his lordship's kennel and that of his nephew, the late Lord Ilchester. The Right Hon. Lewis Harcourt has made this interesting variety a speciality, but it is alleged that for want of fresh blood his strain contains an outcross of some sort'. It was the sort of story which must have appealed to Cruft's tastes and what did it matter that it wasn't true? These dogs were the forerunners of the Golden Retriever, and would be given their own register, as Retrievers (Golden or Yellow), by the Kennel Club in the following year. It was true that the breed had been developed by Lord Tweedsmouth not from imported dogs from Russia but, more mundanely, by judicious crossing between yellow Flat Coat puppies which appeared from time to time and the local liver Tweed-water Spaniels.

Royalty again supported the show with entries, Queen Alexandra

London hotels in 1911 were pleased to welcome Cruft's exhibitors and their dogs.

making several entries which, however did not appear at the show due to the death of the Duke of Fife, the Queen's son-in-law.

In 1913, with clouds of war gathering over Europe, Cruft, for the first time, achieved more than 4000 entries though with an increase in the number of classes by 232. One interesting point about the show was that Arthur Heinemann, a prolific sporting journalist, whose often inconsistent opinions delivered under the pseudonym 'Peep-out', have encouraged the belief that he was vehemently opposed to all dog shows, judged the classes for working terriers. It seems that, like the Rev. Jack Russell before him his objection to dog shows is something which, in the face of all the evidence, exists entirely and only in the imagination of those who themselves harbour such an antipathy. The existence of these classes also points to some concern that terriers were perhaps already losing contact with their plebeian ancestry and of an early recognition of the need to preserve the old working types.

In 1914 Queen Alexandra again paid a visit to Cruft's, once more breaking all records with 4239 entries. She was escorted to the Royal box, this time decked in French grey silk, Louis XV furniture and cut glass bowls of flowers. Classes for Working terriers were again scheduled but with a mere seven entries it was apparent that owners of working terriers were otherwise engaged in mid February. Sealyhams, still very much a genuine working terrier though used principally for badger digging which did not recognise a fixed season of activity, mustered 173 entries to rival the 178 achieved by Smooth Fox Terriers and beating the Airedales by 170. Black-and-tans though were in a poor state with just two entries and Old English Whites even worse with none at all. With 300 entries Wire Fox Terriers were the most popular breed at the show. Dachshunds whose popularity had suffered because of the War were down to 72 entries.

The 1915 Cruft's Show took place in a nation which was at war but which, as had already been demonstrated at the Birmingham Show, was in no mood to have its enjoyment curtailed. In the circumstances an entry of 3447 was a great achievement. It wasn't much helped by two Italian Greyhounds and the same number of Working Terriers, even Wire Fox Terriers, though still with the highest entry in the show, were down to 196. All eyes were on the Sealyhams now with 122 entries and fully justifying their status as the 'coming breed'. It would have been most unlike Cruft to miss an opportunity to make some suitable and noticeable patriotic gesture at the show. This he did by persuading the Editor of *John Bull*, Mr Horatio Bottomley, to make his debut as an exhibitor in the Old English Mastiff ring, a move which might also have attracted much needed, if incidental, attention to this neglected breed. Mr Bottomley's dog, Brompton Duke, won all before him and its owner was praised for his attitude towards the war 'which has raised him to a great height of eminence in the estimation of the people of this country, with which he has become an idol almost'.

Horatio Bottomley was the recently re-elected Independent M.P. for Hackney who seemed to thrive on bankruptcy and whose *John Bull* magazine, a sensational and jingoistic publication, blatantly exploited the prevailing public mood. Less patriotically the magazine was also used, by Bottomley, as part of a fraudulent scheme to sell Government Bonds for which he would, in 1922, be sent to jail for seven years. The patriotic idol's clay feet were thoroughly exposed.

Another gesture, which Cruft doubtless saw as a patriotic one, was to drop the Dachshund classes though, such was the public feeling against all things Germanic that the move was also prudent.

The entry in 1916 fell yet again but Cruft was buying himself a great deal of publicity, admiration and future support by his determination to carry on even after the Kennel Club, the Scottish Kennel Club and the Irish Kennel Club had all decided to close down for the duration of the war. Charles Cruft was not going to let a little matter of war prevent him from running his show! By carrying on Cruft was providing, in the face of the very real possibility of financial loss, a service which breeders, exhibitors and the public greatly appreciated and which deserved their admiration.

The 3235 entries he received was the lowest number since 1903 but reflected reduced breeding, the closure of the Kennel Club's registration department so that new puppies could not be registered and shown, and difficulty in travelling rather than any reduced enthusiasm for his show. Bulldogs topped the entry with 220, Wire Fox Terriers had 219 and Basset Hounds had 5. Classes for St Bernards, Newfoundlands and Dandie Dinmonts had followed Dachshunds into oblivion though for different reasons. Queen Alexandra was prevented from attending the show because of a heavy cold and must have been doubly disappointed not to see King George carry off four first prizes with his Labrador bitch, Wolferton Jet. At the post-show Judges' dinner Sir Lindsay Hogg got a round of applause when he 'exhorted Sealyham exhibitors . . . not to forget the utilitarian purposes of the breed, and he despised excessive trimming'. It hadn't been a vintage show but in the circumstances was a remarkable achievement for which Cruft deserved and received great credit.

The year 1917 began with Cruft's under threat not just as a result of hostilities overseas but also from within Britain. A proposal had been put forward that keeping and breeding dogs for exhibition was a waste and an extravagance which should be punitively taxed. The vehemence of fallacious arguments was such as to persuade Government to say that the idea 'might' be considered. It is apparent that neither the anti-dog lobby nor its arguments are recent innovations. Worse still, from Cruft's point of view, was that the Government had recently imposed restrictions on rail travel and although a concession had been won for exhibitors and their dogs they still faced an increase of fifty per cent in rail fares. When, contrary to his usual custom, Cruft failed to announce the entry prior to the show the writing on the wall was apparent. In fact he had received just 2500 entries, the lowest since his very first show in 1891. Even with a much reduced classification and in the face of mounting difficulties the entry must have been bitterly disappointing. Worse still it must have come very close to losing money, even if it didn't actually do so. The problems of finding labour to run the event, the shortage of trade stands and the reluctance of spectators to venture into a building which they regarded as an easy target for zeppelins must have made it an unusually tense event which Cruft was unlikely to repeat in 1918. Patriotism could only be taken so far.

In fact the decision was taken out of Cruft's hands by the army requisitioning the Agricultural Hall as a warehouse for military equipment. Cruft reluctantly followed the example set by other London shows and temporarily went out of business. The next Cruft's would be in 1921.

6.   *From One Interruption to*
Another

Cruft's was now recognised as 'the first great all-round championship fixture of the season – a show noted for the introduction of new features and innovations, and one which specifically caters for novices of all breeds. Moreover, it is a show also noted for the bringing out of new young dogs, who are pitted against the champions of the day for the first time, and who start their careers on the show bench at this great gathering of the clans'. The press, however, seems to have failed to notice that when the series resumed in 1921 it followed the example set by other shows and became a two day event. Only Cruft's and the Kennel Club shows had not adopted the more popular two day format prior to the war.

Judging the breeds was, largely, and usually entirely, still carried out on the first day leaving little other than a few special and often poorly supported variety competitions for the second day. In the past the third and fourth days had merely provided additional opportunity for the public to view the dogs as they sat on their benches. The old arrangement must have been very inconvenient for exhibitors. Only a few would be able to afford the luxury of staying away from home for the entire period of the show and so would have to send their dogs, usually by rail, to be cared for and shown by the show's own attendants. The attention provided at the show was usually reliable, few dogs missed their classes or were returned, after the show, to the wrong address, though such things were not unknown.

Of course show staff would have no time for elaborate, or even any, grooming. Dogs were given basic, though adequate, care but the sort of grooming and preparation which is now regarded as essential in many breeds would simply not be possible. Indeed the Kennel Club was itself continually exercised by ways to prevent grooming and presentation, reaching over into faking and trimming becoming more important than the quality of the dogs.

However, all was not to be plain sailing for the revived show. Classes for returning heroes might well attract some welcome publicity and interest but these same returning heroes by bringing back the pets which had shared their privations in the trenches had also inadvertently re-introduced rabies into Britain. Government restrictions, intended to prevent the spread of rabies, controlled the movement of animals into and out of affected areas and, just before entries closed, these areas were extended to include London, a suspect case of rabies having been reported in Acton.

Deputations from the Kennel Club, Cruft's, the National Terrier Club and a number of breed clubs sought to persuade the government to amend the restrictions in order to allow dogs to travel to shows within restricted areas. These efforts were assisted by the absence of further cases in London and of a lack of evidence to substantiate the initial report. The Government, though making no change to the restrictions themselves, responded by lifting the wider ban on London but left Acton, Ealing, Hammersmith, Brentford and Chiswick within a contracted restricted area. Other restricted areas in different parts of the country remained unaffected. The move was enough to save Cruft's, though not without some effect on the entry which finished, according to Cruft's figures, at 2860 compared with the Kensington Canine Society's 3000 entries for a less well known show held prior to the imposition of restrictions in the London area.

The anti-German feeling which had led to the withdrawal of the Dachshund classes had not only already sufficiently evaporated for the classes to be restored but even for the introduction of another German breed, newly introduced into Britain. This was what was then called the Alsatian Wolf Dog. The anglicised name had been chosen with the intention of obscuring the breed's German origins, apparently association with wolves was deemed more welcome than association with Germany. The breed's debut at Cruft's was a remarkable one, which hinted strongly at its future popularity, with 127 entries placing it fourth in the show behind the two Fox Terrier breeds with 225 entries, Sealyhams with 201 and Pomeranians with 129 entries, which somehow escaped the pre-war anti-German feeling. Another breed making a less impressive Cruft's debut, with just 10 entries, was the Border Terrier.

Overall the entry was a creditable one, though even with a good gate, Cruft said it would 'not leave enough to take him to the Riviera for a sailing holiday'. The show was again supported by entries from King George V, who took the reserve Labrador championship with Wolferton Ben, the King's mother, Queen Alexandra, showed a Smooth Basset Hound, Sandringham Forester, thus introducing to the show ring the Sandringham prefix which the present Queen still uses.

The major attraction of the show, however, as far as the public was concerned, appears to have been the 'Earl Haig classes . . . initiated by our great General (who waded through the war with such dogged determination and distinction). . . . His Lordship is giving a silver cup which is confined to officers and men and women who served in the war . . . and women war-workers, which the war had left wholly unemployed or only partially employed. Major Harding Cox was the appropriate adjudicator of these classes, and announced each competition and subsequent victory to the crowd eight or ten deep which thronged the spacious ring'. The classes were not well supported by exhibitors but Cruft had assessed the public mood and likely interest with typical accuracy.

At the end of the 1921 show Cruft oiled the waters for his next effort by throwing a lavish banquet for all those whose support he valued. After four years absence the goodwill generated before and during the war might have grown rusty and Cruft knew how best to restore its lustre. Another twelve months seems to have been all that dogdom required to get back onto its feet and the 1922 show was able to trumpet 'no fewer than 4587 entries, which is, without doubt, a world record'. All eyes were on the Alsatian Wolf Dogs which had mustered 403 entries, a long way in front of Spaniels with 307, Labradors with 206 and Pomeranians with 203 and all leaving the former favourites Smooth Fox Terriers with 186 entries and Wire Fox Terriers with 155 well behind. At the other end of the scale Afghan Hounds, Basset Hounds, Dalmatians, Elkhounds, Maltese, Poodles, Curly coated Retrievers, Gordon Setters and Working Terriers all failed to reach double figures.

The show, in every respect, was a success. 'Despite the so-called bad times, never before probably did the click of the turnstiles at the Agricultural Hall run along so merrily from morn to night'. At the Cruft's dinner the Minister of Agriculture, Sir Arthur Griffith Boscawen, was, after suitable praise of Cruft and his show, to announce that rabies restrictions throughout the country, in force since 1919, had now been completely withdrawn, though he regretted that he could not do the same for foot and mouth restrictions. At the show he was joined by Mr Kellaway, the Postmaster General, who showed Sealyhams, and both politicians doubtless enjoying the fact that 'the second day of Cruft's show is by no means the "stale, flat, and unprofitable" event that it used to be, and that most second days of shows are. Alive to the spirit of the times, astute Mr Charles Cruft ("King Charles", as he is sometimes dubbed – he certainly is a king of show managers) and his committee provided for the delectation of exhibitors, as well as the public, quite a string of interesting events'.

These included the Gamekeeper, Variety and Toy classes and judging for the specials with which Cruft's abounded, while in this particular year the French judge, Monsieur G. Diemer resumed his task of sorting out the huge entry of Alsatians. It seems that his decisions 'upset the preconceived ideas of many English enthusiasts, not only in type and character, but in some cases even in the details of the dog, which will no doubt form a theme for meditation and discussion by the club that exists to promote the interests of this breed, which has taken Britain by storm'.

The resumption of Cruft's seems to have provoked a bout of nostalgia among the aging enthusiasts who could remember this show and others from the earliest days. Theo Marples was delighted to meet

> 'our old Darlington friend, Mr Tom Swimburne, J.P., an ex-mayor of his native town. . . . He recalled to us two rather remarkable incidents that occurred at the first Dundee dog show, held in 1878. . . . There was a very celebrated Pug in those days – viz., Mr Lewis's (Bristol) Ch. Sooty, – which was entered for the show, which Dr Stables (the judge of Pugs) had had in his charge for a time, but which was not sent to the show. Some wag, however, had put a Pug in Sooty's pen, a dog very far from Sooty's merit as Bristol is from Dundee, which the judge said he had overlooked, and begged an extra 1st prize for it! The other incident referred to Mr Swimburne, who won 1st in Black-and-tan Terriers, but after lunch found that somebody had substituted the 1st and 2nd prizes, his dog being labelled "2nd prize". Of course, Tom Swimburne who was then a tall, hefty young fellow, went to the secretary's office, and demanded to know of the secretary who had transposed the prizes. Getting no satisfaction, his arguments took a practical form, and among those he threw out of the office or over the table was our old friend, Mr Thomson Gray, the author of "Dogs of Scotland". . . . That was in the "good old days".'

Towards the end of 1922 Cruft's claim to having run the largest dog show in the world was quietly eclipsed by the Kennel Club's October show, which had received 4665 entries. Being upstaged was not something which Cruft either liked or was accustomed to and if, in his advancing old age he might have seemed to be rather resting on his laurels, he now had reason to try harder in 1923. 'Mr Charles Cruft and his committee have this year been put on their mettle in the direction of devising some new attraction or other, or inventing some new or novel competition, unearthing new judges, introducing new breeds and avenues of notoriety, or making some departure in keeping with the times, with a view to maintaining this old-established dog show and sports exhibition in its premier and up-to-date position'.

Cruft's first response was what it had always been, to increase the number of classes, which went up to 800, and to introduce yet more special competitions. As far as the breeds were concerned he did very little other than dropping the badly supported classes for Afghans and Bassets. He provided two French judges for the Alsatian classes 'with a view to appeasing, if possible, the susceptibilities of the devotees of the breeders of this breed on the vexed question of type and character, concerning which opinions differ very much among the cognoscenti even'. Apparently some things are immutable.

The tried and trusty methods worked and Cruft was able to announce an entry of 5766 to put him, once more, well ahead of competition from the Kennel Club. But he was beginning to face another problem. The Agricultural Hall could not accommodate many more entries. It must, therefore, have been with some relief that he learned that £25,000 had been set aside to build an extension to the building. The extension came only just in time because the 1924 entry was again up, this time to 6690, to which the small entry produced by Saluki or Gazelle Hounds, appearing at Cruft's for the first time made little difference. Sheer size apart it seems that the most notable feature of the show was the number of absentees among both judges and exhibitors produced by the prevailing epidemic of 'flu.

The trumpets were sounding once more in 1925 for an entry of 8008. Another world record to which 'exhibitors from every class of the community of both sexes, from His Majesty down' had made their contribution. This year Manchester Terriers made their first appearance under that name, there were separate classes for Black and Golden Labradors and for Black and Golden Flat-coated Retrievers and for Sussex and Field Spaniels though, of these, only the Black Labradors with 412 entries made a major contribution to the total. Even that was well behind the Alsatian Wolfdogs with 713.

The show appears to have been a rather quiet affair except that 'a Terrier strangled itself on its bench on Tuesday night, and a Greyhound created a small sensation by having a fit at the side of one of the most crowded judging rings on Wednesday. But there was something like general excitement when Mrs Higgens refused to judge the pocket Cockers, or, in other words of the catalogue, Cockers whose weight does not exceed 19lb. The Cocker Club does not recognise these bantams, and no doubt loyalty to that organisation had something to do with Mrs Higgen's refusal. Eventually Mr Sam Graham made the awards in this officially ignored division'.

The relationship between Cruft's and Spratt's had always been as close as it was mutually supportive and this year was extended by a variety competition in which the first prize, won by Billy Oldershaw's Wire-haired Fox Terrier, was £105.00. Spratt's, of course, were well represented among the trade stands which, since the war, had become an increasingly important feature of the show but they were accompanied by other food manufacturers including Sherley's whose Lactol and newly produced distemper vaccine were of great interest. Spillers' range of Victoria foods were also displayed and Benbows, Gilbertson and Page and Carta Carna were all extolling the virtues of their foodstuffs. Kennel accommodation was displayed by Boulton and Paul, Maggs of Bristol, Grosvenor Workman, F. Pratten and the Berton Boat Company and might be disinfected by Jeyes while its occupants could be

Croxton Smith in 1925.

transported by the London Midland and Scottish Railway Company who were at hand to cater for exhibitors.

In sickness dogs might be treated by the products of the Badminton Distemper Co., Burnett and Godfrey, A. L. Mannings, Reade and Co., Virol and McGuffie and Co. while kennel and show equipment was available from the stands of Duligall and Son, A. Jaffrey, the Titan Dog Requisite Supply Company, Parrishes Patent Cooker, Cooper and Son and the Sussex Basket Company. Canine charities were represented by Our Dumb Friends' League, the National Anti-Vivisection Society and by the Electoral and Parliamentary League which was campaigning against vivisection and for the protection of animals on a world wide basis.

Those who required trophies might obtain them from the Goldsmiths and Silversmiths Company while canine publications were represented by *Our Dogs'* somewhat idiosyncratic four-poster stand. Even better than the large number of stand holders was the number of times the turnstiles clicked during the two days of the show. Over 40,000 on the first day and much the same on the second fell little short of the ninety-odd thousand which Crufts can nowadays expect over a four day period.

In spite of claims that Cruft encouraged new judges he tended to rely on the same small band who often judged the same breeds year after year. Sam Graham judged Border Terriers in three successive years from 1921, and Theo Marples and Harding Cox seemed almost to be fixtures when it came to judging the specials on the second day. In 1928 when a Best in Show winner was first selected the old system was not changed, the same judges appeared year after year, and this doubtless resulted in the same people, often with the same dogs, doing remarkably well.

Inspired by the success of his 1925 show and with the ambition beginning to form in his mind that a show with over 10000 entries would very nicely round off his career as a showman Cruft produced a schedule for the 1926 show which had 1333 classes, far more than anything which had gone before. Entries closed on 25 January and the show took place on 10 and 11 February. The total entry, of 9157, came very close to satisfying Cruft's ambition and within it were some remarkable achievements.

Alsatian Wolfdogs, this year with a Swiss judge, perhaps to demonstrate a degree of neutrality, produced 827 entries and a class average of 22. Cocker Spaniels came next with 593 and 14 a class. In terms of class average, Wire Fox Terriers were second to Alsatians with 18 per class and 370 entries. Only Maltese and Basset Hounds failed to reach double figures and 'the newly classified Keeshonden make a fairly good show for a beginning with 23 nominations; a rationally built dog that looks like "going".'

Cruft had long since demonstrated his ability to get people into his show but this year a new problem presented itself. It had been announced that exhibitors could, on payment of a small fee, remove their dogs at 9 pm. on Wednesday evening. Exhibitors rushed to take advantage of this concession and 'the narrow passage leading to the door was speedily blocked, dogs were trodden on, and exhibitors crushed, and when this was at its height some of the lights became extinguished, and this added to the confusion. Eventually the police had to be requisitioned to regulate the crowd'.

Subsequent to the show the complaints were vociferous, suggesting that the Kennel Club should itself take steps to ensure that arrangements at shows run under its rules were conducive to the comfort and safety of exhibitors. But safety was not the only cause for concern. Cruft had crammed a bigger entry, far more trade stands and far more spectators into the recently enlarged Agricultural Hall than he had ever previously managed. Some of the rings were far too small. That for Airedales, with 23 in the first class, was said to be 'poked away in a small corner about 20 feet square'. On the second day many dogs missed their variety classes because of the crowds and what seems to have been a rather haphazard judging schedule which depended on nothing more than when the appointed judges decided to commence their alloted tasks.

Exhibitors, however, were not deterred by the arrangements and in the following year responded by entering 3433 dogs to produce 9777 entries, again tantalisingly close to the magic 10000. Most exhibitors still travelled by train, making use of the special trains and reduced fares which Cruft negotiated with the various railway companies. More and more, however, were making use of motor cars and Cruft was able to announce that he had made arrangements to park 700 cars close to the show. Safety standards had been improved by making more exits available to exhibitors and the London County Council had made it clear that they 'will not permit dog boxes and hampers to be left in the gangways'. At the close of the show the main talking point seems to have been the certainty that the 1928 show would finally reach the 10000 entry level. In fact it would still be some years and would take something a little special before Cruft's ambition would be realised.

Perhaps, in hindsight, the most significant development at the 1928 show was the introduction of a competition to find the best dog in the show. Previously, although an antique silver trophy had, for a few years, been available for the Best Champion in the Show emphasis had been on breed classes with variety competitions regarded as little more than a means to while away the second day of the show. A number of special awards were available for competition between breeds but these tended to be restricted to related groups of breed, retrievers or spaniels, though one, the Keddell Trophy, for the best conditioned dog in the show, was available for competition between all breeds.

To some extent some of the specials may have anticipated the group system, still some way from becoming formalised, and the Trophy for the Best Champion at the Show anticipated a Best in Show award, as perhaps did the Keddell Trophy. Uncharacteristically the decision to select a Best in Show winner was not heralded by Cruft's usual publicity or given much attention by the press. It seems to have been a development which was regarded as of little significance. Nor was the system of selecting the Best in Show winner free from inconsistencies and contradictions. The winner, 'Mr H. Whitley's wonderful Greyhound bitch, Primley Sceptre' had failed to win the Hound International Challenge Bowl which had been won by Mrs W. Knox's Irish Wolfhound Lady of Raikeshill while the runner up Mr Moorby's Pointer, Stainton Spruce, had taken the Petanelle Challenge Cup for the best conditioned dog in the show, the Sporting International Challenge Bowl and the Cruft Gundog Trophy. It was, to say the least, all a little bit confused and uncharacteristically low key.

On 1 January 1929 new railway fares for dogs travelling with or without their owners were published. These were much cheaper than those they replaced. They meant that a dog, on collar and chain, and, if necessary, with muzzle, could travel from Manchester to London for 7s 3d (36p) and, if the dog was in a box, both weighing not more than 50lb, for 6s 4d (31p).

The new fares must have boosted the entries of shows other than Cruft's but what Cruft's exhibitors might well have appreciated even more was the announcement that a newly installed system meant that the Agricultural Hall could now be 'artificially heated to 60 degrees (F), which is a very great advance on previous totally unheated conditions, when it has earned the reputation of being the coldest, as well as the largest, show on earth'.

The total entry did not match the previous year's by over 300 and a new breed emerged to head the list. Alsatians, for the first time with a German judge, had fallen back to 543 entries while Cocker Spaniels had increased to 698 and Labradors had 524, Wire Fox Terriers, Cairns, Pekingese and Sealyhams all had over 300 entries. English Springers, Smooth Fox Terriers, Golden Retrievers, Flat-coated Retrievers, Bulldogs, Irish Setters, Airedales and Elkhounds all had over 200.

The criticism which Cruft had endured during the early days of the show had now been replaced by praise and affection, though it was being increasingly noticed that his almost legendary vigour was being replaced by experience and guile. Cruft himself had taken on an assistant, Miss E. Hardingham, his son Cecil, who had assisted his father at several of the post-war shows and who, it was generally assumed, would eventually take over the reins, not always being available to provide assistance. The old order was slowly changing and it must have come as a shock to the old man to learn, just a few weeks before his 1929 show, that Sir Humphrey de Trafford, his first President, had died, aged sixty-seven. Sir Humphrey had shown his first dog when he was a twenty-one-year-old student at Oxford, and had subsequently shown several other breeds, as well as being very active in the field, but it was his Wire-fox Terriers shown under the Barton affix which established his fame in the show ring.

The entry once more failed to beat the 1927 total. Cockers again were at the top with 685 entries and Labradors second with 556 while the stiffest competition at the show was found in the Greyhound classes which with 252 entries had a class average of 19.

It was almost beginning to seem as though Cruft's would now do little more than trundle along on the familiar and successful lines which Charles Cruft had laid down. Innovations were becoming less frequent and those which did appear were not heralded with anything like the old energy. The 10000 entry figure was proving to be very elusive and increasingly there was a tendency to look back at former successes. The competition for Best in Show, won in 1929 by Robert Chapman's Scottish Terrier, Heather Necessity, was beaten by Baroness Burton's Cairn for the award for Best Terrier. The judges were Major Harding Cox, the Rev. Needham Davies, R. Heaton and F. Calvert Butler and Theo Marples. In 1930 Mrs Fraser and Croxton Smith replaced Heaton and Davies, the other judges were the same as in the previous year. They were unable to agree about whether the Scottish Terrier should win again or whether Bert Lloyd's blue roan Cocker Spaniel, Luckystar of Ware should be the winner. Even casting lots did not break the deadlock and eventually Theo Marples, acting as referee, cast his vote in favour of the Spaniel. A repeat of this win, under Theo Marples, Harding Cox, Croxton Smith and Walter Glynn, was perhaps the only significant feature of the 1931 show. Once more the runner up was ignored.

Show entries generally were falling as indeed were Kennel Club registrations. The 1930 registrations at 48784 were the lowest since 1924 and were almost 10000 down on the 1926 figure. Cruft, faced with problems caused by his own declining energies and having already used all his best ideas was caught up in a general decline which was itself a product of a general depression. In fact Cruft's had performed remarkably well in the face of falling registrations and national poverty but the elusive 10000 entries seemed further away than ever.

The canine press slightly altered its tone in order to encourage exhibitors to support Cruft's not just, as in the past, because it was the biggest and most publicised show in the world but also out of a sense of loyalty to Charles Cruft himself. Increasingly affection for the aging 'British Barnum' was a feature of most reports. In 1932 an entry of 9216, the lowest since 1926, drew the comment that 'exhibitors have responded nobly to the call, and it now only remains to visitors to flock to the Agricultural Hall to assure Cruft's 1932 venture a complete success'. It seemed almost as though exhibitors and even spectators were regarded as having a duty to give Cruft their support. The exhortations seem to have worked because although a reduced classification inevitably attracted a reduced entry the number of dogs at the show, something which had, in the past, tended not to be discussed, was about 250 more than were benched at the record 1926 show.

> 'Even the largest show of the Westminster Kennel Club, held in New York, U.S.A., did not muster more than 2673 dogs; this was in 1930, the year of the Club's record show, at which the entry was 3557. Cruft's, therefore, has set an example that other show executives should follow if they wish to be successes'.

What was the real nature of this example? Was it to point to entries and ignore the number of actual dogs when that presented the best picture and to change the emphasis when a different picture began to emerge? What had previously been hailed as the largest show in the world, the 1927 Cruft's Show, had about 2400 dogs, over 200 less than the record Westminster Show, though the entry, boosted by multiple entries from the same dog and by counting, none too accurately, brace, team, auction classes and even in the art exhibition, was nearly three times greater than at Westminster.

Once more the panel of Best in Show judges was hardly changed, only Theo Marples being missing from the previous year. This year, however, the choice was a unanimous one and fell on a dog making its debut in the show ring. That dog was Lorna, Countess Howe's Labrador Retriever, Bramshaw Bob. The judges had their legs pulled about putting up an unglamorous 'common barnyard dog' but had the satisfaction of seeing him repeat his Cruft's success at Manchester a few weeks later.

Unprecedented drum banging from the canine press, which seems to have become almost as anxious as was Cruft to see the 10000 entry mark reached, announced the 1933 show.

'The stupendous total of 1138 classes is scheduled – an increase of 39 on the classification of last year, and there is also a colossal special prize list numbering 1362. ... Judges are very cosmopolitan, and, in addition to many of the greatest experts of this country, some of the leading canine authorities in America, Holland, Sweden and Germany will come over specially to adjudicate. ... A special service of luxury motor coaches (toilet and central heated) will run direct to and from Manchester, Altrincham, Newcastle and Coventry and a number of other places in the country'.

In addition Cruft had won a new concession from the railways which enabled his subscribers to travel at much reduced rates. Even those who might be unable to attend the show were exhorted to enter.

'Let it be remembered that this great event has a world-wide fame, that a win there is a sure sign of a dog's excellence, and that even an entry in the catalogue – even if the dog is not a prize winner – is a valuable advertisement. Enter all you can at this show. By doing so you will help yourself and British dogdom, and you may be helping Mr Cruft to achieve his ambition of 10000 entries!'

All that could be done to drum up a massive entry had been done and the signs looked good when the National Terrier Show's entry was bigger than it had been in 1932.

It was not to be. The entry was again down, this time to 8564, the lowest since 1925. Reasons for the drop in entries were quickly put forward 'a 'flu epidemic was raging in this country, the weather was bitterly cold, and, alas, the general financial depression showed but little signs of lifting'. But all was not gloom and despondency, a number of breeds had excellent entries, Cocker Spaniels achieving 703, Labrador Retrievers 495 and both Pekingese and Alsatians comfortably into the 300s. Doubtless too, the newly introduced class for Tibetan Spaniels would exert its novel appeal though it was apparent, from the paltry twenty entries received in the variety classes, that exhibitors themselves were principally interested in breed competitions.

This year Cruft was unable to rely on the attractions exerted by a Royal presence but received some compensation when Amy Johnson visited the show to be escorted round by Arthur Marples whose brother, John Willie, and father, Theo, were both judging at the show. The crowds which attended the show were described as enormous and on the second day so great was the interest that the show had to be kept open well after its advertised time for closing. Even when the lights were extinguished in the Hall people refused to leave the building and Cruft was obliged to bow to popular opinion and allow the exhibition to continue.

The Best in Show Trophy winner was also a popular one with both exhibitors and spectators. 'Lorna Countess Howe's famous Labrador dog, Ch. Bramshaw Bob, which, in superb form, distinguished himself by winning, for the second year in succession, the silver trophy for the best exhibit in show is not only a personal triumph for Lady Howe, but also one for working dogs in general, Bramshaw Bob having proved his all-round excellence by some good wins at field trials in the past season'.

In the following year the eagerness to achieve 10000 entries appears to have subsided a little but Cruft's appetite for records had not in any way diminished and if, by increasing the number of classes and the number of breeds he could not reach his ambition he could at least lay claim to having more dogs at his show than any other had achieved. The 9363 entries were made by 3757 dogs 'making Cruft's easily the largest collection of dogs ever assembled'. Among the dogs entered were some owned by King George and others owned by H. H. Maharajah Dhiraj of Patiala.

Once more Cocker Spaniels topped the entry with 708 from 217 dogs, Labradors had 572 entries and 152 dogs, Alsatians, now well below their former numbers, had 338 entries and 171 dogs beaten by Pekingese with 331 entries and 176 dogs. This year Cruft's had a new President in Mr Nigel C. Colman M.P. whose speech at the traditional lunch for judges and officials showed the extent to which Cruft could still tell a good showman's tale, he 'noted that before the war K.C. registrations did not reach 20000. Last year they were 50000. At today's show there were three miles of dog benching, 250 more exhibitors than last year and a catalogue of 600 pages. . . . This was the 47th Cruft's Show (it was the 42nd or 48th if the terrier shows were included) . . and he hoped Mr

Cruft would be spared for many years to come and that he would realise his ambition which was to run his 50th show and reach 10000 entries.'

The Best in Show winner was the Greyhound, Hartland-Worden's Southball Moonstone, with Lloyd further increasing his familiarity with the Best in Show ring by taking reserve with his Cocker Spaniel, Whoopee of Ware. Not for the first time was a Cruft's admirer inspired to burst into verse. The following verses appeared in *Our Dogs*:

'This is the Show
That Cruft built;
These are the dogs
Who wanted a prize, So went to the Show
That Cruft built.

These are the maids
Who groomed the dogs
Who wanted a prize,
So went to the Show
That Cruft built.

This is the cock
That crowed in the morn
To wake the maidens, all forlorn, To take the dogs –
Some hairy, some shorn –
Who wanted a prize
For their style and size,
To be won in the Show
That Cruft built.

These are the judges,
Some tall of form,
Who had to get up
In the early dawn,
To watch the maidens, all forlorn,
Bring in their dogs –
Some hairy, some shorn;
Dogs that got brushed
From daylight to dusk,
To win in the Show
That Cruft built.

This is the Greyhound,
Champion of all,
Who won the cup,

Over large and small,
And went so happily
Back to his stall,
The best in the Show
That Cruft built.

In 1935, for the first time, separate classification was provided for
Pembroke and Cardigan Corgis. The total entry was down on the
previous year, to 9130, though the number of actual dogs increased to
3983, and so, once more, Cruft was able to lay claim to a world record!
He must have been especially grateful to Mrs Elms who had entered no
less than sixty dogs in Bloodhounds, Bassets and Beagles, more than half
the total number in these breeds. Gratitude was due also to Isaac Sharpe
who had drawn a record 170 entry of Pointers. The eventual Best in
Show winner the Pointer, Pennine Prima Donna, was not entered in its
breed classes, though it had won the bitch Challenge Certificate in 1933
and 1934. Apparently Isaac Sharpe was not universally popular.

'The win of the Pointer created considerable controversy and many
argued that according to the latest K.C. rule the bitch was not eligible
to compete for the trophy as she was not entered in the classes for her
own breed. To those who held this opinion we would point out that
this latest K.C. rule did not come into force until Friday, 8 February,
the day after the day on which Prima Donna put up her great win. The
Pointer, therefore, was quite eligible for the best in show competition.
Her winning it, however, brought about a repetition of the very
debatable situation of an exhibit being made best of all breeds in show
after having been beaten by another exhibit at the same show; earlier
in the day in the A.V. Open class, Mr Sidney Simpson, the judge,

*Some Crufts 1935 judges
seen by Mac.*

placed Mr F. Peake's Airedale Terrier Ch. Stockfield Aristocratic first, and the Pointer second. This did not affect her eligibility for the best in show competition, as the K.C. rule only debars those dogs beaten in their breed classes. To give the logically-minded another headache, we would point out that Pennine Prima Donna, a Pointer herself, was not given the distinction of best Pointer (as she was not entered in the breed classes) this honour going to Mr J. R. Bishop's Witherm Queen of Clubs. Of course, we know that these apparently topsy-turvy awards have come about because Prima Donna was judged by different judges, each with his own opinion, and because she was not entered in her breed classes. And, after all in a competition to decide the best exhibit in show the opinion of the judge or judges appointed for this competition is the only one that matters. At the same time we contend that K.C. rules should make it impossible for a beaten exhibit to be awarded the honour of best in show'.

In fact the situation was even more confused than Theo Marples, one of the judges who had made the controversial decision, here describes. The Airedale which had beaten Prima Donna had itself not been entered in its breed. So that the winner of Cruft's Terrier Challenge Bowl was Mrs G. Hayes' Airedale Ch. Aislaby Aethling and the Cruft's Sporting Challenge Bowl was won by Mr T. H. Moorby's Pointer Ch. Stainton Startler. Prima Donna had won the Country Life Challenge Trophy for the best of all sporting breeds and the Lady Howe Perpetual Gundog Trophy for best Gundog. Nor was the situation improved by the fact that the reserve Best in Show winner, Mrs V. A. M. Mannooch's Chow Chow Ch. Choonam Hung Kwong, had not only won its breed but had gone on to take the award for the best conditioned dog in the show and the Best Non-Sporting dog in the show but did not win the Nettie Levy Challenge Cup for the best exhibit owned by a lady, this being won by Mrs Mannooch's Chow Chow Choonam Tao Wang which had failed to win in its breed. Nevertheless Mrs Mannooch felt it necessary to lodge an official complaint.

By the time the contentious 1935 show had passed into history it had become apparent that even the repeated exhortations of his friends were insufficient to enable Cruft to achieve his ambition of running a show with 10000 entries. Something special was going to be required and so Cruft decided that something special would be produced. He would run his Golden Jubilee Show to celebrate fifty glorious years. It was only forty-five years since the first Cruft's Show in 1891 but it was fifty years since the first of his terrier shows and was already twenty-seven years since he had celebrated his Silver Jubilee show. It was as good a time as any to have a Golden Jubilee.

Charles Cruft was now well into his eighties and it was very possible that if his ambition was not achieved at his Golden Jubilee show it might never be achieved. All his experience was devoted to ensuring a huge entry. The number of classes was increased to 1466, new breeds, including Affenschnauzers which produced nineteen entries, Boxers with ten entries, Chesapeake Bay Retrievers with eleven entries, Trail Hounds which failed to attract an entry and Staffordshire Bull Terriers with forty-two entries were added to the schedule. The classes for King Charles Spaniels, once referred to as Toy Spaniels, which in the previous year had yielded seventy-six entries were split to allow for the increasingly popular old type which was referred to as the Cavalier King Charles Spaniel. The King Charles produced sixty-eight entries and the Cavalier thirty-four. Added to all was the offer of 1725 specials, an unprecedented number of which could be won outright, and prize money, already higher than that paid at other shows, at an even higher level made it apparent that Charles Cruft really meant business.

The term Toy Spaniels originally embraced all the colours of the breed, each being given their own Royal name. The King Charles being black and white or black and tan, though black and tans had originally been referred to as King James Spaniels. Tricolours were called Prince Charles, red and whites Blenheims, and reds were called Rubies. This host of names for the same breed, served by the Toy Spaniel Club, prompted the Kennel Club, in 1903 to attempt to rectify the situation by formally accepting the name by which the breed was and would continue to be called, the Toy Spaniel. The Club objected strongly and the ensuing argument was resolved only when King Edward VII made it clear that he preferred the name King Charles Spaniel.

All might then have been well except that there was increasing concern that the shortened faces of the breed were very different from those of the original Toy Spaniels. Criticism of these 'goggle-eyed, pug nosed, pampered little peculiarities', as Col R. Claude Cane described them in 1907 began to increase and, in 1926, Roswell Eldridge, an American who had been disappointed to find nothing but the short nosed variety on display at shows, offered a special prize of £25 to be competed for at Cruft's for Toy Spaniels of the old type. The offer provoked some interest as well as some controversy, especially in 1928 when it was generally agreed that the winner was a small Welsh Spaniel and within a few years Toy Spaniels of the old type were becoming more numerous, so numerous indeed that they were given their own classes at the Jubilee Show.

The result was almost a foregone conclusion.

'Charles Cruft, the world's greatest dog show promoter, has realised the ambition which he has cherished all his life in the amazing total of 10650 entries. . . . This remarkable entry creates a new world record, and easily beats the previous best of 9777 which was made by this same show in 1927. . . . As might be expected, the number of individual dogs (4388) also creates a world record, and is well past the previous record of 3993 which was set up by Cruft's last year. . . . Of the breed entries, the most outstanding is that of Labradors, 200 of which have made the terrific entry of 898, a figure which sets up another world record in that it is the highest entry ever made by one breed at any show. A great compliment to the judge, Lorna Countess Howe, as it nearly doubles last year's entry. . . . Next on the list come Cocker Spaniels with another world-record total, and another compliment to a popular judge in Mr Harry Scott; their 766 entries are 15 better than their previous best entry, which was made at Cruft's in 1927.'

It must have seemed as if there were no more records to be broken and after all the cheering had died down the show itself might have seemed almost an anti-climax. Best in Show, under two of the same judges, was the previous year's runner up, Mrs Mannooch's Chow Chow Ch. Choonam Hung Kwong who had accumulated twenty-five Challenge Certificates under nineteen different judges during a short career.

Cruft continued to protect his valuable monopoly of the Agricultural Hall and refused to relent when, in 1936, the Crystal Palace was burned down making his only serious rival, the Kennel Club's show, homeless. No other venue was available in London and so the Kennel Club was obliged to run an outdoor show, on the Crystal Palace Football Ground, but unfortunately their chosen dates clashed with those of the Roundhay (Leeds) event which, consequently had to be abandoned. In the following year harmony was restored by the Kennel Club taking its show to Olympia in December. Cruft's intransigence cannot have won him many friends. During 1936 King George had died, thus robbing Cruft of any Royal support for his Jubilee Show, but providing him with the opportunity to run Cruft's Great Coronation Show in the following year.

This show saw the totally unpublicised introduction of Obedience Classes, confined to Alsatians, to the Cruft's schedule. Affenschnauzers and Trail Hounds were unceremoniously dropped from the schedule and Pyrenean Mountain dogs, which attracted thirteen entries, Rhodesian Ridgebacks which produced six entries, Rottweilers which produced nine and Miniature Schnauzers which produced eight entries were all, for the first time at Cruft's, given their own classes. The Best in Show award created history by being won, for the third time, by Lorna Countess Howe's Labrador dog, Ch. Cheverell's Ben of Banchory while a newcomer to top honours was Mrs Powys-Lybbe's Elkhound, Kren of the Hollow.

After two such shows it was perhaps inevitable that the 1938 event would be somewhat subdued. King George VI made his debut as a Cruft's exhibitor winning with his home-bred Labrador Sandringham

Barry Webster had a wry look at Charles Cruft after his 1937 show.

Stream and two more breeds, Boston Terriers and Bernese Mountain Dogs made their Cruft's debut. Bert Lloyd's Cocker Spaniel Exquisite Model of Ware beat 755 entries in 80 classes to top its breed, went on to be declared best gundog and eventually Best in Show over Mr J. V. Rank's Great Dane Ch. Ruler of Ouborough. In September Charles Cruft died and the future of what had justly come to be regarded as a national institution was suddenly in doubt. However Charles Cruft's widow rose to the challenge and in 1939 ran a show, with Miss Hardingham's more than able but always unobtrusive, assistance which was every bit as good as any of its predecessors.

Once more Bert Lloyd's Cocker Spaniel Exquisite Model of Ware took her place on the winners' rostrum while Mrs Mannooch's evergreen Chow Chow Ch. Choonam Hung Kwong again stood in reserve place. It was a fitting end to an era. The old winners which Cruft's had made famous were saying goodbye to Cruft's as it was run by Cruft himself. Within a few months Britain would again be at war with Germany and there would be no more national dog shows, though local events somehow contrived to struggle on, for a number of years.

During the 1930s two names stand out in any commentary about Cruft's; one is Bert Lloyd and his 'of Ware' Cocker Spaniels whose reputations would be even further enhanced in years to come. The other was Lorna Countess Howe and her Banchory Labrador Retrievers. Her Bramshaw Bob had won the Best in Show award in 1932 and 1933, she had been one of the Best in Show judges in 1934 and had returned to the Best in Show ring as a winner in 1937 with Ch. Cheverell's Ben of Banchory. A remarkable decade was rounded off when she again joined the panel of Best in Show judges in 1939. Nor was her interest confined to Labradors, her kennels at one time or another also housed Pointers, Spaniels, Border Terriers and Griffons. At a time when ladies were in a small minority in the field, as judges and even as exhibitors she excelled in all three spheres to an extent which has never since been matched.

7.   The Kennel Club Takes Over

*W*hen Charles Cruft died in 1938 the possibility arose that there would be no more Cruft's shows but Mrs Cruft rose magnificently to the challenge and ran the 1939 show with all her husband's flair and attention to detail. Emma Cruft had demonstrated that she and her staff were quite capable of running a very successful dog show and, given the will and the opportunity, could have continued to do so. They may well have run others had not the war interrupted the series. However, there were doubts about Mrs Cruft's desire to continue in the role which her husband had occupied. These doubts meant that others were considering the possibility of acquiring rights to the show. Mrs Cruft was approached by Leo Wilson, well known canine journalist and judge, to see whether she might be prepared to sell him the title. The Kennel Club became aware of this apparently unsolicited approach and their Committee, thereupon, deputed three of its members, Croxton Smith, Chairman of the General Committee, W. F. Holmes and Roger Boulton to discover more about Mrs Cruft's intentions. It was confirmed that Mrs Cruft had already received an offer from a third party, probably Leo Wilson, whereupon the Kennel Club delegates made an offer which Mrs Cruft regarded as acceptable. Only later was this offer approved and confirmed by the General Committee.

The Kennel Club had purchased the title of Cruft's Show for an undisclosed but undoubtedly bargain figure, later alleged to be £4000. It was later suggested that the figure was less than the annual profit yielded by any of the post-war shows. Some of these, however, produced very little profit because it was then the Kennel Club's aim to break even and not to maximise profit. Even so, in later years, when Mrs Cruft saw the commercial success which the show was to achieve in the hands of the Kennel Club she felt very strongly that she had sold it far too cheaply though, obviously, the Kennel Club's acceptable offer was greater than any other she may have received.

The show had made Charles Cruft a wealthy man and there was no reason to suppose that it could not continue to furnish a healthy and even a much increased annual profit. The show's name was well established, internationally known and respected. The show attracted visitors from all over the world and exercised a far greater hold over both visitors and exhibitors than did any other dog show. Mrs Cruft was now an elderly lady and, without her husband, probably no longer wanted the responsibility of this annual event. For its part, the Kennel Club already had its own successful show and so was not in desperate need of Cruft's. Furthermore Cruft's very advantageous monopoly of the Royal Agricultural Hall had been broken, indeed the Hall was no longer available, and it was unlikely that any other venue could be persuaded to offer similar terms to Cruft's. A major advantage had disappeared. Over the years there had also been a Kennel Club policy of refusing to authorise shows run for private profit. Cruft's had slipped under the wire before the policy was properly formulated and remained the only one to have done so. To that extent it was an anachronism which the Kennel Club might have wished to remove.

The Kennel Club's reluctance to authorise shows run for private profit may, during the war years, have hardened into a reluctance to continue to authorise Cruft's in private hands other than Cruft's own. Mrs Cruft would not be left unaware of any changed attitude. She must have

Not every dog may have his day at Cruft's but a boy may dream!

realised that the show could continue as a private and profitable enterprise only with the Kennel Club's approval and support. The Kennel Club could, when shows were again able to be held, refuse to allocate to Cruft's the Challenge Certificates on which its status depended and might even refuse to allow the show to take place at all. Mrs Cruft would not have wanted to see her husband's creation disappear but neither might she have relished the prospect of a difficult and possibly prolonged negotiation with an authority which seemed to hold all the trump cards. She must also have realised that the show's future would always be vulnerable while it remained in private hands and it may well have been concern for the long term future of her husband's creation which led her to accept the Kennel Club's offer.

Cruft's passed out of private control and into the hands of the Kennel Club in 1942. Its future was assured but would the Kennel Club be able to match the flair which had made the show famous? Its own shows had been moderately successful but had failed to capture the imagination of either exhibitors or the public to the same extent as had a number of others. A very different approach would be needed if the charisma of Cruft's was to remain intact.

After Cruft's Show changed hands the first break with established tradition arose out of the Kennel Club's understandable eagerness to run a show as soon as possible. Rather than waiting until February 1949 the decision was taken to run a show in the autumn of 1948. The venue was to be Olympia and the dates the 14th and 15th October. In all ninety-two breeds were scheduled, fifty-six of them to be judged on the first day. The new Cruft's Committee decided that it would not use the group system which a number of major shows had adopted before the war but would select the best from among the Challenge Certificate winners in the Hound, Terrier and Toy Groups at the end of the first day. Since no best of breed winners were to be declared this would mean that two dogs would represent each breed and that there might be ninety-two dogs in the ring at the end of the first day. At the end of the second day the non-sporting and gundog breeds could produce seventy-six dogs for the judges' inspection. The arrangement may appear unwieldy when compared with today's invariable use of the group system which reduces the maximum number of breeds before a judge to about two dozen but, compared with Cruft's customary method of selecting the Best in Show winner from a parade of every Challenge Certificate winner, and in 1939 this had meant that the judges selected from about 180 dogs, it was a vast improvement.

Another significant break with tradition was that all breeds would not be present and judged, as far as was possible, on the first day of the show. Nor would dogs present on the first day be expected to return on the second day, except to compete for Best in Show. The change was one calculated to respond to the convenience of exhibitors though it had the effect of reducing the range of breeds available on either day for public inspection. Another change, again calculated to appeal more to exhibitors than to the public, was that dogs, which could enter the hall at 6 am, could be removed at 8 pm on each day of the show. The much criticised Cruft's system which only allowed subscribers to compete for special prizes was also scrapped. This and a number of other changes passed unnoticed, or at least unremarked, but such were the changes brought about by the new management that, even before the show had taken place it was being hailed as 'the New Look Cruft's'.

During the years immediately prior to the war Kennel Club registration totals had fallen a little short of 60,000 a year. In the war years they had fallen to less than a quarter of this but after the war had begun to climb dramatically so that by 1947 the pre-war totals had been doubled. This increased interest in pedigree dogs was not immediately reflected in a commensurate increase in entries at shows but did indicate, to those who were prepared to see, the potential which existed for the development of dog shows.

At the first Cruft's Show in 1891 forty-five breeds had been scheduled. At the Kennel Club's first Cruft's Show in 1948 there were eighty-four breeds to be seen. A few breeds of British origin, the Clydesdale, Old

In 1948, the Kennel Club's first Cruft's Show, the group system had not been introduced. The Best in Show ring was crowded with nervous exhibitors.

English Black and Tan and Old English White Terriers had disappeared for ever, others had changed their names or been split into several varieties but the largest contribution to the increased number of breeds came from foreign breeds. No less than thirty-two of the forty-five breeds to be seen at the first Cruft's Show were of British origin, a mere thirteen came from overseas. In 1948 Cruft's scheduled thirty-three breeds which had their origins outside the British Isles. Sixteen British breeds had made their Cruft's debut since the first show against twenty from overseas. The trend was one which would continue and increase.

The 1948 show attracted 9,412 entries, over 500 more had been returned by a Committee now strictly adhering to Kennel Club Rules, and there were 4257 dogs entered, easily beating the post-war total, set in April of the previous year by the West of England Ladies Kennel Association with 8881 entries from 3616 dogs, but was still some way short of the total Cruft had claimed for his 1936 'Golden Jubilee' Show.

The show itself somehow managed to satisfy what many might have regarded as unreasonable expectations. The layout, with spacious, well laid out rings, none of which, as in the past, were in dark and secluded corners, came in for special mention. Two days of judging, which meant that every breed did not have to be hurriedly judged on one day, also eased the space problems even if it created problems for the benching contractors who had to rearrange benching overnight. There was some worry that spectators might have been disappointed that they could not see all breeds during a single visit to the show but this did not deter them from flocking through the turnstiles and at the end of the show it was announced that over 50000 people had attended the show, at least 500, who had arrived late having assumed that the show would continue, as in the past, until 10 pm, being allowed in free. A munificent gesture which was another considerable break with Cruft's tradition. Such support took the Committee by surprise, catalogues, of which only 4000 were printed, were quickly sold out. Ring sides were lined six deep and the Best in Show ring twenty or thirty deep.

> 'Chairs, tables and benches were used as grandstands and spectators lined staircases, hung on to every projection and took advantage of any elevated point to get a glimpse of the proceedings. Hundreds of people sought a vantage point on the gallery but owing to L.C.C. regulations they had to be removed'.

It was obvious that Cruft's had lost none of its appeal either for exhibitors or the public.

The Kennel Club had introduced a new method for arriving at the Best in Show winner which avoided all the first day's winners joining those from the second day in the ring. On the first day Hounds, Terriers and Toy dogs were scheduled and from these Ernie Sharpe's Wire Fox Terrier

A SOUVENIR OF CRUFT'S DOG SHOW, OLYMPIA, 1948

KENNEL GAZETTE

TWO SHILLINGS

Mrs Cruft presenting the Keddell Memorial Trophy
to Mr H. S. Lloyd's Cocker Spaniel
'TRACEY WITCH OF WARE'

bitch, Drakehall Dairymaid emerged as the winner, with Miss de Pledge
and Mrs Lunham's Pekingese, Ch. Ku Chi of Caversham runner up. The
judges were Winnie Barber, J. Beynon and H. Sanders. On the second
day Winnie Barber was joined by Baron W. van der Hoop and E. Turner
who selected, from the Non-Sporting and Gundog winners, Bert Lloyd's
Cocker Spaniel Tracey Witch of Ware and J. V. Rank's Great Dane Raet
of Ouborough as the runner up. This left the Best in Show judges, May
Pacey and A. Croxton Smith to choose between the Cocker Spaniel and

the Fox Terrier for their Best in Show winner. Their choice was the Spaniel and such was the rush to congratulate Bert Lloyd on having won Best in Show at Cruft's for the fifth time that he and Tracey Witch had to be given a police escort.

Inevitably, however, there were some complaints. Some judges seemed too old for the task, others seemed not to have the necessary experience, exhibitors were accused of ignoring the requirement to keep their dogs benched when they were not in the ring. But the final verdict was that Cruft's had been a huge success under its new management. Mr Holland Buckley, the Kennel Club Secretary, who also acted as secretary to Cruft's came in for especial praise. He, in his turn, must have been grateful, though the gratitude was not publicly expressed, that his assistant was the same Miss Hardingham who had acted as Charles Cruft's secretary and had been secretary for the 1939 show. Her wealth of experience must have been invaluable and was to remain so for although Miss Hardingham's name would no longer be associated with Cruft's she remained on the Kennel Club staff for a number of years.

Because the 1948 show had taken place in October it was not thought advisable to return to the customary date in 1949 and so it was February, 1950 before the next Cruft's Show took place. The entry eclipsed even that which Cruft had assembled for his 'Golden Jubilee' Show; 12319 entries from 5720 exhibits in 1020 classes easily re-established Cruft's as the largest dog show in the world. Even within the total other minor records were established. In 1913 the Wire Fox Terrier Association Show had produced an entry of 857 to establish a record for the largest number of entries in a single breed. The Cocker Spaniel entry at Crufts 1950 went well beyond this with 1008 entries from 432 individual dogs. Behind the Cockers were Alsatians with 635, and close behind them Labrador Retrievers with 616.

The Kennel Club was also determined that Cruft's should retain and even improve on its reputation for setting new breeds before the public. At the 1950 show seven breeds made their Cruft's debut in breed classes. Miniature Long Haired and Smooth Haired Dachshunds, with seventy-eight and seventy-six entries respectively, had their own classes for the first time. So had Miniature Bull Terriers with fifteen entries. Cavalier King Charles Spaniels, separate since 1948 from the King Charles had eighty entries, while King Charles were left with forty-three. Soft Coated Wheaten Terriers provided the unusual spectacle of a British breed making a belated Cruft's debut though with only six entries. More typically three breeds of foreign origin appeared in their own classes for the first time. Maremmas had sixteen entries, Norwegian Buhunds four, and Dobermann Pinschers, giving little hint of their future popularity, had fifteen.

The 1951 entry failed to increase on the 1950 record. Even the

traditional resilience and enthusiasm of exhibitors was insufficient to combat hard times and shows generally were finding it increasingly difficult to attract entries. Exhibitors were also making fewer entries with each dog, a trend which was to have a profound effect on all dog shows. During the 1920s Cruft could expect each dog to be entered in about three classes; the 1951 entry managed just two classes per dog and by 1989 it would be unusual to find dogs entered in more than a single class. High entry figures, therefore, meant that far more dogs would have to be accommodated and if entries continued to increase more space would be needed to accommodate them. It was partly for this reason that the 1951 Cruft's was the last which would occupy only part of the space available at Olympia.

Tracey Witch and Bert Lloyd were besieged by press photographers after their historic win in 1950.

Perhaps though the 1951 Cruft's was most significant as the show at which the top places were taken not by well known winners from well established large kennels of breeds which were accustomed to the spot light but by small kennels with unfashionable breeds. On the first day May Pacey, Colonel Phipps and J. Beynon chose Captain and Mrs I. Thomas's Welsh Terrier bitch, Twynstra Dyma-Fi as their winner with Mr W. Buglass' Saluki Goldendawn Nadir Nar as the runner-up. On the second day the choice of T. Roger Boulton, A. Nicholls and E. Turner was

As late as 1950 it was customary for exhibitors to wear smart white coats. Here Old English Sheepdogs are judged in a far from spacious ring.

H. Johnson's Alsatian Edana of Combehill with Mr and Mrs R. Howell's Old English Sheepdog Ch. Shepton Indomitable as runner up and the only champion among the four winners. Indeed the Welsh Terrier had only won her second C.C. on the day having won her first at her first show, the National Terrier Show which had taken place in the previous month. The Alsatian had come from Undergraduate to win its first C.C. It was from these two that Winnie Barber and A. Croxton Smith were to select Best in Show and their choice was the Welsh Terrier handled by the diminutive but indomitable professional Georgie Barr.

For the first time since the war the principal prizes were not presented by Mrs Cruft. Her death since the last show had removed the last link, apart from the famous name, which the show had with its founder.

Towards the end of 1951 the Kennel Club Chairman, Air Commodore Cecil Wright seemed to have expressed doubts about Cruft's future profitability. He said that accounts 'show that the last show was satisfactory. But we have also to realise that it compared unfavourably with a far larger surplus for the show in the previous year . . . I think we have to realise that we definitely have passed the peak of large profits on Cruft's.' For all the show's success since the Kennel Club had taken it over in 1948 it appears that it had not the sort of profit which Cruft had regarded as essential and which made him a rich man. There was, however, reason to hope that the 12448 entries from 6040 dogs received in 1952 and the prospect of a substantial gate would guarantee a more profitable outcome. Certainly the entry was an appropriate way to mark the centenary of Charles Cruft's birth which, otherwise, appears to have been allowed to pass unnoticed.

Concern about the dwindling popularity of some British breeds, which had resulted in the formation of a British Breeds Association in the previous year, began to be voiced publically. At Cruft's seven breeds of British origin had twenty or fewer entries while others which had long been among the most popular breeds seemed locked into an accelerating rate of decline.

One innovation which the Kennel Club thoughtfully introduced for the 1952 show allowed exhibitors to queue within Olympia for the veterinary inspection, which was still carried out on each and every one of the 6000 dogs. Previously exhibitors had been obliged to queue outside the building, often in cold and wet weather and for long periods. It was not the best way to get themselves and their dogs into a show looking or feeling at their best. The new arrangement was very welcome.

Most unwelcome was news of the death of the much loved King George VI on the night of Tuesday, 5 February. It seemed doubtful that Cruft's would take place. Only an announcement by the Lord Chamberlain that theatres would close only on 8 February gave the Kennel Club reassurance that the show could take place two days later. The King's death and the accession to the throne of Queen Elizabeth II, who more than once had been heard to express a wish that her Corgis could compete at Cruft's, offered a reason to review the Royal Family's association with Cruft's and with dogs in general. Queen Victoria and her son, Edward the Prince of Wales had been exhibitors at the first Cruft's Show in 1891. They were joined by H.R.H. Princess Henry of Battenburg, Grand Duke Nicholas of Russia and Prince Constantin of Oldenbourg. In 1893 the Princess of Wales, later to become Queen Alexandra, made her debut as a Cruft's exhibitor and, at the same time, introduced the famous Royal Sandringham affix to the show ring. The Tsar was also an exhibitor at the 1893 show. King George V showed at Cruft's under his Wolverton affix which was largely associated with gundogs, principally Labradors and Clumber Spaniels. The Royal association was continued in 1952 when the Princess Royal showed a Smooth Dachshund. No other family has had such a long or extensive connection with Cruft's and it is a connection which remains unbroken.

Those who were becoming worried at the decline in the popularity of

The terrier judging at Crufts 1951 attracted the customary crowds to Olympia.

British breeds must have been cheered by the 1952 results. The winner on the first day was Mr A. Francis's Wire Fox Terrier Ch. Torkard Susan with Julia Curnow's Borzoi Aureola of Woodcourt runner up. The Wire Fox Terrier might not have been everyone's choice because 'she was by no means at her best. Shown woefully short of coat, this was very apparent, even though her handler spent the greater part of the time in the main ring in the final judgement titivating what there was of it'. The second day winners were Mr J. Barnard's Bulldog Ch. Noways Chuckles and Miss M. E. Jarry's English Setter Ripleygate Topnote. For the first time both winners from the first day joined the second day's winners for the Best in Show competition thus giving both runners up a chance to be runner up to the winner which was the Bulldog with the English Setter in second place.

Selection of the second day winners had not been without its element of drama. Tracey Witch, twice a Cruft's Best in Show winner, had missed out in 1951 but was looking well at this show. However, judging in a number of breeds was still going on when Best of Breed winners were called into the big ring. Judges increased the tempo of their judging in order that their Best of Breed winners would not be deprived of the opportunity to compete for Best in Show. One by one their Best of Breed winners hurried to join the assembly until only the Cocker Spaniel was missing. Judging in the big ring continued inexorably and was complete before the Cocker Spaniel winner arrived. When the ringside spectators realised that the dog which had been deprived of the opportunity to compete for Best in Show was none other than Tracey Witch they were quick to voice their appreciation of their favourite and their disappointment that she had been deprived of the opportunity to compete. Olympia's elegant Victorian superstructure rang with their cheerful protests.

Cruft's officials went into a hasty huddle to see if a way could be found to satisfy the crowd's wishes and for justice to be done. Had judging in the big ring itself been delayed or even progressed at a more leisurely pace the problem might easily have been avoided. The decision, however, had been made and was irreversible. Tracey Witch, through no fault of her own or of her owner's, had been deprived of the opportunity to enhance an already illustrious record.

Although Charles Cruft had tentatively introduced an obedience class for Alsatians as long ago as 1936 the Kennel Club had substituted exhibition for competition but, by 1952, seems to have been persuaded

The Pekingese puppy class in 1952 occupied a great deal of table room.

that Cruft's should have an obedience competition. There was consternation, however, when the Cruft's Committee announced that the competition would be by invitation only and restricted to a small number of winning dogs. It was argued that some of the chosen dogs would have been beaten in open competition by dogs which were not chosen; that the Obedience Prizes (which were far higher than those in other classes) would be easily won and that since the Kennel Club did not allow show classes restricted to champions or winners selection would contravene K.C. Rules. It was the first time, though it would not be the last, that Cruft's or, indeed, any show had of its own choice deliberately restricted its entry. Criticism of the decision became more muted during the course of a superb obedience competition which, to a far greater extent than breed judging, held a large audience, perched, not always comfortably or even safely, on every available vantage point in thrall. Some of the criticisms were not without point but who could argue with such a tremendous success?

More general concern was engendered, as Cruft's approached, by the suggestion, put forward by Sir William Darling, Conservative M.P. for

Lady Northesk, herself familiar with the big ring at Crufts both as exhibitor and judge, here presents the 1952 BIS trophy to Ch. Noways Chuckles.

South Edinburgh, that dogs should be taxed at 2 guineas a year, more than the current T.V. licence fee. Sir William said that dogs 'worry sheep, trample down allotments. They dirty the streets. They are dirt eaters. Some are flea-ridden. They trespass in gardens. They eat anything from half a pound to four pounds of food a week each. They may be carriers of disease. They sneeze and they snuffle while children are fondling them'. Like others who have followed him Sir William chose to ignore the fact that Cruft's was an exhibition of dogs which were well kept by responsible owners and which caused none of the problems to which he sought to draw attention. This did not deter him from making use of the attention which Cruft's attracts to further his misguided campaign.

In 1953 all eyes were again on Tracey Witch, who had won her fifty-first C.C. at the show, though rising eight years old, and was competing with Ch. Elch Edler of Ouborough, a Great Dane, Ch. Ashdown Glamorous, a Smooth Dachshund and an Afghan, Ch. Netheroyd Alibaba for the supreme award. The decision cannot have been any easier for the sentimentalists than for the judges. The Great Dane was handled by its owner Bill Siggers who had been kennel manager to the millionaire Mr J. V. Rank. Mr Rank had died during the previous year, his ambition to win Best in Show at Cruft's unfulfilled. Bill Siggers had bought Edler from the estate. The sentimentalists must have been torn between Tracey Witch and Edler. The judges had to take a cooler look and were impressed by the Afghan which had won at both Birmingham shows in 1952. However the dog which most impressed Winnie Barber and Lord Northesk was the Great Dane with the Afghan in Reserve. It is recorded that Bill Siggers required a glass of whisky before he regained his customary composure!

Bert Lloyd had first won in the Cruft's big ring in 1930. He won again in 1931, was reserve in 1934 and 1936, won again in 1938 and 1939 and again in 1948 and 1950. He reappeared, as a judge, in 1960 to round off thirty years of incredible success and establish a record which, alongside that of Lorna, Countess Howe's, is never likely to be matched.

For a number of years Cruft's appears to have been unable to discover any new breed deserving of its own classes. In 1954 Wire Haired Dachshunds made their mark in breed classes with fifty-nine entries and Weimaraners appeared with twenty-nine entries. The top entries had changed hands once more. In Hounds it was Smooth Dachshunds with 323 entries which came first. Toy dogs were led by Pekingese with 389 entries, while the most popular terrier breed was the Cairn with 255 entries. Gundogs still had Cocker Spaniels leading the way with 853 entries and the Non-Sporting breeds, rapidly becoming unmanageable in number were led by Alsatians with 564 entries. Only Soft Coated Wheaten Terriers and Buhunds had fewer than ten entries but Manchester Terriers, Newfoundlands, Smooth Collies, Tibetan Terriers,

Maremmas, Lhasa Apsos, Irish Water Spaniels and Curly Coated Retrievers had fewer than twenty. The overall entry too had fallen from the post-war peak of 12448 to 11835. Perhaps Cruft's 1954 would not be a vintage show but it was set fair to maintain the quality established by its predecessors.

There had been some rumblings of discontent among the electricians who worked at Cruft's and by the Sunday prior to the show this had blown up into what was described as 'guerrilla strike action'. The electricians had refused to disconnect the Hotel and Catering exhibition stands and the equipment used by Bertram Mills Circus both of which had been held at Olympia during the previous week. Olympia could not be cleared to make way for Cruft's and at 1 o'clock on Monday the B.B.C. announced that Cruft's had been cancelled. Previously only the 1926 L.K.A. Show had been abandoned as a result of industrial action. It had taken world wars to prevent Cruft's from taking place.

Cancellation resulting from forces well outside the Kennel Club's control produced an inevitable crop of suggestions that Cruft's should have its own home; unfortunately they came at a time when most major shows, including Cruft's, were facing a spiral of increased costs and falling entries. The climate did not seem right for heavy investment in a property which, while undoubtedly increasing control, would also increase expenditure.

February, 1955 must have arrived to find the Kennel Club and intending Cruft's exhibitors in some trepidation at the possibility of further industrial action forcing cancellation. A railway strike seemed to be looming and unforeseen strike action was always a possibility. The entry, for the third successive year, was again down but the number of dogs, 6127, was higher than ever.

In spite of the Kennel Club's much praised smooth and unruffled organisation the show was not without incident and problems. Efforts to gain a view of dogs in the big ring at Olympia resulted in precarious perches being found on all manner of improvised grandstands. These places were coveted by others and it seems that one Kennel Club member was dragged from his improvised perch by the ankle. His head cracked hard against Olympia's unyielding floor and his assailant, fearing that the blow might have caused serious harm, ran from the scene. He was pursued by another member who, according to leading judge Macdonald Daly, 'collared his man after a chase round half the ring and smacked him such a beauty in the kisser that he not only blacked the hooligan's eye but split the brow as well'. It seems that Macdonald Daly approved of such hooliganism. 'That's,' he said, 'the kind of summary justice for a case like that!'

It was, however, the judges' final decisions which seemed to cause greatest dissent among commentators with pretensions to expertise. Leo

Wilson hailed the show as a 'triumph of the mediocre. It must be a long time,' he said, 'since at the greatest dog show in the greatest dog breeding country in the world, four of what I regard as ordinary dogs were lined up for the best award. . . . If I had been in their (the judges) position I would have been dismayed to see the elimination on both days of great dogs . . . and the survival of dogs which . . . are far from outstanding specimens.'

There can have been few more popular Crufts BIS wins than that of Ch. Elch Edler and Bill Siggers in 1953.

    The dogs which Leo Wilson thought should have been in the big ring included two previous Cruft's Best in Show winners, the Great Dane and the Bulldog and these, among others, he would have placed far higher than the eventual winner Mrs A. Proctor's brown Standard Poodle Ch. Tzigane Aggri of Nashend. Aggri had been the winner on the second day, with a Corgi, Kaytop Maracas Mist, which had yet to win its title, in reserve. On the first day the Poodle had beaten an uncrowned Corgi, Kaytop Maracas Mist, to claim a place in the big ring. The judges, Air Commodore Cecil-Wright and T. Roger Boulton, excited Leo Wilson's sympathy by being obliged to select from such mediocrity but they did the only thing possible, they put the Poodle first and the Borzoi second, and saved the day. However, Leo Wilson's opinion was not the only one. Macdonald Daly took a different view. He quoted, with obvious approval, Cecil-Wright's opinion that the Poodle was one of the best he had ever seen. He quoted Winnie Barber's praise of its head, overall quality and soundness and was not slow to point out that it was she who had judged the breed. He pointed out that it was 'one of the Poodles which still, like its ancestors, works to the gun' and that 'as so often happens at Cruft's this dog that won was a favourite with the ringside crowd.' Two well known judges with very different opinions, not for the first time or the last.

Frank Warner Hill, equally well known as a judge as a canine journalist, was not prepared to accept that the awards had been arrived at in other than 'a highly logical manner and the finalists were all of the highest possible merit. . . . As far as the big ring is concerned I am not

No-one could accuse the 1955 presentation of trophies to Tzigane, the BIS winner, of being over theatrical.

The Wolfhound BOB winner from 1955 seems unimpressed by it all.

accepting any criticism. Good dogs were passed over, naturally, including two previous BIS winners at Cruft's but the finalists I avow were a great credit to British dogdom and well justified the judges' awards'.

The finalists emerged from yet another record number of dogs (6433) and an entry which at 12328 was little short of the 1952 record. On the first day the problems which could arise when breed judges were also employed to select finalists came close to the surface. W. W. Brainard had come from America to judge Wire-haired Fox Terriers, Macdonald Daly had judged Greyhounds and they were joined in the big ring by Hildebrand Wilson. Eventually the contestants were whittled down to Mr P. H. Copley's Ch. Caradochouse Spruce, the Wire Fox Terrier handled by Ernie Sharpe and the Greyhound Judy de Casembroot's and Miss Greenish's brindle and white Treetops Golden Falcon, still under two years old and short of his title. 'There was', reported Warner Hill, 'considerable hesitation with the solid looking Hildebrand carefully assessing the merits of these two top dogs of the other panel judges. There is no better handler of a Greyhound than Miss Greenish and

In 1956 the obedience competition was dominated by Alsatians, nowadays it is the Border Collie's star which is in the ascendancy.

Mr Sharpe, top professional handler last year, could show Spruce on an afternoon tea table. The big ring suited the Greyhound and a storm of applause had the verdict.' The dogs which lined up on the second day were said to be far better in quality than those from the first day and from these Mrs I. M. Tucker's Keeshond Ch. Volkrijk of Vorden emerged as the winner with Vic Smith's Bullmastiff Ch. Ambassador of Buttonoak in second place. From these four Winnie Barber, daughter of Judge Holland Buckley and sister of the K.C. Secretary, joined May Pacey. After a tense duel it was the first day's winners which prevailed.

Once more Cruft's rewrote the record books in 1957, to 12676 entries and 6562 dogs was added the claim that a gate of almost 50,000 was also a record, though it fell a long way short of the 40,000 a day to which Cruft, somewhat improbably, had laid claim at the old Agricultural Hall. It was perhaps appropriate that it was at this particular show that an incident took place which somehow encapsulates what many exhibitors valued about the days when Cruft's was open to all. A young novice Alsatian owner who had previously flown no higher than local shows had been attracted to Cruft's. She faced an entry of 439 and a class average little short of twenty and a judge who knew the breed intimately. It must have been well beyond her wildest dreams when she won the Bitch C.C. The two Alsatian judges then could not decide whether the bitch or the dog should be Best of Breed. After a tense discussion and an even tenser wait the official referee, Leo Wilson, was summoned and after further examination he pronounced in favour of the bitch.

There was, however, another side to the coin which argued that Cruft's policy of running ever bigger shows, irrespective of the quality of the dogs, was perhaps not one which the Kennel Club should continue to follow. This was further underlined when it was revealed that the veterinary surgeons, who had examined all the dogs as they entered a previous show, had conducted an unofficial survey and had discovered that about ten per cent were cryptorchids. The survey underlined existing concern about the quality of the dogs being shown at Cruft's and this, coupled with growing acceptance that Olympia was becoming intolerably crowded, prompted a number of suggestions. These varied from confining the show to established champions, on the lines of the

It was the turn of the Keeshond in 1957.

Dutch Winners Show in Amsterdam, to less draconian measures which would restrict the entry to dogs which had won their way into the K.C. Stud Book. It began to seem that the days of a Cruft's Show open to all were numbered and that there would be few more happy incidents such as had occurred in the Alsatian ring in 1957.

The breeds were split into five groups: Hounds, Gundogs, Terriers, Non-Sporting breeds and Toys. Joe Braddon and the American Stanley Halle judged The Hounds and made an Elkhound Ch. Sian of Deriormond their winner. A Wire Fox Terrier, Francis' Emprise Sensational, still to become a champion, won the Terrier Group and the Toys were headed by Darcy's Maltese Ch. Snowdrop of Beetop. Frank Warner Hill and Bill Siggers chose the Keeshond Tucker's Ch. Volkrijk of Vorden as the winner of the Non-Sporting Group. The same dog had been the best of the second day's winners at Crufts in 1956 and, as often seems to happen, would make further progress in 1957. Indeed Warner Hill and Bill Siggers had the satisfaction of seeing their two winners placed Best in Show and Reserve in the big ring. English's English Setter having won the Gundog Group and then going on to reserve in the show overall.

Cruft's 1958 still had a further small contribution to make to history. Exhibitors, many of whom had arrived at Olympia early on Friday morning and had not since ventured outside, became concerned when spectators began to appear with snow on their boots. By 7 o'clock in the evening, when the groups had been judged but still a couple of hours before exhibitors would normally be allowed to begin their journey home, it became apparent that the weather was deteriorating rapidly and so, in an unprecedented move for Cruft's, the doors were opened early and exhibitors allowed to flood out into a snowy landscape.

The two group judges for the first day, Miss Loughrey and May Pacey, had selected the Pekingese, Ch. Ku Chik Ko of Loofoo, the Lakeland terrier Tithbarn Highlight and the Whippet, Robmayswin Stargazer of Allways as their three first day's winners, they doubtless hardly noticed the weather! On the second day the group judges were Lola Daly and Fred Cross. They had the Non-Sporting Group and the Gundogs to judge. It was a Bullmastiff, Mr and Mrs E. L. Terry's Ch. Ambassadorson of Buttonoak which took the Non-Sporting Group and a Pointer Hilda Parkinson's Ch. Chiming Bells, handled by Bill Parkinson, which led the Gundogs.

The need to increase Cruft's entry fees in 1959 led to all manner of prognostications that the show would be a flop. A few exhibitors for whom Cruft's was an annual and only foray into the show world dropped out and there were fewer 'complimentary' entries but the overall entry (13211) was a new world record. The need to increase entry fees was simply a matter of matching rising costs. Olympia's rental had risen from £1500 in 1948 to £5000 and during this time entry fees had risen from 27/– (£1.35) to 30/– (£1.50).

The Kennel Club had acted quickly and decisively to the survey carried out by Cruft's vets in the previous year. They simply banned all cryptorchids and monorchids from entering the show. As a result of the ban four dogs were turned away from the show. One tried another entrance and another vet but without success!

Otherwise the show ran smoothly and without untoward incident to culminate in Winner Barber and J. A. Cecil-Wright selecting their Best in Show winner from the Beagle, Ch. Derawuda Vixen, the Pekingese, Ch. Acol Ku-Anna, the Welsh Terrier, Ch. Sandstorm Saracen, the Labrador Retriever, Ch. Ruler of Blaircourt and the Standard Poodle, Ch. Frenches Honeysuckle. Their choice was the Welsh Terrier which, they said, they 'could not fault. . . . The best Welsh Terrier we have ever seen; never stopped showing'. Reserve was the Labrador, 'a lovely dog; perhaps just not good enough in movement'. But good enough to go reserve Best in Show at the biggest dog show ever!

Yet another record entry came in 1960 with 7203 dogs making 14297 entries with the biggest increase coming in the Toy Group. 'This', said the experts, 'would certainly seem to be the age of the small dog.' The Toy

No one could have anticipated the impact which Crufts and television would make on one another when MacDonald Daly introduced his first Cruft's TV programme.

Group had increased its entries from 875 in 1959 to 1041, and the Toy and Miniature Poodles, with 410 and 564 entries respectively, confirmed the growing popularity of small dogs.

The show itself was changing. The annual scrabble for seats round the big ring had given way to a grandstand. Nor were the needs of exhibitors forgotten. The Kennel Club made a waiting room available for Best of Breed winners waiting to compete in the groups. Previously they had had to gather in the icy Portcullis Avenue.

'This,' said Lord Northesk, the show's Chairman, 'is only the start of my committee's policy of glamourising Cruft's, we have a lot of new ideas up our sleeves, ideas we think and hope are worthy of the greatest Dog Show in the World.'

Nor were improvements confined to the breed rings. Mr D. Churchman had been invited to judge the obedience classes. He turned up with his own well drilled stewards who carried boards which gave the audience information about the scores achieved in each test and by each dog. The result was that the audience could become involved in and excited by the progress of the competition. It was a tremendous improvement and one which led to an appropriately tremendous result.

Mr Shackleton's Border Collie, Zena, won the bitch obedience and, according to James Baldwin, had even more to crow about than had the Best in Show winner.

'She became an obedience champion when she was two years old, and has competed at Cruft's every year from 1953 to 1960 inclusive, winning twice, second twice, and third once. During that time she was bred from once, but only had one puppy, which is now Obedience Ch. Dash, which has also won twice at Cruft's and has been second once, and he and his mother have won well over 100 obedience certificates between them. And when Zena won last week she was ten years old. No wonder she "brought the house down".'

Response to what had happened in the Best in Show ring tended to be less laudatory. Florence Nagle described the Best in Show winner as a very good young dog who in a year's time would be really excellent. Stafford Somerfield thought 'it was a very moderate year for quality, and the best in show judges must have wished for a finished and exciting animal that appealed to the experts and the general public.'

Enid Nichols and Joe Braddon had judged the Toy Group and had put up Dyke's Pomeranian Pixietown Serenade of Hadleigh. The same judges had put up Nagle and Clarke's Irish Wolfhound Sulhamstead Merman in the Hound Group and the Sealyham Brastedchart Sea Princess in the Terrier Group. None of the three had been champions when they arrived at the show. Henry Fottrell and Stephen Young judged the Non-Sporting and Gundog Groups. They described the Non-Sporting Group as 'fairly strong' and made the Dalmatian Ch. Fanhill

Fleur of Queenwood their winner while in a 'very strong' Gundog Group it was the Labrador Retriever Cairn's Ch. Ruler of Blaircourt which prevailed. Bert Lloyd and Fred Cross judged Best in Show and opted for the Wolfhound with the Pomeranian in reserve place.

Cruft's records seldom last long and that set in 1960 proved to be no exception to the general rule. 7203 dogs in 1960 became 7892 in 1961 and 14297 entries was increased to 15721. Delighted though the Committee undoubtedly was the size of the entry brought problems. Holland Buckley, Cruft's secretary, warned that 'Olympia cannot stretch any more and I envisage a final limit of 8000 dogs'. It was assumed that some way of limiting the entry would be introduced before the 1962 show.

In 1961 Marjorie Couzens and Frank Warner Hill judged the Hound, Toy and Terrier Groups on the first day. Their winners were an Afghan, Major Pede's Bletchingley Ragman of Scheherezade, a Pekingese, Ch. Khognac Patience of Caversham and an Airedale Terrier, Pat McCaughrey and Mrs Schuth's Ch. Riverina Tweedsbairn, Ricky to his friends, presented and handled by Joe Cartledge with the able assistance of Mary Wells, soon to become Mrs Cartledge and to be heard of again in connection with Cruft's. On the second day May Pacey and Cecil-Wright judged the remaining two groups, their winners being an English Setter, Mrs William's Silbury Soames of Madavale, and an Alsatian, Walker's Ch. Sparky of Aronbel.

Winnie Barber and Joe Braddon judged the final and it was on the Airedale, with the English Setter reserve, that their choice was to fall.

Tweedsbairn, they said, was 'three years old, fully matured, and in magnificent form, showed and moved as a Terrier should, he has great bone and muscle and yet has quality, his presentation in the ring was perfect, with no exaggeration or excess of leg-hair and whisker'. Joe Cartledge would have enjoyed that because, with the self-deprecating wit which was one of his hallmarks, he often used to claim that his grooming equipment had been made out of old NAAFI cutlery. He was, it was claimed, only the second professional handler to pilot a dog to the winner's rostrum. The first had been Georgie Barr, who was the first to congratulate Joe on a magnificent win.

At the end of 1961 the Kennel Club announced that registration figures had broken all records to reach 146000, nearly 10000 more than in the previous year and double what had been achieved only five years previously. There could be no denying the growing public interest in pedigree dogs.

In the past industrial action had harmed Cruft's. In 1962 it might be said to have aided the show. A work to rule by Post Office workers had the effect of reducing the entry, something which the Cruft's Committee was not unhappy about. A further increase in entry fees contributed to the same effect. The experts even went so far as to suggest that with a 25/– (£1.25) entry fee against a first prize of £2 10s (£2.50) the optimum had been reached and may even have been passed. How wrong they were!

Sir Richard Glynn and Fred Cross judged the 1962 first day's groups from which the Wire-haired Fox Terrier, Ch. Crackwyn Cockspur, the Maltese, Ch. Vicbrita Spectacular and the Beagle, Cannybuff Barvae Pryer emerged as winners. On the second day Judy de Casembroot and the Earl of Northesk chose the French Bulldog, Phillippa of Elmsleigh, and the Cocker Spaniel, Collinwood Black Eagle, who had to beat Silbury Soames to get the top spot, as their winners.

It was then the turn of May Pacey and Vernon Hirst to make their decisions. They chose a dog which was, they said, 'an outstanding one of the breed; he has such a big refined head and short back and well-made quarters that make him hard to beat. He also was shown very well and was in perfect condition.' The winner was the Wire, handled by Bob Barlow, with the black Cocker, feeling the effects of a long day, in reserve.

In 1961 Joe Cartledge had handled his terrier charge to the top spot. In 1962 Bob Barlow had won with the Wire and 1963 was to make it a hat trick for professional handlers and their terriers. 1963 was to be Les Atkinson's turn with a dog, bought for £5.00, whose journey to the top, even more than most, exemplified the magic of Cruft's and of dog shows in general.

The Hound, Terrier and Toy Groups were judged by Stephen Young and Joe Braddon who commented on the quality of all three groups. The Hound Group was won by the Basenji, Ch. Lograk Lubilash of Littlebreach, yet another Cruft's 'first'. In the Terrier Group it was the Lakeland which prevailed. The Toy Group, another high class group, was won by the Blenheim Cavalier Ch. Amelia of Luguna. On the second day Lola Daly and Frank Warner Hill had no difficulty in sorting their winners out quickly. The Gundog Group was won by William's English Setter, Sh. Ch. Silbury Soames of Madavale and the Non-Sporting winner was Crompton's red Chow Chow Ch. Van Lee of Kai Oko. The stage was set for Cecil-Wright and Sir Richard Glynn to judge Best in Show. Their report expresses appreciation of the quality of the dogs they had to choose from. Both were 'genuinely sorry that we could not give it to that lovely English Setter, Sh. Ch. Silbury Soames of Madavale, who proved what a grand dog he is by attaining Reserve Best in Show for the second year.' Both judges were in fact captivated by the young Lakeland Terrier which they said 'was as near a perfect specimen of its breed as one could imagine' and it was impossible to withhold the premier award from it.

After his win with the thirteen-month-old Lakeland Terrier, Recruit, Les Atkinson was asked one of the less than pertinent questions of which reporters at Cruft's seem exceptionally fond.

'Do you think she is old enough to win Best in Show at Cruft's?'

'Looks like it to me!'

The growing interest in showing dogs, the increasing number of dog shows and, so, the greater opportunities to qualify dogs for Cruft's in 1964 all allied to confidence in the way in which the Kennel Club was developing Cruft's resulted in an entry of 16022 from 8277 dogs. It was the first time, anywhere in the world that a show had attracted more than 8000 dogs. The previous best of 7892 had been set in 1961, inevitably by Cruft's. For the second successive year Alsatians, in the Non-Sporting Group produced the highest entry with 360 dogs. This group now had 35 breeds though the Poodles, with 650 dogs in the three sizes, had been judged on the first day while the rest of the group was judged on the second. Among the Hounds Smooth Haired Dachshunds had 135 representatives. There were 258 Pekingese in the Toy Group and Cocker Spaniels headed the Gundog Group with 293 dogs.

At the other end of the scale only in the Toy group, where Japanese (later Japanese Chins) had attracted twenty-seven dogs, was bottom place occupied by a breed which was not of British origin. There were just four Soft Coated Wheaten Terriers, eleven Mastiffs, nine Sussex Spaniels and twenty-three Deerhounds. It seemed that there was no revival of interest in British breeds.

Cruft's also faced 1964 with a new President, Air-Commodore J. A. C. Cecil-Wright, the Kennel Club's own Chairman. From 1891 to 1907, with a gap in 1905, Sir Humphrey F. de Trafford was Cruft's President. His Grace the Duke of Beaufort had occupied the position briefly in 1905. From 1908 to 1923 the President had been Sir Lindsay Lindsay-Hogg, Bt, from 1924 to 1929 His Grace the Duke of Grafton. There had been no President from 1929 to 1931. In 1932 Dr J. H. Salter was President, he was followed in 1933 by Prof. L. Turton Price and from 1934 to 1939 by Mr, later Sir, Nigel Coleman. The Kennel Club did not appoint a President when it took the show over but by 1964 felt that 'owing to the prominence the Kennel Club has given to the name Cruft's, many people are ignorant of the fact that it is today the Kennel Club show. The General Committee were disturbed by this . . . and felt that the situation would be corrected to some extent if they invited Air-Commodore Cecil-Wright to become President of Cruft's'.

Yet another innovation in 1964 was the much publicised offer of a £500 prize to the Best in Show winner, provided that its owner had paid an insurance premium. It was a commercial gimmick in the very best of Charles Cruft's own tradition.

On the first day Judy de Casembroot and Viscount Chelmsford had judged the Hound, Toy and Terrier Groups and had selected Mrs Hope Water's nine-year-old white Saluki Ch. Burydown Freyha, the Yorkshire

Terrier Mrs S. I. Groom's Ch. Pagnell Peter Pan and Mrs Audrey Dallison's Wire Fox Terrier Ch. Gosmore Kirkmoor Tessa, handled by Vince Mitchell whose father Billy was in America to handle a dog at Westminster on the following day. On the second day Mrs Gwen Broadley and Fred Cross were faced by the Gundog winners from which they selected Mrs A. Williams' English Setter Sh. Ch. Silbury Soames of Madavale while from the huge Non-Sporting Group the victor was Mrs M. R. Franklin's Rough Collie Pattingham Pacemaker. All six finalists, only one of which was not already a champion, were owned by ladies and all had won Best in Show or Reserve Best in Show awards during the preceding months.

Winnie Barber and Stephen Young had the task of selecting the overall winner and, having agreed that rarely had they seen five better dogs, chose the English Setter and the Saluki to occupy the winners' rostrum. And did the winner's owner, who worked as a petrol pump attendant in a Somerset garage, go home clutching a cheque for £500? She did not. In fact none of the five group winners had taken out the necessary insurance, to them the opportunity to compete was enough.

8.   Cruft's Restricted

The continued growth of interest in dog showing, increase in the number of breeds from which exhibitors could choose, ease of travel, more time for leisure pursuits and more money to devote to them all combined with the age old need for people to live their lives without being totally divorced from contact with some species other than their own to make dog showing an even more popular recreational activity. For a number of years it had been apparent that Olympia was becoming uncomfortably, and sometimes perhaps even dangerously, crowded during the course of the three major championship shows which were held there. All three were faced with the same problem which they each eventually solved in a different way. The Ladies Kennel Association Show moved from Olympia to the far bigger and newer indoor venue at the National Exhibition Centre, Birmingham where its size could continue to increase until, in the course of time, it would take over Cruft's mantle as the biggest dog show in the world. The Richmond Championship Dog Show also moved from Olympia but chose to become an outdoor, tented show at the famous Ascot Racecourse in Berkshire where it too could continue to expand.

These moves were to leave Cruft's as the only major championship show in London. Should Cruft's join the exodus from London? It was unthinkable that the capital should have no major dog shows and Cruft's was, in any case, firmly tied to London by almost a century of tradition. Nevertheless the problem of trying to fit a quart, which showed every sign of growing into a gallon or more, into a pint pot remained and the Cruft's Committee was obliged to do something to alleviate the problem. Every possible option was considered but eventually the committee decided to reduce the size of the show by barring puppies under eight months of age from being shown at Cruft's in 1965.

'Never before has any show in this country placed restriction on entries. Never before has any committee planned to reduce the size of a show. Never before has any executive deliberately taken action to reduce its income by approximately £1000. And never before has any decision proved to be so demonstrably correct!' Leo Wilson writing in *Our Dogs* was certain that the decision was the right one. The Committee had planned for about 250 fewer dogs than in 1964, in the event they had to cope with 210 fewer. Their strategy had worked but, inevitably, it was a strategy which, as dog shows continued to increase in popularity, might need revising on an annual basis if the total was to be kept constant at about 8000 dogs. A reduction in the number of puppies, even the total elimination of puppies, offered only a limited room for manoeuvre and one which, many felt, seriously reduced the show's purpose as a shop window for British pedigree dogs.

It soon became obvious that barring puppies from the show only gave the Committee a limited amount of control over the size of the entry. Other methods would have to be considered and eventually the Committee produced the novel idea that all Cruft's exhibits must qualify by winning a prize at a championship show in the previous year. Here was a method which could be, and would be, adjusted to suit changing circumstances and which while offering control over numbers supported regular exhibitors at the expense of those whose only contact with the world of dog shows was an annual excursion to Cruft's with which to impress the neighbours. There was one other consideration which apparently weighed heavily on the Committee and that was the fear that entries in some breeds had reached, and may even already have gone beyond, what one judge could handle in one day. More space or a longer show would not address this problem. The only other possibility seemed to be to restrict the entry in some way.

Even so it was a decision which Stanley Dangerfield felt needed defending. He pointed out that the 1948 entry had produced 4273 dogs but that, less than twenty years later, the 'immediate threat' (perhaps a strange choice of words in the circumstances) was of a 10000 dogs. 'Olympia', he said, 'has a greater usable floor space than any other hall in Great Britain, so alternative sites presented no appeal'.

Already Cruft's occupied Olympia's two largest halls, the Grand and the National. A third hall, the Empire, existed but could not be used in conjunction with the other two to offer an integrated event. The Kennel Club had considered extending Cruft's to three days but had found that Olympia was unavailable for a three day event. In any case they were fearful that the additional costs involved with an extended show might, coupled with what Stanley Dangerfield described as 'three thin days' reduce the show's attraction to exhibitors, spectators and to the trade.

It would have been possible to restrict the entry by price. In 1959 an increased entry fee had reduced the entry by four hundred dogs, a further increase in 1962 had the same effect and it was anticipated that this would again be the case in 1966. These increases had been made necessary by rising costs and were not regarded as a means to control the size of the entry. Indeed the Kennel Club was firmly of the opinion that any restriction should, as far as was possible, protect the regular show goer at the expense of those who showed only at Cruft's for the prestige which an entry could offer.

'The die was cast. The hundred-year-old dog show mentality that the biggest was automatically the best, was deliberately discarded. It was admitted that sheer bulk has no merit. From now on the accent will be on quality and not quantity'.

What had happened since 1965 when a start had been made by barring all puppies under eight months of age could not possibly be regarded as improving quality. Now Cruft's was to insist that dogs should have won a prize at a Championship show during the preceding year. Once a year exhibitors were effectively barred while regular exhibitors, given a modest degree of success, were protected.

Stanley Dangerfield risked a few prophecies. He said that 'in the future, dogs will be advertised as "Qualified for Crufts". . . . Every effort will be made to bring fanciers here from all over the world. . . . Dogs might be allowed to display their qualifying cards over their benches. . . . (and) . . . surely quarantine will not last for ever? . . . Then Cruft's will really have something. The best dogs from a score of countries coming here to have a crack at the top honours that the world of dogs has to offer.' Even though neither veterinary advances nor political complacency have yet made quarantine unnecessary all but one of Stanley Dangerfield's prophecies have come true. Only the display of prize cards from previous shows does not now take place.

W. J. Holmes, one of the Kennel Club team which had negotiated the purchase of Cruft's from Mrs Cruft, had other reservations about the qualifier. He pointed out that Kennel Club rules required every championship show to provide open classes which were open to all and that the qualifier meant that they were not open to all. The Kennel Club's response was that they were open to all which had qualified.

In 1965 Best in Show was judged by two people who had and would continue to have a tremendous influence over Kennel Club affairs. One was Colonel Sir Richard Glynn and the other Air Commodore Cecil-Wright. Both served as Chairmen of the Kennel Club and had before them a Beagle, winner of the Hound Group under Arthur Fullwood, Ch. Forrardon Appeline Beeswing, owned by Mrs Harris and Leonard Pagliero, himself a future K.C. Chairman who had judged the Cruft's Obedience Tests in 1964 and would also judge Best in Show to become the only person with such a wide experience of Cruft's.

Also in the Best in Show ring was the Golden Retriever Raymond's Sh. Ch. Gainspa Florette of Shiremoor, and, two breeds which had not recently been seen in the Cruft's Best in Show ring, the Bedlington Philips' Rathsrigg Little Caesar and the Maltese, White's Ch. Vicbrita Fidelity. It was, however, for the fifth dog, winner of the Non-Sporting Group, the Alsatian Godden's Ch. Fenton of Kenwood which attracted the ringside support.

In the event the two distinguished judges and the ringsiders were in agreement. It was the Alsatian which won the Best in Show award, with the Beagle in reserve place.

In 1966, with Bill Siggers and Fred Cross making the decisions, Best in Show was won by a dog owned by 'a near novice and is not yet even a champion'. That dog was an apricot Toy Poodle, Oakington Puckshill Amber Sunblush which had won from the first section of the Non-Sporting Group. The owner was Mrs C. B. Perry, now better known as Clare Coxall. Runner up, from the Gundog Group, was the Pointer Sh. Ch. Blakeshay Avant Tout with the remaining three groups being won by the Afghan, Ch. Kismati Khan of Tarril, the Pomeranian, Sweet Dreams of Aurum, and the Lakeland Terrier, Stingray of Derryabah. The Pembroke Crogi, Ch. Crawleythorn Miss Poppet was winner of the second section of Non-Sporting Group. Dogs apart it was Mrs Perry's own demeanour at the post-Cruft's press conference which by now had become an obligatory part of the winner's role, which seems most to have impressed Stanley Dangerfield.

> 'Mrs Perry', he said, 'is a cool customer who has learned a lot in her eight years in dogs. As I watched her dealing with the ever penetrating press questions I thought of the intense emotion of some past winners. Of Bill Siggers who was too weak to stand after Elch Edler won for him in 1953. We sat on beer crates in a chill and forgotten corridor, the perspiration streaming off him. . . . Of Bert Lloyd who broke down and wept when he won with Witch in 1950. "No," said Mrs Perry "she is definitely not for sale". "When I bought her I could see the bone structure was perfect". . . . "No it was not a very great surprise. I always knew she was good".'

Stanley Dangerfield also recalled another conversation he had heard some few weeks previously after a well known and respected specialist judge of Poodles had examined Sunblush and declared that though she was sweet and charming, a dear, she was definitely not up to ticket winning standard.

In the following year the name of Stingray of Derryabah, by now carrying the title of Champion, reappeared, this time not just as a group winner but as winner of Best in Show.

The 1967 show found itself being compared with Cassius Clay as 'definitely the greatest' and like Cassius Clay's performances Cruft's too was enlivened by unexpected incidents. One of the dogs competing in the obedience classes rushed into a crowded grandstand to greet an old friend. Margaret Osborne achieved headline status and underlined the dubious value of the qualifier by withholding all the prizes in one class, though the contrary point was made by the entry of over six hundred champions at the show. Less unexpected was the end of compulsory veterinary examination of every dog which came into the show. With the dramatic increase in the number of dogs entered at all shows the examinations had become a real problem. They needed the services of a large number of vets. Exhibitors had to resign themselves to long delays, often standing out in the rain, before they could gain entry to the show and only seldom were dogs refused entry because of their condition. It was felt that improvements in protective vaccines and in the overall health of show dogs now made the veterinary examinations unnecessary.

Cruft's 1967 also saw the introduction of the Working and Utility Groups created out of the thirty-two breeds which had formerly comprised the Non-Sporting Group. Thirty-two breeds was considered to be far too many to compete in a single group. The Hound, Terrier and Toy Groups were judged on the first day by Lola Daly and the American journalist Maxwell Riddle. He had gone on record as saying that 'Cruft's is still almost unbelievable . . . for its calm, courteous, unhurried and unflustered atmosphere'. He ventured the modest prophecy that the qualifier would lead to an increase in entries at other championship shows and concluded his comments by saying that 'For every good dog in the breed at Westminster (the American equivalent of Cruft's), there will be three or four at Cruft's. And for this, the superb British livestock breeder is chiefly responsible in both countries.' It was a compliment which could not have come from a more impeccable source. On the second day Gwen Broadley and Stanley Dangerfield judged the new Utility and Working Groups as well as the Gundog Group.

The six dogs to be brought into the Best in Show ring to face the Viscount Chelmsford and Frank Warner Hill were the Smooth Standard Dachshund Ch. Womack Wrightstarturn, which had beaten the famous Wire-haired Dachshund, Ch. Gisbourne Inca for top spot in the Hound Group, the Pug Ch. Cedarwood Blunshill's Nimrod from the Toy Group and the Lakeland Terrier, already well known to the crowded ringside, Ch. Stingray of Derryabah. The Gundog Group provided a Cocker Spaniel Sh. Ch. Lochranza Quettadene Marksman while the new Working Group produced a Shetland Sheepdog, Deloraine Dilys of Monkswood and the Utility Group a Canadian-bred black Standard Poodle which had taken the show ring by storm since he had emerged from quarantine just five days before the previous Cruft's. He was Ch. Bibelot's Tall Dark and Handsome and on the morning after Cruft's he was on his way back to America to compete at Westminster where a happy ending was not to be. He was beaten in the breed by the eventual Non-Sporting Group winner Ch. Alekai Marlaine who had to give way for Best in Show to the Scottish Terrier Ch. Bardene Bingo. From these six outstanding dogs Lord Chelmsford and Frank Warner Hill chose the previous year's runner up, the Lakeland Terrier, as their winner and the Standard Poodle as their runner up. Immediately after the show Stingray too flew to America and would confirm his greatness by winning Best in Show at Westminster in the following year.

The export business to which dogs made a significant contribution was stressed in the following year when it was revealed that from 577 dogs sold overseas in 1947 the cumulative figure had grown to 84160 with 8327 going overseas in 1967 alone.

Cruft's, 1968 was also the show at which criticism of Olympia's cramped and dreary condition began to surface. The monotonous and repetitive big ring presentation and the absence of window dressing all led to calls for a change of venue. It was even suggested, though not with much hope of a sympathetic hearing that Cruft's might leave London or find a suitable London venue for a mid summer show.

On the first day, Judy de Casembroot, who had taken her Greyhound to the winner's rostrum in 1956, and Max Singleton, a well known Scottish Terrier breeder whose veterinary son, Brian, would eventually become Director of the Animal Health Trust, judged the three sporting groups. On the second day the Non-Sporting breeds were judged by Owen Grindey and Stephen Young. Together they sent six dogs forward for Josephine Creasy and Arthur Fullwood. They were a lemon and white Beagle, Houndsmark Manful, a Scottish Terrier, the previous

At Crufts 1968 Adam Faith was just another hopeful exhibitor.

year's top dog, Ch. Gosmore Eilburn Admaration, a German Short-haired Pointer, Ch. Patrick of Malahide, a Dalmatian, Ch. Fanhill Faune, a Maltese, Ellwyn Victorianna and an eight-year-old Pyrenean Mountain Dog, Ch. Bergerie Diable. Both judges had no hesitation in placing the Dalmatian in first place with the Pyrenean playing the supporting role.

It was in 1968 that the Kennel Club revived an old Cruft's tradition by holding a Cruft's Dinner. Held in Painter's Hall it was described as a glittering affair. 'Marble stairs, Old Masters on the walls, lush carpeting, carved ceilings, the ladies in elegant dresses and tiaras, gentlemen wore medals and, of course, liveried servants.' It must have felt a million miles from Olympia's drab and overcrowded halls.

One guest at the dinner was Her Serene Highness Princess Antoinette of Monaco, a past-President of the Federation Cynologique International who had used her time in London to approach the Ministry of Agriculture and plead for a cessation of quarantine. Her initiative received support from the Kennel Club whose Secretary Charles Binney said that 'Removal of the 67-year-old quarantine laws would be quite reasonable now in view of recent veterinary advances'. The Kennel Club Chairman, Sir Richard Glynn, M.P., added his support to the argument but fortunately the Ministry of Agriculture refused to be swayed and quarantine stayed firmly in place.

The entry for the 1969 show continued the recovery which had been apparent during the previous year but, even so, 13366 entries was still lower than anything since 1959. The show itself was, as usual, well run and without any apparent problems. The six group winners introduced new faces to the Cruft's big ring. The Hound Group, judged by Mrs Whitwell, was won by Holden's Afghan Hound Ranjitsinhji of Jagai, while the Gundogs, judged by L. C. James, were led home by the Cocker Spaniel, MacMillan's Sh. Ch. Lochranza Strollaway. Clifton's Bedlington Terrier, Ch. Vardene Blue Grenadier, won the Terrier Group under Nancy Baylay and the Utility Group, under Fred Parsons, was won by Walne and Coppage's Standard Poodle, Ch. Vulcan Psyche of Gayshaws. It was the Alsatian, always a very popular breed with the ringsiders, which won the Working Group under Bill Siggers, returning to the scene of his triumph with the Great Dane. The Alsatian was White's Ch. Hendrawen Nibelung of Charavigne. Finally the Toy Group, judged by Hermione Warner Hill, produced a breed which in the past had been very much at home in the Cruft's big ring, the Pomeranian Berney's Pandora of Aurum.

Maurice Gilliatt, a very well known and respected judge of Gundogs, was joined in the Best in Show ring by the Australian judge, David Roche, and together they selected the Alsatian as their Best in Show winner with the Cocker Spaniel in the reserve place.

Though Cruft's was approaching its eightieth birthday it was still

German Shepherd Dogs are one of the breeds for which the ringside spectators have a particular affection. In 1969 their hopes were realised when Nibelung won BIS.

capable of producing a few 'firsts'. In 1970 for the first and only time the Groups and Best in Show were judged by one man. That man was Stanley Dangerfield, and, for the first time, Best in Show went to a Pyrenean Mountain Dog, Mr and Mrs Prince's 2½ year old Bergerie Knur. Reserve was Caddy's Cocker Spaniel Ch. Ovaine Chieftain. A Standard Poodle Ashwell's Ch. Vicmar's Follow That, a Norwich Terrier Bradshaw and Finney's Withalder Locksley, an English Toy Terrier, Palmer's Ch. Stealaway Golden Girl, and Harris and Pagliero's Beagle Ch. Forrardon Foxtrot won the remaining groups. Foxtrot, who had quite a Cruft's pedigree, also created another first by being owned and handled at Cruft's by the Kennel Club Chairman. In 1965 Ch. Forrardon

Appeline Beeswing had been reserve BIS at Cruft's, in 1967 her daughter had represented Beagles in the Hound Group and in 1970 her adversary for Best of Breed had been her litter brother, Frolic.

Rather oddly, in view of Cruft's history, the way in which the Kennel Club made use of the press to boost their show's attractions was described as 'deplorable'. But the critic, Bill Rasbridge had a point when he said that 'each year as Cruft's comes round we can now expect to be regaled in the newspapers and/or over the air with attacks on pedigree dogs and their breeders. Cruft's seems to be regarded by certain sections as a heaven sent opportunity and an appropriate occasion to pull Dogdom's skeletons, real and imaginary, out of the cupboard.' The same old skeletons continue to be rattled each year as public interest in pedigree dogs generally and in dog shows in particular grows from strength to strength.

Her Majesty Queen Elizabeth, the Kennel Club's Patron, visited the show in 1969.

The 1970 BIS winner was Bergerie Knur, one of relatively few winners large enough to dwarf the trophy.

In 1971 Catherine Sutton and Judy de Casembroot were canvassing support for the idea of holding a Cruft's Week, not with a week-long show, two days was regarded as plenty long enough, but with a show supported by a variety of canine activities. Her Royal Highness Princess Anne, by her presence at the show, extended her family's connection with Cruft's.

Bill Rasbridge returned to his criticism of the effect of Cruft's publicity which he still believed would not only attract criticism to pedigree dogs but would also have the effect of making the show intolerably crowded.

In order to contain the steady increase in the number of Cruft's exhibits, produced by a growing determination to qualify and greater opportunity to do so as more championship shows appeared, more breeds achieved championship status and championship shows provided more classes in which exhibitors could qualify their dogs the qualifier for Cruft's 1972 was made far stiffer than anything which had applied during the previous seven years. Only dogs which had won a first prize at a championship show during the previous year would be eligible for entry. For the first time the claim that the qualifier led to an increased quality of entry as was revealed when the *Kennel Gazette* analysed the entry and found that twenty-eight per cent of the dogs already held challenge certificates. Unfortunately this meant that many of the lower classes were poorly filled and minor puppy classes, in particular, because of the passage of time between qualifying, were particularly badly hit.

Problems with the qualifier apart the majority opinion was that the Kennel Club's new Secretary, Commander John Williams, got off to an excellent start at his debut as a Show organiser. He did, however, face a problem which was perhaps a sign of times to come. Each year there were threats to disrupt the show, sometimes by violent means, and always from unidentified sources. Judgement was needed to decide just how seriously these threats should be treated. The appropriate authority was always informed, sometimes rings were changed, judges withdrawn

Lord Snowdon behind the camera at Crufts.

Princess Anne appears to have posed some difficult questions during her visit to Crufts.

and sniffer dogs employed. Action was taken to nullify the threat without causing alarm or providing the culprit with gratuitous publicity. There are more facets to organising Cruft's, or any major public event, than the participants and the public are aware of.

Criticism, however, was not entirely stifled. Yves Bentinck, Chairman of the Kennel Club's Ladies Branch, was critical of the absence of ladies from the Cruft's Committee. She pointed out that 'Two of the biggest and best run shows in the country, the LKA and WELKS, are entirely run by the ladies committees' but stopped short of following her argument to its logical conclusion when she said that 'the really serious minded of us I am sure are not of the opinion women should take over or even have a say on the General Committee of the Kennel Club.'

Catherine Sutton judged the Hound Group and found her winner in

Anne Knight's Whippet Ch. Dondelayo Duette a daughter of a famous dam to which Mrs Sutton had given the CC and BIS at Bournemouth in 1969. George Down judged the Toy Group and placed the Yorkshire Terrier Beech's Ch. Deebees Beebee first. In the Terrier Group it was Joe Cartledge, who had piloted the Airedale, Ch. Riverina Tweedsbairn, to the winner's rostrum in 1961, who helped to make history when Miss Violet Drummond Dick's Bull Terrier Ch. Abraxas Audacity became his winner. No Bull Terrier had previously won a Group at Cruft's. Joe Braddon judged the Gundogs for which he could find no higher praise than 'quite a strong group'. The winner was an American Cocker Spaniel, another Cruft's first, Am. Ch. Dreamridge Delegate with a seven-year-old English Setter, Sh. Ch. Iriquois Rainbow, in reserve place. The run of firsts continued when Thelma Gray, who had done so much to popularise the breed, placed a Pembrokeshire Welsh Corgi, Ch. Kaytop Marshall, first in the Working Group and finally the indomitable Miss Loughrey placed Mrs N. Creed's Standard Poodle, Ch. Greekmyth Aphrodite, to win the Utility Group.

The stage was set for a new breed to occupy the winner's rostrum and Arthur Westlake, dispensing with the ritual of telephoning his decisions to an announcer first led the Whippet to the reserve place and then indicated that the Bull Terrier was his winner. It was a popular choice and Stafford Somerfield captured the dog's appeal when he wrote: 'Well called Audacity this one, a wicked boy obviously with a twinkle in his eye and courage deep in his heart. I go for him. The crowd love him too, and cheer when he shakes himself and sends the white chalk flying.'

All the criticisms which had been building up for several years appear to have surfaced at Cruft's 1973. The organisation was, as ever, impeccable but even loyal Kennel Club stalwarts such as Harry Glover and Yves Bentinck added their voices to the growing criticism. Harry Glover said that he had 'never seen Olympia looking more untidy and scruffy'. Yves Bentinck said that she had 'seldom heard more grumbling around the ringside, in fact all over the show'. Even the President of Cruft's and the Kennel Club Chairman, J. A. Cecil-Wright had to admit that the show 'was probably the most controversial Kennel Club Championship Show'. The dilapidated venue, the absence of puppies, the big ring lighting, the use of telephones to transmit the judge's decision to a distant commentary box, the domination by trade stands and the crowds all came in for their share of criticism but it was an incident which occurred in the big ring which cast the biggest cloud over the event.

The Hound Group, judged by Harry Glover, had been won by the Greyhound Odell's Ch. Shalfleet Sir Lancelot. Margaret Osborne had placed Nan Butler's Pembroke Welsh Corgi, Ch. Georgetter of Wey at head of the Working Group. Judy de Casembroot had favoured the

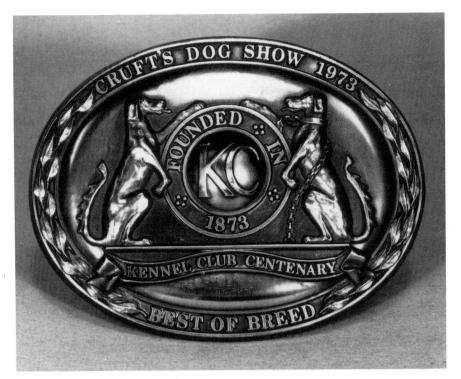

Cavalier King Charles, Hall and Evan's Alansmere Aquarius in what she described as an outstanding Toy Group. A Bulldog, Ch. Portfield-So-Small had won the Utility Group under Felicia Price while a Kerry Blue Terrier, Int. Ch. Sheenon Fusilier, had won under Tom Horner. The six finalists were completed by Mrs Parkinson's Pointer Sh. Ch. Daviam Titus Lartius handled by Bill Parkinson and sent through from the Gundog Group by Fenton Fitzgerald. Best in Show was judged by Owen Grindey who, after examining each of the six dogs, discarded the Corgi and then indicated the Pointer and the Bulldog. The crowd roared their approval, Bill Parkinson leapt in the air, he was congratulated, but he hadn't won. It was the Cavalier, which had won through from a special Junior class in its breed, which Owen Grindey chose as his Best in Show winner. The Pointer was reserve and the Bulldog was left to relish its group win.

The 1974 winter of discontent, with its repeated power cuts resulting from industrial action, gave a new committee, headed by Sir Dudley Forwood, and including a few ladies, a veritable baptism of fire and this was compounded by a strike which delayed the dismantling of the Boat Show and put real doubts on whether Cruft's 1974 could take place. It did take place and the new team avoided all the criticisms which had been directed at previous shows, even Olympia was spared, perhaps the subdued lighting made necessary by energy restrictions obscured its dilapidations. Even an abbreviated catalogue, made necessary by a three day working week, was accepted with philosophical good humour. As one commentator put it there was no discussion of a forthcoming General Election, of Britain's pending economical suicide, of oil crises or of inflation 'for two days, every visitor was able to forget the troubles of the world' and enjoy the greatest of all dog shows.

Apart from national gloom Crufts, 1974 faced a reason for domestic sadness in that this was to be Fred Lawrence's last show as Cruft's manager. He had joined the Kennel Club staff in 1946 and, since 1948, had been the one constant figure in the Cruft's organisation. He provided a changing committee, not always consisting entirely of people with great expertise about show management, headed by a new Chairman and served by a new Secretary, with the benefit of his long experience, meticulous organisation and attention to detail. In a way his role was much the same as had been Miss Hardingham's during Charles Cruft's time: unsung but vital to the show's continued success.

Nor was Fred Lawrence's departure the only loss which Cruft's was to sustain in 1974. Another was self inflicted and of minor proportions. During 1973 the Cruft's Committee had decided to update the style of their schedule and catalogue. The Kennel Club's restrained house colours of light and dark green were substituted for the more eye catching if rather garish red and yellow livery which Charles Cruft had always used. When the Committee came to examine the new designs it occurred to them that the apostrophe, which had always signalled Charles Cruft's proprietorial rights over Cruft's Dog Show, was no longer appropriate. They decided that, henceforth, the show would be Crufts Dog Show.

As though national gloom, the departure of a valued and valuable servant and a stylistic break with tradition were not enough 1974 saw a very unwelcome change. For the first time ever bomb threats had been made against the show. There was no way of knowing whether they had been made by some irresponsible crank or whether they carried a real threat from political or animal rights organisations. Precautions were taken and the show carried on with a barely susceptible sense of public stress in the air though behind the scenes the stress and anxiety must have been considerable.

In 1974 Crufts contrived to find yet another 'first' to achieve. This was the first show at which the destination of the Best in Show award was decided by a single judge who herself had experience of owning a Crufts Best in Show winner. The judge was Judy de Casembroot. The Lhasa Apso Sefton and Cross-Stern's Ch. Cheska Alexander of Sternroc had won the Utility Group under the previous year's Best in Show judge Owen Grindey. It was the first time that any of the Tibetan breeds had captured the Crufts spotlight. From the Hound Group Bobby James sent the Long-haired Dachshund Jensen's Ch. Albaney's Red Rheinhart forward while the top winning dog of 1974 was sent forward by Glen Broadley from the Gundog Group. He was the English Springer Spaniel Hancock and Cudworth's Sh. Ch. Hawkshill Connaught. From the Terrier Group Stanley Dangerfield sent in, from what he described as the best terrier line up he had seen for some time, the Skye Terrier Atkinson's Ch. Silhill Silver Secret. The Hound Group, under Bobby James was won by Jensen's Long-haired Dachshund Ch. Albaney's Red Rheinhart and the Toy Group, under Yves Bentinck, by Lister's Yorkshire Terrier Ch. Blairsville Most Royale. The sextet was completed by George Leatt's selection from the Working Group, Miss Hinde's St Bernard Ch. Burtonswood Bossy Boots. Judy de Casembroot's practiced eye assessed the finalists and rested on the stately St Bernard and the diminutive Yorkshire Terrier which perhaps only lost the top spot because tumultuous ringside applause had disturbed her usual composure. But how do winners react? On receiving the award Miss Hinde murmured to the judge 'I feel ill'.

Crufts, 1975 was different in a number of ways from its predecessors. Bill Edmond made his debut as the show manager and, for the first time, it was possible to make use of all three of Olympia's Halls. The extra space made the show less crowded, less dominated by trade stands and allowed rings to be more spacious. One commentator even went so far as to suggest that the show 'at last, reverted in appearance to a dog show and looked less like the Temple in Jerusalem from which, nearly 2000 years ago, there were cast out "all then that sold and bought".' The main innovation, however, resulted from an attempt to introduce more activity, interest and excitement into the activities which took place in the big ring and to use this to give some of the dogs which provide such valuable service to the community an opportunity to show their paces. The Personality Parade was organised by John Varley, a Kennel Club member who worked in the theatre. A commentary, provided by actor Frank Windsor, introduced Beagles from the Surrey and North Sussex, the champion foxhounds and harriers from the Royal Peterborough Hound Show, police dogs and working gundogs, including the Queen's Labrador Field Trial Champion Sandringham Sydney. It had been a long time since the Royal Family's dogs had been represented at Crufts. How many people noticed that Soft Coated Wheaten Terriers and Pharaoh Hounds were appearing for the first time to compete for Challenge Certificates?

Inevitably and rightly, however, the competition for Best in Show provided a fitting climax to the show. Bill Pinches judged the Hound Group and made Wright's Whippet Beseeka Knight Errant of Silkstone the winner. Violet Yates sent Mills-de-Hoog's German Shorthaired

Pointer, Wittekind Igor forward to the big ring. Judy de Casembroot selected Shaw's Bulldog Ch. Beechlyn Golden Nugget of Denrough to represent the Utility Group while from the Working Group, judged by Stanley Dangerfield, it was Crick's Dobermann Ch. Flexor Flugelman which caught the judge's eye. The Toy Group, judged by Fred Chandler, produced the Maltese, Turner's Ch. Quantos Con-Vivacita, a Tibetan Terrier, and from the Terrier Group Joe Braddon sent forward the Italian owned Wire Fox Terrier, Guiseppe Benelli and Paola Dondina's Ch. Brookewire Brandy of Layven, handled by Albert Langley. In arriving at a difficult decision Thelma Gray ignored the rather stereotyped military ritual to which judges were expected to conform. She moved her candidates several times and in different directions before deciding that the Wire, still on its toes, and the very sound and active Bulldog should be her winners.

In many ways the 1975 winner was not unexpected. The same could not be said of 1976, though it may fairly be said of most dog shows that 'the inevitable never happens and the unexpected invariably occurs'. The entry was appreciably larger than it had been in the past and, even with Olympia's three halls in use, questions were being asked about whether, rather than continually tightening the qualifier the Crufts Committee should accept the need to look for a larger venue.

Perhaps not entirely coincidentally by 1976 Harry Glover, an influential member of the Kennel Club Committee and sometime Crufts commentator, was enthusiastically extolling the virtues of the newly built National Exhibition Centre. He pointed out that just one of its halls was as large as Olympia and Earls Court put together and recommended it as a place to hold dog shows. However, he stopped short of suggesting that Crufts should move to this new venue, though others were certainly less reticent.

Cecil-Wright ended his term as Crufts President in 1976.

The Gundog Group was judged by Maurice Gilliat, the Show's Vice-Chairman, who was well into his task when Mr G. William's rising five-year-old Cocker Spaniel, Ch. Bournehouse Starshine, entered the ring. It was Starshine he chose as his group winner with the Labrador Ch. Geannie in reserve. Tedd's Saluki Almanza Kafiat won the Hound Group under Fred Curnow who said the Group was 'one of the best seen for quite a long time'. The Terrier Group, judged by Diana Hamilton, was won by the West Highland White Terrier Mrs K. Newstead's Ch. Dianthus Button, handled by Geoff Corish. Elizabeth Somerfield said the St Bernard, McMurray's Ch. Snowranger Cascade, was outstanding in the Working Group. Owen Grindey judged the Toy Group and his winner was the Maltese bitch Clarke's Ch. Maytheas Delila. Stanley Dangerfield judged the Utility Group and selected the Keeshond, Purdon's Ch. Ledwell Dutchman as his winner.

So the stage was set for Joe Braddon to make the final decisions of Cruft's 1976 and his choice was the West Highland White Terrier with the Maltese in reserve place.

By the time 1977 came round Crufts was certainly running short of 'firsts' to be achieved. Even so yet another was found when both the Best in Show winner and the Reserve came from the same town, Sutton Coldfield. Silver Prize cards were on offer as a modest celebration of the Queen's Silver Jubilee.

One of the aspects of Crufts which, over the years, had been both infuriating and endearing was its ability to surprise. Certain winners regularly fell at the first fence and 'no-hopers' found themselves on the winner's rostrum. In 1932 Countess Howe's Bramshaw Bob was making its show debut when it won Best in Show. In 1967 the Lakeland Terrier, scarcely more than a puppy, had stood on the winner's rostrum. In other years dogs of an age when their owners might have thought that success at the highest level was a thing of the past had taken the winner's spot. There had been a number of years in which the winner was not a champion and several when neither the winner nor the reserve had gained their titles. Indeed there would even be some who would never achieve that distinction. Crufts had an apparently infinite capacity to surprise.

Even so as each show arrived there would be people who knew, with absolute certainty, what the winner would be. Sometimes these certain winners were not even at the show, most often they were beaten by another dog.

During 1977 one dog, Brian Lister's Yorkshire Terrier, Ch. Blairsville Royal Seal had steadily drawn away from all the competition. By any assessment this was the outstanding dog of 1977.

Owen Grindey judged the Hound Group and his winner was Anderson's Borzoi Ch. Waycross Roksana. L. C. James, judging the Gundogs, with which he was so much at home, preferred William's English Setter Bournehouse Dancing Master. Reg Gadsden liked Lisa Attwood Parker's Kerry Blue Terrier Ch. Binate Plantagenet and Ferelith Hamilton chose Gee's Miniature Poodle Ch. Beritas Banacheke as the winner of a strong Utility Group. Percy Whitaker judged the Working Group and selected the fine old English Bullmastiff Newton's Ch. Craigylea Sir Galahad as his winner. Finally the Toy Group judged by Bob Russell-Roberts produced Appleton's Pug Ch. Dingleberry Vega. The 'knowing money' had been proved wrong once more, it would not be Royal Seal's year.

Stanley Dangerfield's report of Crufts 1978 described it and its predecessors as:

'the greatest dog show on earth. It is run in the wrong hall at the wrong time of year. It's run by the wrong people (the KC should not compete against its own customers) in the wrong way. We all hate it,

criticise it and grumble about it. Good judges who get a job there all too often leave their wits at home for this special occasion. . . . Good dogs start getting the chopper from the moment the show starts. Too many people. Too many catch-pennys. Too many gimmicks. Too much ballyhoo. But it's still a great dog show. The great dog show. The greatest dog show on earth.'

The demonstration of gundog work gives the crowd entertainment as well as an insight into an aspect of dogs which very few will have the opportunity to experience.

His criticism repeated much of what many had been saying about Cruft's almost since 1891. The change from Charles Cruft's stewardship to that of the Kennel Club may have altered the direction in which much of the criticism was aimed but the criticism itself seems to have remained remarkably consistent. More importantly so did recognition of the show's unique ability to attract attention and interest and to generate excitement. Stanley Dangerfield's criticisms may well have contained an element of journalistic hyperbole but his recognition that Crufts was the greatest dog show on earth was nothing more than the simple truth.

He also drew attention to a trend which was, if not new, at least one with which Cruft himself did not have to contend. That was the way in which reports in the general press tended to concentrate on negative aspects of the show and the world of dog shows. Whereas newspapers in Cruft's day carried detailed and well informed reports about the show, often, it is true, laced with well aimed criticism but also appreciating the positive aspects of the event, it seemed that newspapers were either not at all interested in Crufts or were interested only in sensational stories, true or false, critical of the show and those who gave it their support.

Herbert Essam judged the Utility Group, under what he described as 'ideal conditions in a huge ring with a full gallery of ringsiders'. His winner was the Bulldog Cotton's Ch. Aldridge Anenome. Lilly Turner judged the Working Group, some of whose representatives were showing signs of having endured a long, weary day though not the winner the well known German Shepherd Dog, White's Ch. Spartacist of Hendrawen. In the Toy Group it was Mr and Mrs Brian Lister's Yorkshire Terrier Ch. Blairsville Royal Seal, perhaps one of the most successful show dogs which won under Bob Flavell. Under Percy Whitaker the Hound Group winner was Dagmar Kenis' Greyhound Ch. Solstrand Double Diamond and under Walter Bradshaw the winning Gundog was MacMillan and Gillespie's Sh. Ch. Lochranza Man of Fashion. The Terrier Group contained the Wire Fox Terrier Miss E. Howles's Ch. Harrowhill Huntsman which finished in the top spot.

Huntsman had a number of claims to fame, not least of which was that he was handled by his owner. The Terriers which had been successful at Crufts tended to be in professional hands. He had won Best of Breed in both 1976 and 1977 but at 4½ years old was perhaps over the top. Attempts had been made to buy him, all of which Miss Howles firmly rejected. One last effort had been made in the previous year, again Miss Howles refused to sell. The bidder said he wouldn't try again because the dog was too old.

He went into the Best in Show ring in 1978 to compete with an outstanding line-up under Gwen Broadley and it was he that emerged as the winner. The Yorkshire Terrier, perhaps the biggest certainty to win Crufts there had been for years, was reserve.

9.   *At Earl's Court*

*I*n 1959 Lord Northesk, Chairman of Cruft's, Ted Buckley, the Kennel Club Secretary and Stanley Dangerfield, Cruft's Chief Steward, had visited Earl's Court in order to assess its potential as a dog show venue. Their official report was unanimous that Earl's Court must be considered a totally unsuitable venue for a dog show.

In 1979 Crufts moved from Olympia to Earl's Court, only its third home in eighty-eight years. The move from the Agricultural Hall had been tempered by a gap of several years and by the architectural

The indefinable Crufts atmosphere at Olympia was created by dogs and people in their thousands.

similarities between the two venues. No such factors eased the move to Earl's Court. The 1978 show was held in Olympia's three halls, with their elegant wrought iron structures, their rectangular forms, their large open spaces and their comfortable familiarity for exhibitors. Earl's Court, a building distinguished only by its external and internal ugliness was a complicated triangular building broken up by internal columns and staircases. It was a difficult building for exhibitors to become familiar with and must have been a difficult one in which to plan a major dog show. Inevitably there were problems but, under the guidance of Sir Dudley Forwood and the able management of Jaqueline Hollis, the move was made without major discernible difficulties.

Inevitably, however, the move had a major effect on the character of the show itself. In Olympia the Grand Hall had housed the breed rings. Exhibitors made occasional forays among the trade stands in the National Hall which really only came alive when group judging began in the evening. It was the elegant Grand Hall, dominated by dogs and their owners which established the character of Crufts at Olympia.

At Earl's Court the centre stage was dominated by the trade stands and the huge main ring, in which the obedience and new agility competitions were held before a parade of canine personalities made way for the group judging. Breed rings somehow seemed to be less apparent than they had been at Olympia.

But, architectural impediments notwithstanding, it was the dogs which dominated Crufts, 1979 and in particular one dog. That dog was Wendy Streatfield's Kerry Blue Terrier English and American Ch. Callaghan of Leander who was handled to win Best in Show by Don Munro. Cal was not only the first Kerry Blue Terrier to win Best in Show at Crufts but the first foreign born dog to do so.

Cal had been born in America where he won seventy-six Best of Breed and nine Best in Show awards. He was seen, bought and brought to England by John Streatfield. Emerging from quarantine in June, 1978 he quickly won his British title and made some impression in the big ring by taking reserve in the Terrier Group at the City of Birmingham Show and winning reserve Best in Show at Midland Counties.

At Crufts Cal, having won the Terrier Group under Lavinia Graham Weall, faced competition from five other group winners. Pam Cross-Stern had sent the Smoothcoat Chihuahua Ch. Belmuriz Brevier from a really strong Toy Group. Lily Turner had chosen the Miniature Poodle, Mrs J. Porter's Ch. Jolanta By Jove from the Utility Group. The German Shepherd, Mr and Mrs E. J. White's Ch. Spartacist of Hendrawen had won the Working Group under Bobby James and the Gundog Group, judged by Rene Parsons, was won by Mrs M. Wood's Golden Retriever Brensham Audacity. The Best in Show judge L. C. James defined a truly great dog as one with 'that indefinable quality of personality, ring presence and complete balance. . . . Absolute soundness with true type are pre-requisites, together with superb condition and presentation. All these attributes I found in the Kerry Blue Terrier.' Reserve to the Kerry was the Chihuahua who, Cal's owner said would have been her winner.

After the overall outstanding quality of the 1979 finalists 1980 proved to be something of a disappointment but what they may have lacked in quality they more than made up for by offering the certainty that Crufts would achieve another 'first'. None of the six breeds in the final had ever provided Crufts with a Best in Show winner.

Fred Curnow had sent Mr and Mrs B. Griffiths' Ch. Folkdance at Forgeman, a Bernese Mountain dog, forward from the Working Group. Ken Bullock, judging the Utility Group, had chosen a Miniature Schnauzer Mr and Mrs F. Morley's Ch. Castilla Linajudo and the Toy Group, judged by Catherine Sutton, had produced the Hon. Anna Leigh's Italian Greyhound Ch. Tamoretta Tailormade with the previous year's reserve Best in Show in second place. Mollie Garrish judged the Hound Group and sent Ch. Jubilant Lady of Tygreen and Lowerdon a Whippet forward to the final. The Terrier Group, judged by Audrey Dallison, produced Anderson's Bedlington Birkonbrae Bronze Bachique and Miss Pat Chapman's Flatcoat Retriever Ch. Shargleam Blackcap won the Gundog Group under Margaret Lindsay Smith. He went on to win Best in Show under Harry Glover.

Miss Chapman then had to face the press who were ready with their less than perceptive questions.

Had she expected to win?

'I hoped I might win the breed.'

'How much would you charge if you were to sell him?'

'He will never be sold.'

'Is he an especial pet?'

'They are all special pets.'

Miss Chapman revealed that Brett was not just a pretty face but also a good worker.

'What at?'

'Picking up.'

'Picking up what?'

'Pheasants.'

The changes which had been visited on Crufts as a result of its move to Earl's Court and because of the way in which the Crufts Committee were developing activities in the big ring and a more obvious emphasis on commerce all had their critics. However, the 1981 Best in Show judge, Bobby James, was not one of these critics.

'Crufts, and no matter what anyone may say, is the greatest show on earth. I have never missed a Crufts since the war, either as a spectator, exhibitor or judge and for me it has never lost its vital attraction, its atmosphere or its magic. The big ring is like no other in all the world, the sheer electricity, the excitement of being in there, well the feeling is indescribable, ask anyone.'

Crufts has always had both its critics and its supporters, neither have had a monopoly of right or wrong but, perhaps, Bobby James had put his finger on one major change. He spoke of the big ring, its excitement and magic and he took its importance for granted. That importance did not exist at all during the show's early days and only slowly developed as judging by groups became formalised and as Crufts emphasised the drama and glamour of the big ring. The contrast between what happened in the big ring and what happened in the breed rings became more and more marked.

The big ring laid out in readiness for the Agility competition. Soon the stands will be full of spectators cheering on their favourites.

Owen Grindey described the Hound Group as tremendously strong and chose Mr P. Tutchener's Beagle Ch. Beacott Buckthorn as his winner. Ernie Froggatt, with Blackcap before him in a strong Gundog Group, favoured Tuite's Irish Setter Ch. Astley's Portia of Rua. With twenty-four breeds representing 2198 dogs the Working Group was by far the largest. The winner, under Reg Gadsden, was Di Johnson's Great Dane Ch. The Contender of Dicarl. The Utility Group also produced a previous Crufts Best in Show winner, Ch. Grayco Hazelnut, but Percy

Whitaker's choice was the Standard Poodle, Sablecomb White Polar at Leander. Linda Beak, judging the Terrier Group, chose the Scottish Terrier, Ch. Mayson Monopoly and from a Toy Group which Joe Braddon described as 'very good indeed . . . one of the very best seen for many years' the winner was the Cavalier King Charles Spaniel Ch. Jia Laertes of Tonnew.

These were the six from which Bobby James was to select his winner. He later said 'for me it just had to be the Irish Setter. Her head is classical with that dreamy "Irish" expression, a most lovely head, neck and shoulder, just the right amount of body and beautifully conditioned coat.' But once more the glamorous winner was also a worker, already qualified in the field for her full title, whose owner's ambition was to win a major award in a Field Trial.

Crufts, 1982 was a three day show, another reluctant move to ease the ever growing pressure on limited and inconvenient space. Once more the show's character was perceptibly changed. In 1981 a brown Toy Poodle, Ch. Grayco Hazelnut, had been in the last half dozen in the Utility Group. Her owner's husband, a London cabby, ensured that the 1982 rail strike did not cause too much inconvenience for a dog which went to Crufts as dog of the year 1980 and with seven Best in Show wins behind her. Her owner, Lesley Howard thought she had a chance but favourites had been beaten before.

Not for the first time some of the breed judging had given rise to comment. Owen Grindey, whose decisions in the big ring had led to confusion in 1973, had placed Mr and Mrs Haig's Groenendael, Hadley Polar Star, fourth in Limit bitch and subsequently, without indicating that he intended to change his mind, first in Open with the Limit winner in third place. Then he gave the CC to Polar Star. Judging Toy Poodles Mr Grindey found that a number of dogs in the first two dog classes would not pass under the measure. It was then found that he had been issued with a ten inch measure used in America and not the British eleven inch measure. He changed to the correct measure but could not rejudge the first two classes in which dogs had been penalised because they did not pass under an incorrect measure. Subsequently a formal complaint was made to the Kennel Club, not a usual occurrence.

Walter Bradshaw judged what he described as a 'first class' Terrier Group from which Stuart Plane's Scottish Terrier Stuane Highland Empress emerged as the winner. In contrast Catherine Sutton, judging the Gundog Group, said 'this was one of the poorest groups I have judged for a long time'. The group was won by the Best in Show winner of 1980 the Flatcoat Retriever, Pat Chapman's Ch. Shargleam Blackcap, who had matured and improved since his win. Gardener's German Shepherd, Kenmil's Bellisima of Danala had won the Working Group. The Hound Group produced an outstanding example and a well known winner from a breed which has not been regarded as regular group winners. This was Nora Hartley's Deerhound Ch. Betsinda of Rotherwood. Finally Bill Taylor had chosen Ellis Hulme's Papillon Ch. Tongemoor Miss Peppermint to win the Toy Group. In the subsequent interview the press were, as ever, anxious to equate Hazelnut's win with a sum of money.

'Winning the supreme championship,' said Jan Leeming, 'brings enormous prestige as well as thousands and thousands of pounds in breeding fees.'

She did not go on to explain how a bitch with its one and only litter behind it was going to earn these breeding fees.

Just as Charles Cruft had staged an exhibition of obedience which had grown into a major and very popular activity so in 1978 Crufts had staged an exhibition, conceived by John Varley and staged by Peter Meanwell, of canine agility, a competitive exercise very similar in its skill and potential appeal, though not its cost, to show jumping. In 1983 what had begun at Crufts returned as a very popular competitive activity. Eight teams, who had qualified at regional heats during the previous year, went through their paces in the big ring and gave the crowds thrills, spills and a demonstration of yet one more facet of the way in which dogs and people can combine to have fun. The winning team were the Waldridge Fell Team.

Sponsorship has always been an important and integral part of Crufts. Here the Agility competition features the well known name of its sponsor.

In 1983 Crufts also had its shady side exposed when two ladies were found to have smuggled boxes containing Yorkshire Terrier puppies, which were being offered for sale, into the building. In Charles Cruft's day an annual auction of dogs was held but the event was well regulated and certainly the Kennel Club could not accept the show being casually used to offer puppies for sale. The two ladies subsequently found themselves before a Kennel Club disciplinary committee. It is, perhaps, one of the more remarkable but lesser known aspects of Crufts, indeed of the entire show world that, though competition is intense and the participants numbered in their thousands, there is very seldom a need to evoke Kennel Club disciplinary procedures. The thousands of shows and other events run each year under Kennel Club rules generate no more than a handful of cases and it is most unusual for Crufts to produce any.

The terrier group tidily arranged in alphabetical order by breed nervously await the judge's decision.

Bill Parkinson, who as an exhibitor had known both triumph and disappointment in Crufts big ring, was the 1983 Best in Show judge. Marian Fairbrother had sent forward McAlpine's Great Dane Ch. Dicarl Tendellie. Harold Wright had preferred Jenkin's and Nock's Welsh Terrier Ch. Puzzle of Kenstaff to the previous year's winning Scottish Terrier in the Terrier Group and 'Beefey' Sutton chose the Afghan Gibbs' Ch. Montravia Kaskarak Hitari. It was the Keeshond, Luckhurst's Ch. Gavimir Nighthawk which Pam Cross-Stern sent forward from the

Utility Group while Owen Grindey said he had no hesitation in sending the Irish Setter Bryden and Levick's Corriecas Fagan forward. The Toy Group winner to complete the sextet of finalists was the Maltese, Herrief's Ch. Snowgoose Valient Lad. Bill Parkinson too denied any hesitation when he placed the Afghan first and the Irish Setter reserve.

A number of different and unrelated problems arose at Crufts 1984: one concerned dogs being left overnight in Earl's Court in their travelling boxes, another was that the usual number of catalogues proved to be inadequate and the third was that judging in Briards and St Bernards was so delayed that their Best of Breed winners were denied an opportunity to compete in the groups. Nor, even with the luxury of three days, did Crufts totally escape uncomfortable crowding. Over 75,000 people went through the turnstiles and to these must be added the exhibitors, judges and stewards, their friends and supporters who

The winner of the Kennel Club Junior Organisation's Obedience competition here receives the trophy from the Crufts' President Prince Michael of Kent.

had concessionary tickets who would have taken the Crufts audience to over the 100,000 mark during the show's three days.

The Groups produced their usual dramas. Under Mary Roslin Williams a Sussex Spaniel, Mr and Mrs Ifor Williams' Brytonian Aelwyn won the Gundog Group in the Sussex Spaniel Association's jubilee year. Another winner from Wales came from the Working Group, Messrs Taylor and Jones' Pembroke Corgi, Ch. Belroyd Lovebird, chosen by Joe Braddon. Owen Grindey, judging the Terrier Group, favoured Mr and Mrs Ron Armstrong's West Highland White Ch. Jaimont of Whitebriar. Mr and Mrs Richard's Bloodhound Ch. Chasedown Hopeful won the Hound Group under Leonard Pagliero but it was the Utility and Toy Groups which were to provide the show's stars.

Bobby James judged the Utility Group and made Jean Blyth's Lhasa Apso, Ch. Saxonsprings Hackensack, handled by Geoff Corish, his winner. It was only the second time Geoff Corish had handled a Crufts Group winner and last time, with the West Highland White Terrier, Bertie Buttons, he had gone all the way. In the Toy Group Averil Cawthera Purdy's Pomeranian, Ch. Lireva's Shooting Star was sent forward by Gwen Broadley. Molly Garrish judged Best in Show and was confronted by some breeds which do not regularly win groups – the Bloodhound and the Sussex Spaniel – but it was to Hackensack, already with eight group wins and two Best in Shows that she turned with the Pomeranian in reserve place.

After a record-breaking gate in 1984 atrocious weather in February, 1985 ensured that one record would remain intact for another year but while the cost of staging the show over three rather than four days and the inexorable march of inflation were increasing costs, income too was increasing. In 1984 Crufts had produced a surplus of £78,000 but this seemed likely to be reduced to something nearer £50,000 in 1985. The Kennel Club's attitude had changed, perhaps out of necessity combined with sound business acumen. At least one Kennel Club Chairman regarded Crufts as a service to breeders and exhibitors which should not produce a profit. Now it was regarded both as a service and a useful, if not vital, source of revenue.

The Terrier Group was judged by Catherine Sutton whose winner was the Kerry Blue Terrier, Miss B. Brennan's Ch. Arkama Take By Storm. The Gundog Group saw Leslie Page making the decisions and giving the final nod to Mr and Mrs Miller's liver and white English Springer Spaniel Sh. Ch. Graftonberry Genghis Khan who had won the Crufts dog CC in his breed on four successive occasions. Perhaps not a record but certainly a considerable achievement. The Hound Group saw the judge Joe Braddon at his theatrical best, transforming a routine process into a real drama, full of interest and excitement. Perhaps the hint of theatre especially suited Chris Amoo, lead singer of The Real Thing, handling his and his wife's Afghan Hound Ch. Ashihna Raoul. The Toy Group, judged

A recent feature of Crufts is the range of imaginatively decorated stands which are taken by breed clubs in order to encourage interest in the breed.

by Nora Down, saw Mr and Mrs Jack Mitchell's Pekingese Ch. Micklee Roc's Ru-Ago as the winner while in the Working Group, judged by Mrs Augustus Riggs IV from America, it was the Dobermann Mr and Mrs J. D. Banforth's Ch. Hughroyds Man of the Year.

Harold Spira, an Australian veterinary surgeon, was the Best in Show judge and he favoured the Standard Poodle with the Pekingese in reserve. The decision was one which many had predicted. Tommy Gun had arrived at Crufts with two reserve and five Best in Show awards already under his belt but to win at Crufts would not be easy. First of all he had to beat eleven other Standard Poodle Champions in an impressive breed entry which included six of his own offspring. Then under George Down he had to win the Utility Group over even stiffer opposition. Only then would the chance of achieving a remarkable double, of two Crufts Best in Show awards in three years for the Montravia kennel, be reduced to reasonable odds. Against greater opposition and a wider variety of judges to be satisfied, the achievement perhaps supersedes that of previous doubles but a strategic change in Tommy Gun's ownership means that the record books remain unchanged.

The talking point among foot weary exhibitors at Crufts 1985 was what would happen when, in 1986, Crufts was spread over four days. The prospect was not one which anyone could anticipate with pleasure but first Crufts 1985 had to be survived. One which didn't survive was Mr J. Hamilton's Samoyed Ch. Hurkur Jingles who, in the breed, beat his son Mrs Fox's Ch. Zamoyski Lucky Star for the dog CC, his forty-fifth. Jingles became unwell during the day and after visiting the show vet was

A traditional feature of Crufts, for which the Kennel Club turns a blind eye to its own rules, are the decorated benches used by the dogs competing in the obedience competition.

Barbara Banfield is the present Crufts' Secretary and is seldom seen without a smile.

taken home. His condition worsened during the journey. He was rushed straight to his own vet who immediately operated to relieve a twisted gut, sadly Jingles died some hours later. The event did, however serve to draw attention to one aspect of Crufts, indeed of all dog shows, which receives little notice.

After Jingles' untimely death his owners were inundated with the condolences of their rivals.

In 1988 a story which was more to the taste of the press was pushed to the fore. A Shetland Sheepdog which had no realistic hope of success was fed a tranquilliser in a piece of liver.

A former member of the Kennel Club's General Committee, Wilson Stephens was quoted as saying that 'Nobbling is not unknown nowadays to make a fancied animal miss its class'. Certainly there had been accusations, not all in recent years, of nobbling, though none had ever been substantiated. Furthermore there was no evidence that the dog had been nobbled. It was far more likely to have been doped by someone who disliked all dogs or by an animal rights activist.

More than 92,000 people passed through the turnstiles at Crufts' first four day show. Add the exhibitors and their friends, Kennel Club members and associates with concessionary tickets and the total would exceed 110,000. Crufts was not just the most popular dog show but the most popular show of any sort to be staged at Earl's Court.

The winner in 1988 was Joe and Val Watkin's elegant English Setter Sh. Ch. Starlite Express of Valsett and had been sent through to the big ring by breed specialist Marion France who had handled Gordon William's English Setter, Dancing Master, to its place on the winner's rostrum.

After Bonnie's win, as after almost each year's win, the Press were easily able to find someone who would introduce a totally unnecessary sour note into the proceedings by suggesting that the win would lead to an increase in the popularity of the breed – in this case of English Setters. In fact there is very little evidence that wins at shows, even wins at Crufts, have any significant effect on popular appeal. If Crufts wins are compared with the prior and subsequent popularity of a breed and all other factors which affect popularity are ignored it would be much easier to make out a case for a win at Crufts reducing rather than increasing a breed's popularity. Furthermore the Best in Show record of breeds which enjoy great popularity is not good.

In fact Beefey Sutton had a line up of which less popular breeds predominated from which to select his winner. Fox's Samoyed Ch. Zamoyski Lucky Star of Ostyak, Bassett's Borzoi Ch. Colhugh Caminickers, McPherson and Hutchinson's Border Terrier Ch. Brannigan of Brumberhill, Sameja's Yorkshire Terrier, Ch. Ozmilion Dedication and, most remarkable, the nine-and-a-half year old Lhasa Apso, for whom the Crufts Best in Show ring was familiar territory, Corish's Ch. Saxonsprings Fresno but at the end of the day it was the English Setter which was chosen to occupy the winner's rostrum.

The 1989 Crufts show hit the headlines for all the wrong reasons. One of Crufts' stand-holders had decided that they could not accept the conditions which were imposed on and accepted by all stand-holders and which required that they should not exhibit material which, in the opinion of the Crufts' Committee, was offensive. Unfortunately the stand-holder in dispute with Crufts was the Royal Society for the Prevention of Cruelty to Animals. They had been conducting a campaign using posters which depicted piles of dead dogs and dead dogs in black plastic bags. They wanted to display these posters at Crufts and the Crufts' Committee said they were offensive. Rather than finding a way to solve the problem the RSPCA used it to create publicity and the result was that Crufts 1989 took place under a cloud of dispute and recrimination.

But such matters were of trivial consequence in comparison with what Crufts is, and always has been, essentially about: competitions to find the

Best in Show Crufts 1987 and Mr and Mrs Chris and 'Gable' Amoo are content.

best dogs in a widening variety of competitions. The unaccustomed luxury of space provided by four days had encouraged Crufts to introduce classes for veterans, for dogs over the age of seven years. A number had always appeared at Crufts, indeed an eight-year-old Saluki had got as far as reserve Best in Show in 1964, but they were at a disadvantage against younger animals. Their own classes not only gave them an opportunity to compete on equal terms but also gave breeders and spectators an opportunity to see dogs which had made their impact in the past.

The oldest exhibit to appear was a Miniature Poodle, Pooghans Nicholas, owned by Majorie McCarthy, which had last been seen at Crufts in 1972. He was seventeen years old. In his heyday he had won a

CC and this was to be his key to a reappearance at Crufts in 1989.

Anne Wynyard judged the Utility Group and found her winner in Barnes' and Dainty's white Standard Poodle Ch. Davlen the Beloved, with a name from Crufts recent history, Geoff Corish's Lhasa Apso Ch. Saxonsprings Fresno, in reserve. In the Toy Group Ellis Hulme found his winner in Easdon and Martin's Pekingese Ch. Yakee For Your Eyes Only. It was the Bearded Collie Brenda White's Ch. Potterdale Classic of Moonhill which attracted Andrew Thomson's eye in the Working Group while, for the first time ever, the Crufts Terrier Group, judged by Maurice Marshall, was won by a Staffordshire Bull Terrier, McKnight's Belnite Dark Huntsman while the previous year's reserve Best in Show, the Border Terrier, finished in the last six in the group. The Hound Group was judged by Joan Wells-Meacham and the winner was the Elkhound Lee's Kestos Aderyn, fifteen months old and sired by an import from Norway.

Best in Show Crufts 1989 and her owner share a moment of mutual satisfaction.

The Gundog Group winner was the Irish Setter which had won twenty-five CCs in its breed but had previously made no great impression in the big ring. Indeed, worthy winners though they undoubtedly were on the day, of the six finalists only the Staffordshire Bull Terrier had previously won a group. The Elkhound, indeed, had won its way from the Puppy and Junior classes in its breed. It had been quite a journey and was a considerable achievement.

It was, however, the Bearded Collie, making Crufts and breed history, and the Pekingese which stood on the winners' rostrum.

Anticipation for the 1990 show began to mount early in the New Year when it was realised that the entry was, in spite of the imposition of even tighter qualifying standards and which meant that neither puppies nor veterans would be represented at the show, going to be a big one as exhibitors grasped the last opportunity to show at a London Crufts. The show itself was preceded by a period of wet and stormy weather which made the journey to Crufts unusually difficult and even hazardous for many but it certainly didn't deter them any more than it deterred the spectators. From the first day Earl's Court had never been more crowded for Crufts, 96,794 people passed through the turnstiles and, including those with concessionary passes, must have meant that well over 150,000 people were able to enjoy, not just London's last Crufts but what might well be the last major dog show to be held in the capital.

One interesting sidelight on Crufts spanned 1989 and 1990. In 1990 the Government had decided, apparently against all the evidence, that

The team from Dundee won the Crufts agility competition in 1987 and here receive their rewards from the show's Chairman Sir Dudley Forewood.

Britain had too many veterinary surgeons. It was proposed that two veterinary schools should be closed. Two petitions, which together attracted 197000 signatures, were circulated at Crufts, and formed the basis of a popular and professional protest which, by the time Crufts 1990 came round, resulted in Government acceptance of a need to increase veterinary training in Britain.

With the centenary show less than a year away and with the problems caused by continued rebuilding work at Earl's Court the Crufts Committee might have been expected to do no more than rely on their established routine but, in fact, even at this last London Crufts a few innovations were introduced. Some additional excitement was introduced to the big ring programme by the terrier racing, a popular pastime at shows run outside the Kennel Club system but now, for the first time, seen at a KC Show. The sixteen terriers and their Cumbrian owners put on a display which quickly had the crowd on its feet cheering. Crufts

Agility competitions demand a high level of obedience and fitness from the dog as well as concentration and fitness from the handler.

Terrier Racing was a success and would doubtless be added to the big ring's existing attractions which included individual and regional obedience competitions, an inter-club agility competition, and gundog demonstrations.

Since 1955 when the Cruft's Obedience Test had been introduced as a Championship event it had been subject to a strict qualifying standard which required that every competitor had to have achieved a winning score in excess of 290 out of 300 at Test C level during the previous year. Even so this had produced twenty-eight bitches for judge Mr R. Page to assess, more than enough to keep him fully occupied during a long and intensely demanding day. At the end of the day, almost as though Crufts was determined to leave London having once more made history, it was Gavin's Obedience Champion Lady Gessler of Bryan which had won in bitches, the first time ever that a Dobermann had won a Crufts Obedience test. In dogs the winner was Ray's Border Collie Ob. Ch. Red Hot Toddy, a breed which, along with Working Sheepdogs has tended to dominate the Crufts tests.

For the first time the Best in Show judging was being transmitted live on television. This meant that all the working breeds and the group itself had to be complete by a precise time so that the six finalists could parade before the cameras in the big ring. Whatever apprehension might have been caused by this strict new requirement was shown to be groundless as the six group winners came into the ring for judge Ferelith Somerfield's opinion.

The Toy Group on the first day had been judged by Tom Horner and had produced one of those moments of magic for which Crufts is renowned. The winner, Mr and Mrs J. Wiggins' Whyteplace Apollo, a Cavalier King Charles Spaniel, had not only won its first Challenge Certificate on the day but it was also the owner's first Challenge Certificate. That alone would have been an impossible dream come true but to go on to win the Toy Group and be in the last six for Best in Show could not even have been contemplated in dreams. Yet similar things had happened in the past and there had even been dogs which had won Best in Show which were not and would not become Champions.

The Utility Group winner, judged by Jean Lanning, was Liz Holmes' stylish Miniature Poodle Ch. Navarre's Executive, an owner and breed already accustomed to appearing in the big ring. On the second day, when Gundogs were judged, Peggy Grayson sent forward the Welsh Springer Spaniel Hunton Morgan's Sh. Ch. Dalati Sarian. Vincent Mitchell, who judged the Terrier Group, found his winner in Derek Tattersall's West Highland White Terrier Ch. Olac Moon Pilot, one of the top winning dogs of the previous year. The Hound Group, judged by Barbara Wilton Clark on the same day also produced one of the previous year's top winners, in Editha Newton's Whippet Ch. Nutshell of

Nevedith. Two such well known dogs might have been regarded as likely favourites to take the ultimate award but on the last day they were joined by another, equally illustrious, dog from the Working Group. Mrs D. Anderson's Dobermann Ch. Sallate's Ferris was judge Leonard Pagliero's choice. He, too, took the opportunity to introduce his own Crufts innovation by shaking hands with all those who did not reach the Group's final line-up, a courteous, sporting and thoughtful gesture appreciated by exhibitors and spectators alike which encapsulated much of the essence of dog showing.

With the final group complete the stage was set for Best in Show. Whippets, Dobermanns and Cavalier King Charles Spaniels had each appeared in the Crufts Best in Show ring four times since 1948, West Highland White Terriers and Miniature Poodles had each appeared three times while Welsh Springer Spaniels were making their Crufts big ring debut. Right up to the very last London Crufts the ability to produce

Charles Cruft's grandson and namesake was a visitor to the 1990 show.

something new was very much in evidence.

The six winners paraded before Ferelith Somerfield and she had no hesitation in signalling the West Highland White Terrier to the winner's rostrum with the Whippet in Reserve place. The beaten finalists were among the first to congratulate the winners. Dog showing, at all levels maintains the traditions of courteous sportsmanship which seem to have disappeared from some other competitive pastimes.

Crufts was moving into a new home, a new era, but the links with its history were recognised and confirmed when Charles Cruft, the seventy-nine-year-old grandson of Charles, accepted the Kennel Club's invitation to be present at the 1990 Crufts Show, the last London Show, and so was able to join all those tens of thousands of people who, in many different ways, each year enjoy the benefits of his grandfather's remarkable creation – Crufts Dog Show.

10. The Trophies

In 1985 John Williams, former Secretary of the Kennel Club and a former Crufts Show Manager, wrote, for the Crufts Souvenir which OUR DOGS *had introduced in 1984, a detailed history of the Trophies which were on offer at Crufts. I am grateful for permission from the Editor of* OUR DOGS *and from John Williams to reproduce that article here.*

TROPHY: a memorial of a victory; a memorial of success, glory, etc.; a piece of plate or suchlike awarded as a prize.

These are but three of the dictionary definitions. I like the first two.

They smack of proud owner and happy dog standing together to receive the just reward of their combined efforts to win. 'A piece of plate or suchlike. . . ?' – all right, accept it gratefully even if it doesn't sound quite so majestic.

But just wait until you see that 'piece of plate or suchlike'. Many of Crufts Show trophies are really something to behold. A great number will not fit on the average mantleshelf, and even the sideboard will have to be of a certain size to accommodate some of them – if your dog is good enough to win.

The trophies presented by Crufts Show are an amalgam of the cups, vases, bowls and tankards from the original show when it was organised by Charles Cruft and from the Kennel Club Show, which until 1938 was held annually too. Both were blessed with impressive trophies and neither gave a cup for all the breeds that were classified. Some breeds relied on club trophies presented on the results of the show.

At this year's Crufts, nearly 120 cups and trophies will be awarded, to be held, after engraving, until one month before the next show. The co-ordination of the return of the trophies from last year's winners, checking that they are still in good order, making sure that there is still room on the plinths for further engraving, listing the names of the new winners for engraving, packing and posting to the new custodians is an established routine, carried out by Crufts staff and Garrard and Co., silversmiths, every year. It is, when considered together with insurance premiums, an expensive operation, but surely a tradition to be enjoyed, even in these days of cost-cutting and recession.

Prize money is fine, but it quickly loses its identity in the pocket or handbag along with the other pound notes. The red card is great but you cannot with all modesty make it the centerpiece of the table when friends come for dinner. One way of recognising a win permanently is by the engraving on a trophy which will be presented and re-presented in the years to come – and on which memories reside.

Thirty-one breeds classified this year at Crufts will not have a trophy. Many of them are comparatively new to separate classification and Challenge Certificates, the last major reshuffle of trophies was carried out in 1969 and the years since then have seen a fair number of new breeds with CCs, Briards, Bernese Mountain Dogs and Pharaoh Hounds to name but a few.

Nevertheless, 96 breeds have their own trophies and altogether with group winners and reserves, a few other specials and the Best-in-Show cup, there are 130 trophies to be won, not outright but to be held by the winners until just before the next Crufts. They all have interesting connections, they were all presented either to the Kennel Club or to Crufts Show with good reason and with warm-hearted intent.

Inevitably, with the development of shows and breeds, there have been some adjustments to the allocation of the available trophies, but in general the original connections have remained. Some cups must feel that they belong to individuals rather than to Crufts. The Coval Cup for the best Irish Wolfhound, for instance, presented by Mr K. P. Strohmenger in 1952, has been won, either in partnership or on her own, by Mrs Florence Nagle no fewer than 16 times, much to the doubtless frustration of her great rivals for the trophy, Mr and Mrs L. S. Jenkins of the Eaglescrag affix.

A number of the trophies were presented by commercial firms, many more by owners of famous dogs and others by friends of personalities in the breeds.

The Lassie Cup for the best Rough Collie could only have been, and was, presented by Metro-Goldwyn-Mayer Pictures Ltd. The best St Bernard each year holds the – what better – Hennessy Trophy, and the best Sealyham Terrier wins the Pearson Tankard, not originally intended for Sealyhams alone but presented to the Kennel Club in 1920 for the best Sporting dog or bitch in the show, and accompanied in those days by a memento for the winner in the form of a five-gallon drum of Pacolin (Pacolin? . . .). Even the commercial changes in dog food brand leaders can be seen in the two Pedigree Chum Challenge Cups presented for the Obedience championships – they were first known as the 'Chappie' and 'Lassie' Challenge Cups presented by Chappie Ltd.

The names of many of the Kennel Club Committee chairmen of the past are commemorated by trophies – the Shirley Memorial Bowl, the Sidney Turner Memorial Challenge Cup, the Francis Redmond Cup, the McCandlish Bowl.

At the Kennel Club Show in 1938, there were 10 trophies available to be won by an entry of 14 St Bernards, 23 Irish Terriers competed for 21 trophies. Admittedly, many of these were breed club awards, but the near 200 Irish Setters at this year's Crufts apparently have only the Lonsdale Cup to do battle over. Elkhounds are best off with four trophies for the breed.

Each of the Group winners receives a similar trophy, a Send Gold Vase. Five of these elegant pieces were presented to the Kennel Club in 1930 by Mr Gordon Stewart, owner of the Send Kennel of Great Danes. They were for the best exhibit in the following sections: (1) Sporting, other than Gundog or Terrier, (2) Gundog, (3) Terrier, (4) Non-Sporting other than Toy and (5) Toy. Mr Stewart's splendid Great Dane Ch. Mavis of Send won the vase for best exhibit in the Non-Sporting other than Toy section, and Mr H. S. Lloyd's Cocker Spaniel Luckystar of Ware was the best Gundog.

The vases were presented annually until 1938 but for some reason were not allocated at all when the Kennel Club started to organise Crufts Show after the war; in fact, they did not reappear until 1964. A further vase was added in 1967 when the Non-Sporting Group was split into Utility and Working. Should the decision ever be made to split the Working Group, it could prove a little costly if yet another Send Gold Vase has to be added to the present collection.

The trophies awarded to the reserves in the groups are somewhat more of a mixed bag and they bear some illustrious names. Two, the Theo Marples Sporting and Non-Sporting Trophies were donated by him to the Kennel Club, having been presented to him in 1926 following a nationwide subscription in recognition of his services to dogdom. They are now awarded to the reserve best Hound and the reserve best Working respectively. The reserve best of the Utility Group receives the Trayshill Challenge Bowl, which recalls the great kennel of Mrs Lee Booker, and Mrs Helen Pilkington and that outstanding American dog-person Mrs Geraldine Dodge, are remembered by the trophies for the reserve best of the Toy and the Gundog breeds.

At last, after having beaten some 9000 dogs, the Best in Show, affectionately known world-wide as the Crufts Supreme Champion, will be presented with the Keddell Memorial Trophy, which is without doubt the best-known trophy in dogdom. It was first presented at Crufts Show in 1925 and was then allocated to a different breed each year. The Keddell really is a most impressive piece of silver and was chosen as the Best-in-Show award for the 1948 Crufts Show, the first organised by the Kennel Club.

In that year, it was won by H. S. Lloyd with his memorable Cocker Tracey Witch of Ware. This was not the first time that Lloyd had held the Keddell Trophy, for he first won it in 1928 when it was allocated to the

Best Spaniel. Indeed, the irrepressible H. S. Lloyd, with his Cocker Luckystar of Ware, also won the first-ever-cup presented at Cruft's for Best-in-Show in 1930, a 'Sterling Silver Trophy'. (The first two winners of that title went trophy-less for their effort.)

There were a few years, between 1968 and 1972, when the Keddell was demoted and presented for the reserve best Terrier, but it came into its own again in 1973 when the Daytona Cup was withdrawn from circulation.

Cups and trophies in the world of dogs must represent a small fortune in weight of precious metal. To club secretaries they are something of a worry, with thoughts of safe-keeping, insurance, engraving and so on always in the back of the mind.

But for the recipients, they are always a delight to hold, albeit for one short year only, and each trophy is in itself a small piece of history.

Appendix 1

CRUFT'S TOTAL ENTRIES

Date		Entries	Date		Entries	Date		Entries	Date		Entries
1891	1	2437	1916	26	3235	1942		—	1968	65	12541
1892	2	3025	1917	27	2500	1943		—	1969	66	13686
1893	3	2791	1918		—	1944		—	1970	67	14425
1894	4	2628	1919		—	1945		—	1971	68	13726
1895	5	2849	1920		—	1946		—	1972	69	10065
1896	6	3164	1921	28	2860	1947		—	1973	70	11203
1897	7	3072	1922	29	4587	1948	47	9412	1974	71	11824
1898	8	2907	1923	30	5766	1949		—	1975	72	11860
1899	9	3488	1924	31	6690	1950	48	12319	1976	73	13354
1900	10	2889	1925	32	8008	1951	49	11265	1977	74	12329
1901	11	3162	1926	33	9157	1952	50	12448	1978	75	13165
1902	12	2898	1927	34	9777	1953	51	11869	1979	76	10619
1903	13	3129	1928	35	9466	1954		—	1980	77	11914
1904	14	3537	1929	36	9682	1955	52	11869	1981	78	12312
1905	15	3854	1930	37	9565	1956	53	12328	1982	79	12090
1906	16	3888	1931	38	9389	1957	54	12676	1983	80	10981
1907	17	3473	1932	39	9216	1958	55	13085	1984	81	12215
1908	18	3888	1933	40	8564	1959	56	13211	1985	82	13075
1909	19	3563	1934	41	9363	1960	57	14297	1986	83	13826
1910	20	3477	1935	42	9130	1961	58	15721	1987	84	17059
1911	21	3682	1936	43	10650	1962	59	14317	1988	85	18222
1912	22	3950	1937	44	9949	1963	60	15205	1989	86	16025
1913	23	4007	1938	45	9109	1964	61	16022	1990	87	16315
1914	24	4239	1939	46	8839	1965	62	15561	1991	88	
1915	25	3447	1940		—	1966	63	14913			
			1941		—	1967	64	12302			

Appendix 2

CRUFT'S GROUP & BEST IN SHOW WINNERS, OWNERS & JUDGES:

Prior to 1906 there were no Cruft's competitions which could be regarded as selecting the best dog in the show. In 1906 a new Challenge Bowl for the Best Champion in the Show was introduced and this might be seen as equivalent to a Best in Show award. However like similar bowls awarded to the best Sporting dog, which was confined to Gundogs, best Hound, best Terrier, best Pet dog and best Non-Sporting dog, the Bowl does not appear to have been awarded every year. It was not until 1928 that the competition for Best Champion in the Show became a competition for the Best in Show and reserve Best in Show Awards. A question mark indicates that the author has not been able to ascertain the result.

AWARD JUDGE(S)	BREED	NAME OF OWNER & NAME OF DOG
1906		
BEST CHAMPION	Rough Collie	Tait's Ch. Wishaw Leader
SPORTING	Flat Coat Retriever	Cooke's Ch. High Legh Blarney
NON-SPORTING	Rough Collie	Tait's Ch. Wishaw Leader
HOUND	Deerhound	Rawson's Ch. St Ronan's Rhyme
TERRIER	Dandie Dinmont	Lucas's Ch. Milverton King
PET DOG	Pomeranian	Vale Nicolas' Ch. Shelton Sable Atom

F. Gresham, Elias Bishop, E. B. Joachim, H. Hewlock, H. Sawtrell, J. Edkins, F. C. Hignett, L. P. C. Astley, W. H. Reeves

1907		
BEST CHAMPION	Pomeranian	Vale Nicolas' Ch. The Sable Mite
NON-SPORTING	Poodle	Crouch's Orchard Postboy
HOUND	Deerhound	Rawson's Ch. St Ronan's Rhyme
TERRIER	Skye	Alexander's Wee Mac of Adel
PET DOG	Pomeranian	Vale Nicolas' Ch. The Sable Mite

Theo Marples, Nicol, Chris Houlkner

1908		
BEST CHAMPION	Newfoundland	Vale Nicholas' Ch. Shelton Viking
GUNDOG	Irish Setter	Judd's Ch. Strabane Sally
NON-SPORTING	Newfoundland	Vale Nicholas' Ch. Shelton Viking
HOUND	Deerhound	Rawson's St Ronan's Roderick
TERRIER	Welsh	Greene's Ch. Landore Boy
PET DOG	Pekingese	Cross's Ch. Chu erh of Alderbourne

AWARD JUDGE(S)	BREED	NAME OF OWNER & NAME OF DOG

1909

BEST CHAMPION	Field Spaniel	Rouse's Ch. Clareholm Dora
SPORTING	Field Spaniel	Rouse's Ch. Clareholm Dora
NON-SPORTING	Bulldog	Mayor's Ch. Silent Duchess
HOUND	Borzoi	Borman's Ch. Ramsden Rajah
TERRIER	Wire Fox	Redmond's Ch. Dusky Dairymaid
PET DOG	Pug	Hopkins' Ch. Deodora Model

Col. C. S. Dean, F. Gresham, Theo Marples, L. P. C. Astley, Lefroy-Dean, E. B. Withers, E. Bowers, J. R. Culshaw, Robert Leighton

1910

BEST CHAMPION	Greyhound	Chapman's Ch. Broadwater Banker
SPORTING	Flat Coat Retriever	Cooke's Ch. Jimmy of Riverside
NON-SPORTING	Bulldog	Hopkins' Deodora Delilah
HOUND	Greyhound	Chapman's Ch. Broadwater Banker
TERRIER	Scottish	Deane-Willis's Bapton Warrior
PET DOG	Pomeranian	Hopkins' Malwood Marcorona

Theo Marples, F. McKrill, L. C. R. Cameron, E. B. Joachim

1911

BEST CHAMPION	Wire Fox	Way's Ch. Collarbone of Notts
SPORTING	Flat Coat Retriever	Cooke's Ch. Jimmy of Riverside
NON-SPORTING	Bobtail	Charter's Ch. Brentwood Hero
HOUND	Deerhound	Doxford's Ch. The Laird of Abbotsford
TERRIER	Smooth Fox	Tudor-Crosthwaite's Ch. Donna's Double
PET DOG	Pekingese	H.H. Princess Toussoun's Puck of Alderbourne

Theo Marples, Blatspiel Stamp, C. W. Wharton

1912

BEST CHAMPION	St Bernard	Stocken & Samuel's Ch. The Pride of Sussex
SPORTING	Flat Coat Retriever	Cooke's Ch. Jimmy of Riverside
NON-SPORTING	Bulldog	Hopkins' Ch. Deodora Monarch
HOUND	Greyhound	Decies' Ch. Larchmont King
TERRIER	Wire Fox	Way's Ch. Collarbone of Notts
PET DOG	Pomeranian	Geddes' Offley Blackthorn

W. B. Stamp, J. S. Cowell, Harding Cox

1913

BEST CHAMPION	?	?
GUNDOG	Flat Coat Retriever	Cooke's Ch. Jimmy of Riverside
NON-SPORTING	Old English Sheepdog	Phillips' Ch. Home Farm Shepherdess
HOUND	Greyhound	Decies' Scotswood Sylph
TERRIER	Wire Fox	Way's Ch. Collarette of Paignton
PET DOG	Pekingese	Ashton-Cross's Ch. Choo-tai of Egham

Harry Haylock, Arthur Maxwell, Blatspiel Stamp

AWARD JUDGE(S)	BREED	NAME OF OWNER & NAME OF DOG
1914		
BEST CHAMPION	Greyhound	Beadon's Ch. St Blaise
SPORTING	Flat Coat Retriever	Cooke's Kaffir of Riverside
NON-SPORTING	Old English Sheepdog	Oakman's Ch. Shepton Laddie
HOUND	Greyhound	Beadon's Ch. St Blaise
TERRIER	Irish	Pritchard's Rumney Ruth
PET DOG	Pekingese	Ashton-Cross's Ch. Chu-ty of Alderbourne
W. B. Stamp, Harding Cox, R. Everill		
1915		
BEST CHAMPION	Rough Collie	van Huttum's Sonneburgh Squire
SPORTING	Flat Coat Retriever	Cooke's Pike
NON-SPORTING	Newfoundland	Goodall's Ch. Gipsy Baron
HOUND	Greyhound	Beadon's Ch. St Blaise
TERRIER	Wire Fox	Duchess of Newcastle's Ch. Cocoatina of Notts
PET DOG	Pekingese	Ashton-Cross's Ch. Chu-ty of Alderbourne
Theo Marples, Harding Cox		
1916		
BEST CHAMPION	Wire Fox	Duchess of Newcastle's Ch. Chequebook of Notts
SPORTING	Curly Coat	Fish's Ch. Penwortham Sportsman
NON-SPORTING	Rough Collie	Stansfield's Ch. Laund Luminous
HOUND	Borzoi	Vlasto's Ch. Nizam of Addlestone
TERRIER	Wire Fox	Duchess of Newcastle's Ch. Chequebook of Notts
PET DOG	Pekingese	Ashton-Cross's Ch. Chu-ty of Alderbourne
Theo Marples, Harding Cox, W. B. Stamp		
1917		
BEST CHAMPION	?	?
SPORTING	Flat Coat Retriever	Cooke's Pike
NON-SPORTING	Chow Chow	Scaramanga's Ch. Pagoda Kwong
HOUND	Greyhound	Beadon's Ch. St Blaise
TERRIER	Wire Fox	Duchess of Newcastle's Ch. Olcliffe Tea Rose
PET DOG	Pekingese	Ashton-Cross's Tien Joss of Greystones
Theo Marples, Harding Cox, W. B. Stamp		
1918		
No Show		
1919		
No Show		
1920		
No Show		

AWARD JUDGE(S)	BREED	NAME OF OWNER & NAME OF DOG
1921		
BEST CHAMPION	?	?
SPORTING	Labrador Retriever	Dick's Ch. Banchory Rando
NON-SPORTING	St Bernard	Thompson's Ch. King's Mark of Tynebank
HOUND	Deerhound	Doxford's Ch. Noel of Ruritania
TERRIER	Irish	Montgomery's Ch. War Bonus
PET DOG	Pomeranian	Franklin's Ch. Morceau d'Or
1922		
BEST CHAMPION	?	?
GUNDOG	Labrador Retriever	Dick's Ch. Grateley Ben
NON-SPORTING	Rough Collie	Stansfield's Laund Lauder
HOUND	Bloodhound	Hylden's Ch. Dark of Brighton
TERRIER	Irish	Montgomery's Ch. Celtic Patriot
PET DOG	Pomeranian	Wilson's Ch. Flashaway of Dara
Theo Marples, Harding Cox		
1923		
BEST CHAMPION	Skye Terrier	Alexander's Ballochmyle Lightening
SPORTING	Labrador Retriever	Dick's Ch. Grateley Ben
NON-SPORTING	Bulldog	Nichols' Ch. Hefty Master Grumpy
HOUND	Greyhound	White's Fortune's Wheel
TERRIER	Irish	Montgomery's Ch. Celtic Patriot
PET DOG	Pekingese	Calley's Ch. Kuan of Burderop
Harding Cox, Theo Marples, Harry Haylock, T. Whaley		
1924		
BEST CHAMPION	?	?
SPORTING	Flat Coat Retriever	Cooke's Sadie of Riverside
NON-SPORTING	Bulldog	Hubbard's Ch. Caulfield Monarch
HOUND	Great Dane	Rank's Pride of Ouborough
TERRIER	Wire Fox	Duchess of Newcastle's Ch. Chipped Tip of Notts
PET DOG	Pekingese	Cowell's Ch. Tai Yang of Newnham
Harding Cox, A. B. Montgomery, Sam Crabtree		
1925		
BEST CHAMPION	?	?
SPORTING	English Setter	Turton Price's O' by Jingo
NON-SPORTING	Bulldog	Rousseau's Ch. Oakville Supreme
HOUND	Irish Wolfhound	Hudson's King Shane of Brabyns
TERRIER	Irish	McDaid's Ch. Celtic Timothy
PET DOG	Yorkshire Terrier	Marshall's Little Comet
Harding Cox, Croxton Smith, Harry Haylock		

AWARD JUDGE(S)	BREED	NAME OF OWNER & NAME OF DOG
1926		
BEST CHAMPION	?	?
SPORTING	Labrador Retriever	Dick's Ch. Banchory Danilo
NON-SPORTING	Chow Chow	Mannooch's Ch. The Lotus Flower
HOUND	Irish Wolfhound	Hudson's Ch. King Shane of Brabyns
TERRIER	Smooth Fox	Bishop's Ch. Selecta Ideal
PET DOG	Pomeranian	Langdon-Thomas's Ch. Perivale Dainty June

Sam Crabtree, Major Carrell, Harding Cox

1927		
BEST CHAMPION	?	?
SPORTING	Cocker Spaniel	Scott's Vivary Crusader
NON-SPORTING	Bulldog	Wheatley's Kippax Victoria
HOUND	Great Dane	Mansell's Ch. Maurice of Cuddington
TERRIER	Wire Fox	Homer Gage's Ch. Newmarket Brandy Snap
PET DOG	Pekingese	Fraser's Ch. Faraline Yang

Mrs Quintin Dick, Mrs Harry Cowell, Harding Cox, Calvert Butler, Harry Haylock

(From 1928 Best in Show was open to all whereas competition for the specials available was confined to Cruft's subscribers, hence the occasional apparent discrepancy between winners)

1928		
BEST IN SHOW	Greyhound	Whitley's Primley Sceptre
RESERVE	Pointer	Moorby's Stainton Spruce
GUNDOG	Pointer	Moorby's Stainton Spruce
NON-SPORTING	Chow Chow	Mannooch's Ch. Choonam Brilliantina
HOUND	Irish Wolfhound	Knox's Lady of Raikeshill
TERRIER	Cairn	Baroness Burton's Ch. Firring Fionn
PET DOG	Pomeranian	Langdon-Thomas's Ch. Perivale Pimento

Theo Marples, Major Harding Cox, Harry Haycock, Will Hally

1929		
BEST IN SHOW	Scottish Terrier	Chapman's Heather Necessity
RESERVE	English Setter	Moorby's Stainton Spruce
SPORTING	Irish Setter	Carbery's Ch. Sarsfield of Boyne
NON-SPORTING	Dalmatian	Newman's Pongo the Warrior of Hyders
HOUND	Great Dane	Rank's Ch. Vivien of Ouborough
TERRIER	Cairn	Baroness Burton's Dochfour Dhuran
PET DOG	King Charles Spaniel	Raymond-Mallock's Ch. Ashton Moro Barritone

Theo Marples, Major Harding Cox, F. Calvert Butler

1930		
BEST IN SHOW	Cocker Spaniel	Lloyd's Luckystar of Ware
RESERVE	Scottish Terrier	Chapman's Heather Necessity
SPORTING	Cocker Spaniel	Lloyd's Luckystar of Ware
NON-SPORTING	Chow Chow	Mannooch's Ch. Choonam Brilliancy
HOUND	Greyhound	Peace's Pilot of Devoir
TERRIER	Cairn	Baroness Burton's Dochfour Timothy
TOY DOG	King Charles Spaniel	Raymond-Mallock's Ch. Ashton-More Wild Flowers

Mrs H. Fraser, Messrs F. Calvert Butler, Theo Marples, A. Croxton Smith, Major Harding Cox

AWARD JUDGE(S)	BREED	NAME OF OWNER & NAME OF DOG

1931

BEST IN SHOW	Cocker Spaniel	Lloyd's Luckystar of Ware
RESERVE	Pointer	Rowe's Ch. Nancolleth Markable
SPORTING	Cocker Spaniel	Lloyd's Luckystar of Ware
NON-SPORTING	Dalmatian	Proctor's Silver Wings
HOUND	Great Dane	Stewart's Ch. Mavis of Send
TERRIER	?	Not awarded
TOY DOG	Pomeranian	Bentley's Minegold Justit

Major Harding Cox, Messrs Theo Marples, A. Croxton Smith, Walter S. Glynn

1932

BEST IN SHOW	Labrador Retriever	Lorna Countess Howe's Bramshaw Bob
RESERVE	Kerry Blue Terrier	Toft's Another Prince of the Chevin
SPORTING	Labrador Retriever	Lorna Countess Howe's Bramshaw Bob
NON-SPORTING	Chow Chow	Rotch's Ch. Rochow Dragoon
HOUND	Great Dane	Rank's Ch. Record of Ouborough
TERRIER	Smooth Fox	Pearson's Kipyard Jakin
TOY DOG	King Charles Spaniel	Raymond-Mallock's Ch. Ashton-More Cupid

Major Harding Cox, Messrs A. Croxton Smith, Walter S. Glynn

1933

BEST IN SHOW	Labrador Retriever	Lorna Countess Howe's Ch. Bramshaw Bob
RESERVE	Scottish Terrier	Sharp's Ch. Rose Marie of Rookes
SPORTING	Labrador Retriever	Lorna Countess Howe's Ch. Bramshaw Bob
NON-SPORTING	?	?
HOUND	Irish Wolfhound	Rank's Farnoge of Ouborough
TERRIER	Smooth Fox	Tansey's Avon Peddlar
TOY DOG	Pomeranian	Jemson's Ch. Woodfield May King

Major Harding Cox, W. S. Glynn, A. Croxton Smith

1934

BEST IN SHOW	Greyhound	Hartland-Worden's Ch. Southball Moonstone
RESERVE	Cocker Spaniel	Lloyd's Whoopee of Ware
SPORTING	Cocker Spaniel	Lloyd's Whoopee of Ware
NON-SPORTING	French Bulldog	Osborne's Ch. Rangeworthy Roulette
HOUND	Irish Wolfhound	Rank's Fonab of Ouborough
TERRIER	Kerry Blue	Handy's Princeton Hell-of-a Fellow
TOY DOG	Pomeranian	Gatehouse's Jewel of Blackacre

Lorna Countess Howe, Major Harding Cox, A. Croxton Smith

1935

BEST IN SHOW	Pointer	Eggleton's Pennine Prima Donna
RESERVE	Chow Chow	Mannooch's Ch. Choonam Hung Kwong
GUNDOG	Pointer	Moorby's Ch. Stainton Startler
NON-SPORTING	Chow Chow	Mannooch's Ch. Choonam Hung Kwong
HOUND	Greyhound	Marchetti's Ch. Jasmine of Harrowins
TERRIER	Airedale	Haye's Ch. Aislably Aethling
TOY DOG	Pomeranian	Ch. Montacute Radiant (withdrawn)

Major Harding Cox, A. Croxton Smith, Major P. C. G. Hayward

AWARD JUDGE(S)	BREED	NAME OF OWNER & NAME OF DOG
1936		
BEST IN SHOW	Chow Chow	Mannooch's Ch. Choonam Hung Kwong
RESERVE	Cocker Spaniel	Lloyd's Silver Templa of Ware
GUNDOG	Cocker Spaniel	Lloyd's Silver Templa of Ware
NON-SPORTING	Chow Chow	Mannooch's Ch. Choonam Hung Kwong
HOUND	?	?
TERRIER	Airedale	Handy's Ch. Princeton Hell-of-a-Fellow
TOY DOG	Black and Tan Terrier	Darling's Lilliput Lysette
Major Harding Cox, A. Croxton Smith, Chris Houlkner		
1937		
BEST IN SHOW	Labrador Retriever	Lorna Countess Howe's Ch. Cheverell's Ben of Banchory
RESERVE	Elkhound	Powys-Lybbe's Kren of the Hollow
GUNDOG	Labrador Retriever	Lorna Countess Howe's Ch. Cheverell's Ben of Banchory
NON-SPORTING	Old English Sheepdog	d'Arcy Thompson's Ch. Bouncer of Pickhurst
HOUND	Bloodhound	Sadleir's Ch. Barset of Barchester
TERRIER	Cairn	Townley's Ch. Fear Nil of Carysfort
TOY DOG	Pomeranian	Bromehead's Ch. Sherdon Starette
Major Harding Cox, A. Croxton Smith, Chris Houlkner		
1938		
BEST IN SHOW	Cocker Spaniel	Lloyd's Exquisite Model of Ware
RESERVE	Great Dane	Rank's Ch. Ruler of Ouborough
GUNDOG	Cocker Spaniel	Lloyd's Exquisite Model of Ware
NON-SPORTING	Bulldog	Palmer's Cloverley Blissful
HOUND	Great Dane	Rank's Ch. Ruler of Ouborough
TERRIER	Airedale	Stewart's Int.Ch. Sheltercock Merry Sovereign
TOY DOG	Pug	Swainston Goodger's Thunder Cloud of Swainston
Major P. C. G. Hayward, A. Croxton Smith, Chris Houlkner		
1939		
BEST IN SHOW	Cocker Spaniel	Lloyd's Exquisite Model of Ware
RESERVE	Chow Chow	Mannooch's Ch. Choonam Hung Kwong
GUNDOG	Labrador Retriever	Gilliatt's Ch. Holton Joyful
NON-SPORTING	Old English Sheepdog	Flower's Pastorale Mate o'Mine
HOUND	Afghan Hound	Wood's Ch. Westmill Ben Havid
TERRIER	Wire Fox	Fielding's Ch. Whitecastle Conqueror
TOY DOG	Yorkshire Terrier	Lady Windham's Ruby of Soham
Lorna Countess Howe, A. Croxton Smith, Chris Houlkner		

1940
No Show

1941
No Show

1942
No Show

AWARD JUDGE(S)	BREED	NAME OF OWNER & NAME OF DOG

1943
No Show

1944
No Show

1945
No Show

1946
No Show

1947
No Show

1948

BEST IN SHOW	Cocker Spaniel	Lloyd's Tracey Witch of Ware
RESERVE	Wire Fox	Sharpe's Drakehall Dairymaid

May Pacey, Croxton Smith

SPORTING	Cocker Spaniel	Lloyd's Tracey Witch of Ware
RESERVE	Wire Fox	Sharpe's Drakehall Dairymaid

Winnie Barber, J. W. Beynon, H. G. Sanders

NON-SPORTING	Great Dane	Rank's Raet of Ouborough
RESERVE	Pekingese	de Pledge and Lunham's Ch. Ku Chi of Caversham

Winnie Barber, Baron W. van der Hoop, E. E. Turner

1949
No Show

1950

BEST IN SHOW	Cocker Spaniel	Lloyd's Tracey Witch of Ware
RESERVE	Min. Poodle	Coventon's Ch. Adastra Magic Beau

Leo Wilson, Croxton Smith

SPORTING	Cocker Spaniel	Lloyd's Tracey Witch of Ware
RESERVE	West Highland White	Finch's Ch. Shiningcliff Simon

Winnie Barber, Aubrey Ireland, H. R. Phipps

NON-SPORTING	Min. Poodle	Coventon's Ch. Adastra Magic Beau
RESERVE	Pekingese	de Pledge and Lunham's Ch. Ku Chi of Caversham

J. W. Beynon, E. E. Turner

1951

BEST IN SHOW	Welsh Terrier	Thomas's Twynstar Dyma-Fi
RESERVE	Alsatian	Johnson's Edana of Combehill

Winnie Barber, Croxton Smith

SPORTING	Welsh Terrier	Thomas's Twynstar Dyma-Fi
RESERVE	Saluki	Buglass' Ch. Goldendawn Nadir Nar

May Pacey, Col. H. Phipps, J. W. Beynon

NON-SPORTING	Alsatian	Johnson's Edana of Combehill
RESERVE	Old English Sheepdog	Howell's Ch. Shepton Indomitable

Roger Boulton, E. Turner, A. G. Nichols

AWARD JUDGE(S)	BREED	NAME OF OWNER & NAME OF DOG
1952		
BEST IN SHOW	Bulldog	Barnard's Ch. Noways Chuckles
RESERVE	English Setter	Jarry's Ripleygate Topnote
Roger Boulton, Croxton Smith		
SPORTING & TOY	Wire Fox Terrier	Francis' Ch. Torkard Susan
RESERVE	Borzoi	Curnow's Aureola of Woodcourt
Roger Boulton, Croxton Smith		
NON-SPORTING &		
GUNDOG	Bulldog	Barnard's Ch. Noways Chuckles
RESERVE	English Setter	Jarry's Ripleygate Topnote
Roger Boulton, Croxton Smith		
1953		
BEST IN SHOW	Great Dane	Sigger's Ch. Elch Edler of Ouborough
RESERVE	Afghan Hound	Abson's Ch. Netheroyd Alibaba
Winnie Barber, the Earl of Northesk		
SPORTING & TOY	Afghan Hound	Abson's Ch. Netheroyd Alibaba
RESERVE	Smooth Dachshund	Pilkington's Ch. Ashdown Glamorous
Winnie Barber, the Earl of Northesk		
NON-SPORTING &		
GUNDOG	Great Dane	Sigger's Ch. Elch Edler of Ouborough
RESERVE	Cocker Spaniel	Lloyd's Ch. Tracey Witch of Ware
Winnie Barber, the Earl of Northesk		
1954		
No Show		
1955		
BEST IN SHOW	Standard Poodle	Proctor's Ch. Tzigane Aggri of Nashend
RESERVE	Borzoi	Milston's Melba of Quernmore
Cecil-Wright, Roger Boulton		
SPORTING & TOY	Borzoi	Milston's Melba of Quernmore
RESERVE	Pomeranian	Buttery's Ch. Colwyn's Toy Drum Major
May Pacey, Col Phipps, MacDonald Daly		
NON-SPORTING &		
GUNDOG	Standard Poodle	Proctor's Ch. Tzigane Aggri of Nashend
RESERVE	Welsh Corgi	Moore's Ch. Kaytop Maracas Mist
Winnie Barber, the Earl of Northesk, Tom Scott		
1956		
BEST IN SHOW	Greyhound	de Casembroot & Greenish's Treetops Golden Falcon
RESERVE	Wire Fox Terrier	Copley's Ch. Caradochouse Spruce
May Pacey, Winnie Barber		
SPORTING & TOY	Greyhound	de Casembroot & Greenish's Treetops Golden Falcon
RESERVE	Wire Fox Terrier	Copley's Ch. Caradochouse Spruce
W. W. Brainard, Hildebrand Wilson, Macdonald Daly		
NON-SPORTING &		
GUNDOG	Keeshond	Tucker's Ch. Volkrijk of Vorden
RESERVE	Bullmastiff	Terry's Ch. Ambassador of Buttonoak
Capt S. Bower, Vernon Hirst, Bert Lloyd		

AWARD JUDGE(S)	BREED	NAME OF OWNER & NAME OF DOG

1957

BEST IN SHOW	Keeshond	Tucker's Ch. Volkrijk of Vorden
RESERVE	English Setter	English's Ch. Shiplake Dean of Crombie
The Earl of Northesk, Roger Boulton		
HOUND	Elkhound	Thomas' Ch. Sian of Deriormond
Joe Braddon, Stanley Halle		
GUNDOG	English Setter	English's Ch. Shiplake Dean of Crombie
Frank Warner Hill, Bill Siggers		
TERRIER	Wire Fox	Francis' Emprise Sensational
Joe Braddon, Stanley Halle		
NON-SPORTING	Keeshond	Tucker's Ch. Volkrijk of Vorden
Frank Warner Hill, Bill Siggers		
TOY	Maltese	D'Arcy's Ch. Snowdrop of Beetop
Joe Braddon, Stanley Halle		

1958

BEST IN SHOW	Pointer	Parkinson's Ch. Chiming Bells
RESERVE	Bullmastiff	Terry's Ch. Ambassadorson of Buttonoak
McNab Cassells, George Trueman Hewitt		
HOUND	Whippet	Jones' Robmaywin Stargazer of Allways
May Pacey, Miss Loughrey		
GUNDOG	Pointer	Parkinson's Ch. Chiming Bells
Lola Daly, Fred Cross		
TERRIER	Lakeland	Ashton's Tithebarn Highlight
May Pacey, Miss Loughrey		
NON-SPORTING	Bullmastiff	Terry's Ch. Ambassadorson of Buttonoak
Lola Daly, Fred Cross		
TOY	Pekingese	Jones' Ch. Ku Chik Ko of Loofoo
May Pacey, Miss Loughrey		

1959

BEST IN SHOW	Welsh Terrier	Thomas & Leach's Ch. Sandstorm Saracen
RESERVE	Labrador Retriever	Grant Cairn's Ch. Ruler of Blaircourt
The Earl of Northesk, Col Richard Glyn		
HOUND	Beagle	Watson's Ch. Derawuda Vixen
Winnie Barber, Air-Com. Cecil-Wright		
GUNDOG	Labrador Retriever	Grant Cairn's Ch. Ruler of Blaircourt
May Pacey, McNab Chassels		
TERRIER	Welsh	Thomas & Leach's Ch. Sandstorm Saracen
Winnie Barber, Air-Com. Cecil-Wright		
NON-SPORTING	Standard Poodle	Price-Jones' Ch. Frenches Honeysuckle
May Pacey, McNab Chassels		
TOY	Pekingese	Silcock's Ch. Acol Ku-Anna
Winnie Barber, Air-Com. Cecil-Wright		

1960

BEST IN SHOW	Irish Wolfhound	Nagle & Clarke's Sulhamsted Merman
RESERVE	Pomeranian	Dyke's Ch. Pixietown Serenade of Hadleigh
Bert Lloyd, Fred Cross		

AWARD JUDGE(S)	BREED	NAME OF OWNER & NAME OF DOG

1960 cont'd

HOUND	Irish Wolfhound	Nagle & Clarke's Sulhamsted Merman
Enid Nicholls, Joe Braddon		
GUNDOG	Labrador	Cairn's Ch. Ruler of Blaircourt
H. Fottrell, Stephen Young		
TERRIER	Sealyham	Forsyth's Brastedchart Sea Princess
Enid Nicholls, Joe Braddon		
NON-SPORTING	Dalmatian	Woodyatt's Ch. Fanhill Fleur of Queenwood
H. Fottrell, Stephen Young		
TOY	Pomeranian	Dyke's Ch. Pixietown Serenade of Hadleigh
Enid Nicholls, Joe Braddon		

1961

BEST IN SHOW	Airedale Terrier	McCaughrey & Schuth's Ch. Riverina Tweedsbairn
RESERVE	English Setter	William's Silbury Soames of Madavale
Winnie Barber, Joe Braddon		
HOUND	Afghan	Pede's Bletchingly Ragman of Scheherezade
Marjorie Couzens, Frank Warner Hill		
GUNDOG	English Setter	William's Silbury Soames of Madavale
May Pacey, Air-Com. Cecil-Wright		
TERRIER	Airedale	McCaughrey & Schuth's Ch. Riverina Tweedsbairn
Marjorie Couzens, Frank Warner Hill		
NON-SPORTING	Alsatian	Walker's Ch. Sparky of Aronbel
May Pacey, Air-Com. Cecil-Wright		
TOY	Pekingese	Tom's Ch. Khognac Patience of Caversham
Marjorie Couzens, Frank Warner Hill		

1962

BEST IN SHOW	Wire Fox Terrier	Gill's Ch. Crackwyn Cockspur
RESERVE	Cocker Spaniel	Collin's Collinwood Black Eagle
May Pacey, Vernon Hirst		
HOUND	Beagle	Crowther-Davies' Cannybuff Barvae Pryer
Sir Richard Glynn, Fred Cross		
GUNDOG	Cocker Spaniel	Collin's Collinwood Black Eagle
Judy de Casembroot, the Earl of Northesk		
TERRIER	Wire Fox	Gill's Ch. Crackwyn Cockspur
Sir Richard Glynn, Fred Cross		
NON-SPORTING	French Bulldog	Gibson's Phillippa of Elmsleigh
Judy de Casembroot, the Earl of Northesk		
TOY	Maltese	White's Ch. Vicbrita Spectacular
Sir Richard Glynn, Fred Cross		

1963

BEST IN SHOW	Lakeland Terrier	Roger's Ch. Rogerholm Recruit
RESERVE	English Setter	William's Sh. Ch. Silbury Soames of Madavale
Air Com. Cecil-Wright, Col Sir Richard Glynn		
HOUND	Basenji	Percival's Ch. Lograk Lubilash of Littlebreach
Stephen Young, Joe Braddon		
GUNDOG	English Setter	William's Ch. Silbury Soames of Madavale
Lola M. Daly, Frank Warner Hill		

AWARD	BREED	NAME OF OWNER & NAME OF DOG
JUDGE(S)		

1963 cont'd

TERRIER   Lakeland   Roger's Ch. Rogerholm Recruit
Stephen Young, Joe Braddon
NON-SPORTING   Chow Chow   Crompton's Ch. Van Lee of Kai Oko
Lola M.Daly, Frank Warner Hill
TOY   Cavalier King Charles Spaniel   Cryer's Ch. Amelia of Luguna
Winnie Barber, Stephen Young

1964

BEST IN SHOW   English Setter   William's Sh. Ch. Silbury Soames of Madavale
RESERVE   Saluki   Waters' Ch. Burydown Freyha
Winnie Barber, Stephen Young
HOUND   Saluki   Waters' Ch. Burydown Freyha
Judy de Casembroot, Viscount Chelmsford
GUNDOG   English Setter   William's Sh. Ch. Silbury Soames of Madavale
Gwen Broadley, Fred Cross
TERRIER   Wire Fox   Dallison's Ch. Gosmore Kirkmoor Tessa
Judy de Casembroot, Viscount Chelmsford
NON-SPORTING   Rough Collie   Franklin's Pattingham Pacemaker
Gwen Broadley, Fred Cross
TOY   Yorkshire Terrier   Groom's Ch. Pagnell Peter Pan
Judy de Casembroot, Viscount Chelmsford

1965

BEST IN SHOW   Alsatian   Godden's Ch. Fenton of Kenwood
RESERVE   Beagle   Harris & Pagliero's Ch. Forrardon Appeline Beeswing
Air Com. Cecil-Wright, Col Sir Richard Glynn
HOUND   Beagle   Harris & Pagliero's Ch. Forrardon Appeline Beeswing
Arthur Fullwood
GUNDOG   Golden Retriever   Raymond's Sh. Ch. Gainspa Florette of Shiremoor
Frank Warner Hill
TERRIER   Bedlington   Philips' Rathsrigg Little Caesar
Arthur Fullwood
NON-SPORTING   Alsatian   Godden's Ch. Fenton of Kenwood
TOY   Maltese   White's Ch. Vicbrita Fidelity
Josephine Creasey

1966

BEST IN SHOW   Toy Poodle   Perry's Oakington Puckshill Amber Sunblush
RESERVE   Pointer   Baxter's Sh.Ch. Blakeshay Avant Tout
Bill Siggers, Fred Cross
HOUND   Afghan   Pollock's Ch. Kismati Khan of Tarril
Winnie Barber, Stanley Dangerfield
GUNDOG   Pointer   Baxter's Sh.Ch. Blakeshay Avant Tout
Joe Braddon, Maurice Gilliat
TERRIER   Lakeland   Postlethwaite's Ch. Stingray of Derryabah
Winnie Barber, Stanley Dangerfield
NON-SPORTING
Section 1   Toy Poodle   Perry's Oakington Puckshill Amber Sunblush
Joe Braddon, Maurice Gilliat

AWARD JUDGE(S)	BREED	NAME OF OWNER & NAME OF DOG

1966 cont'd

Section 2	Pembroke Corgi	Duckworth's Ch. Crowleythorn Miss Poppet
Joe Braddon, Maurice Gilliat		
TOY	Pomeranian	Berney's Sweet Dreams of Aurum
Winnie Barber, Stanley Dangerfield		

1967

BEST IN SHOW	Lakeland Terrier	Postlethwaite's Ch. Stingray of Derryabah
RESERVE	Standard Poodle	Fraser's Int. Ch. Bibelot's Tall Dark & Handsome
Viscount Chelmsford, Frank Warner Hill		
HOUND	Smooth Standard Dachshund	Gale's Ch. Womack Wrightstarturn
Lola M. Daly, Maxwell Riddle		
GUNDOG	Cocker Spaniel	Macmillan's Sh.Ch. Lochranza Quettadene Marksman
Gwen Broadley, Stanley Dangerfield		
TERRIER	Lakeland	Postlethwaite's Ch. Stingray of Derrybah
Lola M. Daly, Maxwell Riddle		
UTILITY	Standard Poodle	Fraser's Int. Ch. Bibelot's Tall Dark & Handsome
Gwen Broadley, Stanley Dangerfield		
WORKING	Shetland Sheepdog	Davis & Knight's Deloraine Dilys of Monkswood
Gwen Broadley, Stanley Dangerfield		
TOY	Pug	Thorp's Ch. Cedarwood Blunshill's Nimrod
Lola M. Daly, Maxwell Riddle		

1968

BEST IN SHOW	Dalmatian	Woodyatt's Ch. Fanhill Faune
RESERVE	Pyrenean Mountain Dog	Prince's Ch. Bergerie Diable
Josephine Creasey, Arthur Fullwood		
HOUND	Beagle	Field's Houndsmark Manful
Judy de Casembroot, Max Singleton		
GUNDOG	G.S. Pointer	Ward's Sh.Ch. Patrick of Malahide
Judy de Casembroot, Max Singleton		
TERRIER	Scottish	Dallison's Ch. Gosmore Eilburn Admaration
Judy de Casembroot, Max Singleton		
UTILITY	Dalmatian	Woodyatt's Ch. Fanhill Faune
Owen Grindey, Stephen Young		
WORKING	Pyrenean Mountain Dog	Prince's Ch. Bergerie Diable
Owen Grindey, Stephen Young		
TOY	Maltese	Lewin's Ellwyn Victorianna
Owen Grindey, Stephen Young		

1969

BEST IN SHOW	Alsatian	White's Ch. Hendrawen's Nibelung of Charavigne
RESERVE	Cocker Spaniel	MacMillan's Sh.Ch. Lochranza Strollaway
Maurice Gilliat, David Roche		
HOUND	Afghan	Holden's Ranjitsinhji of Jagai
Mrs F. D. Whitwell		
GUNDOG	Cocker Spaniel	MacMillan's Sh.Ch. Lochranza Strollaway
L. C. James		
TERRIER	Bedlington	Clifton's Ch. Vardene Blue Grenadier
Nancy Baylay		

AWARD JUDGE(S)	BREED	NAME OF OWNER & NAME OF DOG
1969 cont'd		
UTILITY *Fred Parsons*	Standard Poodle	Walne & Coppage's Ch. Vulcan Psyche of Gayshaws
WORKING *Bill Siggers*	Alsatian	White's Ch. Hendrawen's Nibelung of Charavigne
TOY *Hermione Warner Hill*	Pomeranian	Berney's Pandora of Aurum
1970		
BEST IN SHOW RESERVE *Stanley Dangerfield*	Pyrenean Mountain Dog Cocker Spaniel	Prince's Bergerie Knur Caddy's Sh.Ch. Ovaine Chieftain
HOUND *Stanley Dangerfield*	Beagle	Harris & Pagliero's Ch. Forrardon Foxtrot
GUNDOG *Stanley Dangerfield*	Cocker Spaniel	Caddy's Sh.Ch. Ovaine Chieftain
TERRIER *Stanley Dangerfield*	Norwich	Bradshaw & Finney's Withalder Locksley
UTILITY *Stanley Dangerfield*	Standard Poodle	Ashwell's Ch. Vicmar's Follow That
WORKING *Stanley Dangerfield*	Pyrenean Mountain Dog	Prince's Bergerie Knur
TOY *Stanley Dangerfield*	English Toy Terrier	Palmer's Ch. Stealaway Golden Girl
1971		
BEST IN SHOW RESERVE *Air Com. Cecil-Wright*	Alsatian Smooth Chihuahua	Prince Ahmed Hussain's Ch. Ramacon Swashbuckler Gray's Ch. Rozavel Tarina Song
HOUND *Stanley Dangerfield*	Elkhound	Winter's Ch. Fourwents Gretel of Eskamere
GUNDOG *Judy de Casembroot*	English Setter	Tate's Trodgers Scot's Oat
TERRIER *Jack Abbott*	Lakeland	O'Donoghue's Blackdale Handful
UTILITY *Catherine Sutton*	Chow Chow	Egerton's Ch. U-Kwong King Solomon
WORKING *Peggy Haslam*	Alsatian	Prince Ahmed Hussain's Ch. Ramacon Swashbuckler
TOY *Bill Hindley Taylor*	Smooth Chihuahua	Gray's Ch. Rozavel Tarina Song
1972		
BEST IN SHOW RESERVE *Arthur Westlake*	Bull Terrier Whippet	Drummond Dick's Ch. Abraxas Audacity Knight's Ch. Dondelayo Duette
HOUND *Catherine Sutton*	Whippet	Knight's Ch. Dondelayo Duette
GUNDOG *Joe Braddon*	American Cocker Spaniel	Caine's Sh. & Am. Ch. Dreamridge Delegate

AWARD JUDGE(S)	BREED	NAME OF OWNER & NAME OF DOG
1972 cont'd		
TERRIER *Joe Cartledge*	Bull	Drummond Dick's Ch. Abraxas Audacity
UTILITY *Miss Loughrey*	Standard Poodle	Creed's Ch. Greekmyth Aphrodite
WORKING *Thelma Gray*	Pembroke Welsh Corgi	Moore's Ch. Kaytop Marshall
TOY *George Down*	Yorkshire Terrier	Beech's Ch. Deebees Beebee
1973		
BEST IN SHOW	Cavalier King Charles Spaniel	Hall & Evan's Alansmere Aquarius
RESERVE *Owen Grindey*	Pointer	Parkinson's Sh.Ch. Daviam Titus Lartius
HOUND *Harry Glover*	Greyhound	Odell's Ch. Shalfleet Sir Lancelot
GUNDOG *Fenton Fitzgerald*	Pointer	Parkinson's Sh.Ch. Daviam Titus Lartius
TERRIER *Tom Horner*	Kerry Blue	Connolly's Int.Ch. Sheenon Fusilier
UTILITY *Frank Warner Hill*	Bulldog	Goddard's Ch. Portfield So Small
WORKING *Margaret Osborne*	Pembroke Welsh Corgi	Butler's Ch. Georgette of Wey
TOY *Judy de Casembroot*	Cavalier King Charles Spaniel	Hall & Evan's Alansmere Aquarius
1974		
BEST IN SHOW	St Bernard	Hinde's Ch. Burtonswood Bossy Boots
RESERVE *Judy de Casembroot*	Yorkshire Terrier	Lister's Ch. Blairsville Most Royale
HOUND *Bobby James*	Long-haired Dachshund	Jensen's Ch. Albaney's Red Rheinhart
GUNDOG *Gwen Broadley*	English Springer Spaniel	Hancock & Cudworth's Sh.Ch. Hawkhill Connaught
TERRIER *Stanley Dangerfield*	Skye Terrier	Atkinson's Ch. Silhill Silver Secret
UTILITY *Owen Grindey*	Lhasa Apso	Sefton & Cross-Stern's Ch. Cheska Alexander of Sternroc
WORKING *George Leatt*	St Bernard	Hinde's Ch. Burtonswood Bossy Boots
TOY *Yves Bentinck*	Yorkshire Terrier	Lister's Ch. Blairsville Most Royale

AWARD JUDGE(S)	BREED	NAME OF OWNER & NAME OF DOG
1975		
BEST IN SHOW	Wire Fox Terrier	Benelli & Dondina's Ch. Brookewire Brandy of Layven
RESERVE	Bulldog	Shaw's Ch. Beechlyn Golden Nugget of Denbrough
Thelma Gray		
HOUND	Whippet	Wright's Beseeka Knight Errant of Silkstone
Bill Pinches		
GUNDOG	German Short-haired Pointer	Mills-de-Hoog's Ch. Wittekind Igor
Violet Yates		
TERRIER	Wire Fox	Benelli & Dondina's Ch. Brookewire Brandy of Layven
Joe Braddon		
UTILITY	Bulldog	Shaw's Ch. Beechlyn Golden Nugget of Denbrough
Judy de Casembroot		
WORKING	Dobermann	Crick's Ch. Flexor Flugelman
Stanley Dangerfield		
TOY	Maltese	Turner's Ch. Quantos Con-Vivacita
Fred Chandler		
1976		
BEST IN SHOW	West Highland White	Newstead's Ch. Dianthus Buttons
RESERVE	Maltese	Clarke's Ch. Maytheas Delila
Joe Braddon		
HOUND	Saluki	Tedd's Almanza Kafiat
Fred Curnow		
GUNDOG	Cocker Spaniel	William's Ch. Bournehouse Starshine
Maurice Gilliatt		
TERRIER	West Highland White	Newstead's Ch. Dianthus Buttons
Diana Hamilton		
UTILITY	Keeshond	Purdon's Ch. Ledwell Dutchman
Stanley Dangerfield		
WORKING	St Bernard	McMurray's Ch. Snowranger Cascade
Elizabeth Somerfield		
TOY	Maltese	Clarke's Ch. Maytheas Delila
Owen Grindey		
1977		
BEST IN SHOW	English Setter	William's Bournehouse Dancing Master
RESERVE	Kerry Blue	Attwood Parker's Ch. Binate Plantagenet
Catherine Sutton		
HOUND	Borzoi	Anderson's Ch. Waycross Roksana
Owen Grindey		
GUNDOG	English Setter	William's Bournehouse Dancing Master
L. C. James		
TERRIER	Kerry Blue	Attwood Parker's Ch. Binate Plantagenet
Reg Gadsden		
UTILITY	Miniature Poodle	Gee's Ch. Beritas Banacheke
Ferelith Hamilton		
WORKING	Bullmastiff	Newton's Ch. Craigylea Sir Galahad
Percy Whitaker		
TOY	Pug	Appleton's Ch. Dingleberry Vega
Bob Russell-Roberts		

AWARD JUDGE(S)	BREED	NAME OF OWNER & NAME OF DOG
1978		
BEST IN SHOW	Wire Fox Terrier	Howle's Ch. Harrowhill Huntsman
RESERVE	Yorkshire Terrier	Lister's Ch. Blairsville Royal Seal
Gwen Broadley		
HOUND	Greyhound	Kenis' Ch. Solstrand Double Diamond
Percy Whitaker		
GUNDOG	Cocker Spaniel	MacMillan & Gillespie's Sh.Ch. Lochranza Man of Fashion
Walter Bradshaw		
TERRIER	Wire Fox	Howles Ch. Harrowhill Huntsman
Fred Dempster		
UTILITY	Bulldog	Cotton's Ch. Aldridge Anenome
Herbert Essam		
WORKING	German Shepherd Dog	White's Ch. Spartacist of Hendrawen
Lily Turner		
TOY	Yorkshire Terrier	Lister's Ch. Blairsville Royal Seal
Bob Flavell		
1979		
BEST IN SHOW	Kerry Blue	Streatfield's Eng. & Am.Ch. Callaghan of Leander
RESERVE	Smooth Chihuahua	Murray's Ch. Belmuriz Brevier
L. C. James		
HOUND	Wire-haired Dachshund	Farrand & Naylor's Krystona Augustus
Badanach Nicholson		
GUNDOG	Golden Retriever	Wood's Brensham Audacity
Rene Parsons		
TERRIER	Kerry Blue	Streatfield's Eng. & Am. Ch. Callaghan of Leander
Lavinia Graham Weall		
UTILITY	Miniature Poodle	Porter's Ch. Jolanta by Jove
Lily Turner		
WORKING	German Shepherd Dog	White's Ch. Spartacist of Hendrawen
Bobby James		
TOY	Smooth Chihuahua	Murray's Ch. Belmuriz Brevier
Pamela Cross Stern		
1980		
BEST IN SHOW	Flatcoat Retriever	Chapman's Ch. Shargleam Blackcap
RESERVE	Miniature Schnauzer	Morley's Ch. Castilla Linajudo
Harry Glover		
HOUND	Whippet	Marshall's Ch. Jubilant Lady of Tygreen and Lowerdon
Mollie Garrish		
GUNDOG	Flatcoat Retriever	Chapman's Ch. Shargleam Blackcap
Margaret Lindsay Smith		
TERRIER	Bedlington	Anderson's Birkonbrae Bronze Bachique
Audrey Dallison		
UTILITY	Miniature Schnauzer	Morley's Ch. Castilla Linajudo
Ken Bullock		
WORKING	Bernese Mountain Dog	Griffith's Ch. Folkdance at Forgeman
Fred Curnow		
TOY	Italian Greyhound	Leigh's Ch. Tamoretta Tailormade
Catherine Sutton		

AWARD JUDGE(S)	BREED	NAME OF OWNER & NAME OF DOG
1981		
BEST IN SHOW	Irish Setter	Tuite's Ch. Astley's Portia of Rua
RESERVE	Standard Poodle	Streatfield, Stanley & William's Sablecomb White Polar at Leander
Bobby James		
HOUND	Beagle	Tutchener's Ch. Beacott Buckthorn
Owen Grindey		
GUNDOG	Irish Setter	Tuite's Ch. Astley's Portia of Rua
Ernest Froggatt		
TERRIER	Scottish	Gaskell's Ch. Mayson Monopoly
Linda Beak		
UTILITY	Standard Poodle	Streatfield, Stanley & William's Sablecomb White Polar at Leander
Percy Whitaker		
WORKING	Great Dane	Johnson's Ch. The Contender of Dicarl
Reg Gadsden		
TOY	Cavalier King Charles Spaniel	Newton's Ch. Jia Laertes of Tonnew
Joe Braddon		
1982		
BEST IN SHOW	Toy Poodle	Howard's Ch. Grayco Hazelnut
RESERVE	German Shepherd	Gardener's Kenmil's Bellisima of Danala
Reg Gadsden		
HOUND	Deerhound	Hartley's Ch. Betsinda of Rotherwood
GUNDOG	Flatcoat Retriever	Chapman's Ch. Shargleam Blackcap
Catherine Sutton		
TERRIER	Scottish	Plane's Stuane Highland Empress
Walter Bradshaw		
UTILITY	Toy Poodle	Howard's Ch. Grayco Hazelnut
Rita Price Jones		
WORKING	German Shepherd	Gardener's Kenmil's Bellisima of Danala
Judy de Casembroot		
TOY	Papillon	Hulme's Ch. Tongemoor Miss Peppermint
Bill Taylor		
1983		
BEST IN SHOW	Afghan Hound	Gibbs' Ch. Montravia Kaskarak Hitari
RESERVE	Irish Setter	Levick's Corriecas Fagan
Bill Parkinson		
HOUND	Afghan Hound	Gibbs' Ch. Montravia Kaskarak Hitari
Beefey Sutton		
GUNDOG	Irish Setter	Levick's Corriecas Fagan
Owen Grindey		
TERRIER	Welsh	Hunt's Ch. Puzzle of Kenstaff
Harold Wright		
UTILITY	Keeshond	Luckhurst's Ch. Gavimir Nighthawk
Pamela Cross Stern		
WORKING	Great Dane	McAlpine's Ch. Dicarl Tendellie
Marian Fairbrother		
TOY	Maltese	Herrief's Ch. Snowgoose Valient Lad
Ena Bassett		

AWARD JUDGE(S)	BREED	NAME OF OWNER & NAME OF DOG
1984		
BEST IN SHOW	Lhasa Apso	Blyth's Ch. Saxonsprings Hackensack
RESERVE	Pomeranian	Cawthera-Purdy's Ch. Lireva's Shooting Star
Mollie Garrish		
HOUND	Bloodhound	Richards' Ch. Chasedown Hopeful
Leonard Pagliero		
GUNDOG	Sussex Spaniel	Williams' Brytonian Aelwyn
Mary Roslin Williams		
TERRIER	West Highland White	Armstrong's Ch. Jaimont of Whitebriar
Owen Grindey		
UTILITY	Lhasa Apso	Blyth's Ch. Saxonsprings Hackensack
Bobby James		
WORKING	Pembroke Corgi	Taylor & Jones Ch. Belroyd Lovebird
Joe Braddon		
TOY	Pomeranian	Cawthera-Purdy's Ch. Lireva's Shooting Star
Gwen Broadley		
1985		
BEST IN SHOW	Standard Poodle	Gibbs' Ch. Montravia Tommy Gun
RESERVE	Pekingese	Mitchell's Ch. Micklee Roc's Ru-Ago
Harold Spira		
HOUND	Afghan	Amoo's Ch. Ashihna Raoul
Joe Braddon		
GUNDOG	English Springer	Miller's Sh.Ch. Graftonberry Genghis Khan
Leslie Page		
TERRIER	Kerry Blue	Brennan's Ch. Arkama Take By Storm
Catherine Sutton		
UTILITY	Standard Poodle	Gibbs' Ch. Montravia Tommy Gun
George Down		
WORKING	Dobermann	Banforth's Ch. Hughroyds Man of the Year
Riggs IV		
TOY	Pekingese	Mitchell's Ch. Micklee Roc's Ru-Ago
Nora Down		
1986		
BEST IN SHOW	Airedale Terrier	Livraghi's Ch. Ginger Xmas Carol
RESERVE	Bulldog	Bruton & McHale's Ch. Tyegarth Jacob of Kelloe
Ena Bassett		
HOUND	Saluki	Merchant Gile's Ch. Shamal Kharaz
Terry Thorn		
GUNDOG	Pointer	Sh.Ch. Stonebridgelees Sultana
Rae Furness		
TERRIER	Airedale	Livraghi's Ch. Ginger Xmas Carol
Ronnie Irving		
UTILITY	Bulldog	Bruton & McHale's Ch. Tyegarth Jacob of Kelloe
Joe Braddon		
WORKING	Rottweiler	Bromley's Rottsann Classic Centurian
Gwen Broadley		
TOY	Pomeranian	Hill's Ch. Derronnill's Maxamillion
Audrey Dallison		

AWARD JUDGE(S)	BREED	NAME OF OWNER & NAME OF DOG
1987		
BEST IN SHOW	Afghan Hound	Amoo's Ch. Viscount Grant
RESERVE	Wire Fox Terrier	Baxter's Ch. Killick of the Mess
Bill Pinches		
HOUND	Afghan Hound	Amoo's Ch. Viscount Grant
Ann Argyle		
GUNDOG	Flatcoat Retriever	Brady's Ch. Bordercot Guy
Bill Parkinson		
TERRIER	Wire Fox	Baxter's Ch. Killick of the Mess
Mary Blake		
UTILITY	Shih Tzu	Rawlings' Ch. Harropine Chaka Khan at Antarctica
Bill Jobson		
WORKING	Dobermann	Bevan's Ch. Sallate's Ferris
Jean Lanning		
TOY	Bichon Frise	Coad's Ch. Tiopepi Mad Louie at Pamplona
Jack Mitchell		
1988		
BEST IN SHOW	English Setter	Watkin's Sh.Ch. Starlite Express of Valsett
RESERVE	Border Terrier	MacPherson & Hutchinson's Ch. Brannigan of Brumberhill
Beefey Sutton		
HOUND	Borzoi	Bassett's Ch. Colhugh Caminickers
Audrey Dallison		
GUNDOG	English Setter	Watkin's Sh.Ch. Starlite Express of Valsett
Jimmy Cudworth		
TERRIER	Border	MacPherson & Hutchinson's Ch. Brannigan of Brumberhill
Jane Miller		
UTILITY	Lhasa Apso	Corish's Ch. Saxonsprings Fresno
Tom Horner		
WORKING	Samoyed	Fox's Ch. Zamoyski Lucky Star of Ostyak
Ferelith Somerfield		
TOY	Yorkshire Terrier	Sameja's Ch. Ozmilion Dedication
Bobby James		
1989		
BEST IN SHOW	Bearded Collie	White's Ch. Potterdale Classic of Moonhill
RESERVE	Pekingese	Easdon & Martin's Ch. Yakee For Your Eyes Only
Lionel Hamilton-Renwick		
HOUND	Elkhound	Lee's Kestos Adheryn
Joan Wells-Meacham		
GUNDOG	Irish Setter	Smith's Reddins Ferdinand
TERRIER	Staffordshire Bull	McKnight's Belnite Dark Huntsman
Maurice Marshall		
UTILITY	Standard Poodle	Barnes & Dainty's Ch. Davlen The Beloved
Ann Wynyard		
WORKING	Bearded Collie	White's Ch. Potterdale Classic of Moonhill
Andrew Thompson		
TOY	Pekingese	Easdon & Martin's Ch. Yakee For Your Eyes Only
Ellis Hulme		

AWARD JUDGE(S)	BREED	NAME OF OWNER & NAME OF DOG
1990		
BEST IN SHOW	West Highland White	Tattersall's Ch. Olac Moon Pilot
RESERVE	Whippet	Newton's Ch. Nutshell of Nevedith
Ferelith Somerfield		
HOUND	Whippet	Newton's Ch. Nutshell of Nevedith
Barbara Wilton-Clark		
GUNDOG	Welsh Springer Spaniel	Hunton Morgan's Sh.Ch. Dalati Sarian
Peggy Grayson		
TERRIER	West Highland White	Tattersall's Ch. Olac Moon Pilot
Vince Mitchell		
UTILITY	Miniature Poodle	Holmes' Ch. Navarre's Executive
Jean Lanning		
WORKING	Dobermann	Anderson's Ch. Sallate's Ferris
Leonard Pagliero		
TOY	Cavalier King Charles Spaniel	Wiggins' Whyteplace Apollo
Tom Horner		

Appendix 3

CRUFT'S ENTRIES

HOUND GROUP	1891	1902	1920	1936	1948	1965	1971	1990
AFGHAN HOUND	–	–	–	94	105	209	280	270
BASENJI	–	–	–	–	43	77	82	81
BASSET HOUND	13	40	–	12	10	180	210	128
BEAGLE	–	36	–	8	38	196	225	184
BLOODHOUND	24	31	27	51	18	55	84	35
BORZOI	36	86	40	122	100	98	78	146
DACHSHUND	47	68	32	–	–	–	–	–
DACHSHUND (L/H)	–	–	–	114	161	119	75	104
DACHSHUND (MIN L/H)	–	–	–	–	78	182	137	144
DACHSHUND (S/H)	–	–	–	252	336	206	149	75
DACHSHUND (MIN S/H)	–	–	–	–	76	154	128	64
DACHSHUND (W/H)	–	–	–	90	31	78	76	76
DACHSHUND (MIN W/H)	–	–	–	–	–	55	64	79
DEERHOUND	30	51	24	77	58	92	68	105
ELKHOUND	–	8	3	132	101	119	132	70
FINNISH SPITZ	–	–	–	42	–	69	56	51
GREYHOUND	19	11	15	51	47	24	34	60
IBIZAN HOUND	–	–	–	–	–	–	–	29
IRISH WOLFHOUND	–	50	26	106	32	94	77	146
OTTERHOUND	–	–	–	–	–	–	–	39
PETIT BASSET GRIFFON VENDEEN	–	–	–	–	–	–	–	64
PHARAOH HOUND	–	–	–	–	–	–	–	34
RHODESIAN RIDGEBACK	–	–	–	–	52	39	48	99
SALUKI	–	–	–	31	52	123	90	171
WHIPPET	23	15	31	83	105	219	278	210

GUNDOG GROUP	1891	1902	1920	1936	1948	1965	1971	1990
BRITTANY	–	–	–	–	–	–	–	46
ENGLISH SETTER	–	–	15	143	98	185	151	228
GERMAN SHORTHAIRED POINTER	–	–	–	–	35	110	119	177
GERMAN WIREHAIRED POINTER	–	–	–	–	–	–	–	51
GORDON SETTER	–	–	8	82	47	86	68	174
GORDON & ENG. SETTERS	61	83	–	–	–	–	–	–

Gundog Group cont'd	_1891_	_1902_	_1920_	_1936_	_1948_	_1965_	_1971_	_1990_
HUNGARIAN VISLA	–	–	–	–	–	–	20	67
IRISH RED AND WHITE SETTER	–	–	–	–	–	–	–	87
IRISH SETTER	–	–	40	252	187	234	255	312
ITALIAN SPINONE	–	–	–	–	–	–	–	76
LARGE MUNSTERLANDER	–	–	–	–	–	–	–	70
POINTER	25	35	28	179	117	153	124	129
RETRIEVER (CHESAPEAKE BAY)	–	–	–	–	–	–	–	35
RETRIEVER (CURLY COATED)	–	–	5	28	24	51	44	39
RETRIEVER (FLAT COATED)	–	–	35	127	53	103	135	214
RETRIEVERS (FLAT & CURLY)	51	108	–	–	–	–	–	–
RETRIEVER (GOLDEN)	–	–	45	226	252	479	404	321
RETRIEVER (LABRADOR)	–	–	90	898	308	682	387	285
SPANIEL	–	180	–	–	–	–	–	–
SPANIEL (AMERICAN COCKER)	–	–	–	–	–	–	54	96
SPANIEL (CLUMBER)	8	–	21	48	16	47	44	87
SPANIEL (COCKER)	85	–	91	766	647	728	482	274
SPANIEL (ENGLISH SPRINGER)	–	–	–	239	145	227	175	159
SPANIEL (FIELD)	22	–	–	31	–	13	18	74
SPANIEL (IRISH WATER)	–	–	25	74	18	21	13	48
SPANIEL (SPRINGER)	–	–	36	–	–	–	–	–
SPANIEL (SUSSEX)	7	–	–	47	–	13	21	43
SPANIEL (WELSH SPRINGER)	–	–	–	41	45	54	98	134
WEIMARANER	–	–	–	–	29	54	63	189

TERRIER GROUP

	_1891_	_1902_	_1920_	_1936_	_1948_	_1965_	_1971_	_1990_
AIREDALE TERRIER	69	63	75	132	101	178	85	81
AUSTRALIAN TERRIER	–	–	–	39	45	42	27	36
BEDLINGTON TERRIER	31	44	50	97	90	83	56	79
BORDER TERRIER	–	–	10	57	94	119	92	122
BULL TERRIER (inc. Min)	36	27	45	175	–	–	–	–
BULL TERRIER	–	–	–	–	210	111	66	76
BULL TERRIER (MIN)	–	–	–	–	17	23	14	37
CAIRN TERRIER	–	–	64	296	304	273	205	112
DANDIE DINMONT TERRIER	96	46	8	100	95	58	53	79
FOX TERRIER (both coats)	353	316	295	–	–	–	–	–
FOX TERRIER (SMOOTH)	–	–	–	166	227	145	103	62
FOX TERRIER (WIRE)	–	–	–	281	232	178	90	77
IRISH TERRIER	61	79	50	59	84	63	43	49
KERRY BLUE TERRIER	–	–	–	64	93	80	55	84
LAKELAND TERRIER	–	–	–	81	92	70	52	42
MANCHESTER TERRIER	–	–	–	18	–	24	35	49
NORFOLK TERRIER	–	–	–	–	–	45	40	33
NORWICH TERRIER	–	–	–	35	54	60	39	25
SCOTTISH TERRIER	82	130	45	230	181	169	127	57
SEALYHAM TERRIER	–	–	201	213	112	103	57	42

	1891	1902	1920	1936	1948	1965	1971	1990
SKYE & CLYDESDALE TERRIERS	32	39	—	—	—	—	—	—
SKYE TERRIER	—	—	17	40	112	24	44	54
SOFTCOATED WHEATEN TERRIER	—	—	—	—	6	35	24	41
STAFFORDSHIRE BULL TERRIER	—	—	42	166	117	****	183	240
WELSH TERRIER	51	43	27	71	82	77	41	44
WEST HIGHLAND WHITE TERRIER	—	—	47	111	85	138	171	146
WHITE ENGLISH TERRIER	13	10	—	—	—	—	—	—
WORKING TERRIER	—	—	12	—	—	—	—	—

UTILITY GROUP

	1891	1902	1920	1936	1948	1965	1971	1990
BOSTON TERRIER	—	—	—	34	61	98	75	55
BULLDOG (inc French & Min)	—	224	—	—	—	—	—	—
BULLDOG (inc Min.)	—	—	121	—	—	—	—	—
BULLDOG	60	—	—	250	203	182	157	108
CHOW CHOW	6	102	70	371	220	145	129	114
DALMATIAN	20	24	—	200	138	204	222	140
FRENCH BULLDOG	—	—	47	68	83	84	115	64
GERMAN SPITZ (KLEIN)	—	—	—	—	—	—	—	50
GERMAN SPITZ (MITTEL)	—	—	—	—	—	—	—	28
JAPANESE AKITA	—	—	—	—	—	—	—	152
JAPANESE SPITZ	—	—	—	—	—	—	—	82
KEESHOND	—	—	—	139	113	127	105	93
LHASA APSO	—	—	—	—	—	41	72	186
MIN SCHNAUZER	—	—	—	—	24	100	86	87
POODLE (STANDARD)	—	—	—	—	82	83	105	139
POODLE (MINIATURE)	—	—	—	66	207	459	303	131
POODLE (TOY)	—	—	—	—	262	373	274	125
POODLE (all sizes)	—	—	47	66	—	—	—	—
SCHIPPERKE	57	44	36	51	59	56	49	51
SCHNAUZER	—	—	—	105	39	50	50	61
SHAR PEI	—	—	—	—	—	—	—	44
SHIH TZU	—	—	—	17	—	107	104	182
TIBETAN SPANIEL	—	—	—	11	—	62	89	139
TIBETAN TERRIER	—	—	—	17	11	12	41	115

WORKING GROUP

	1891	1902	1921	1936	1948	1965	1971	1990
ALASKAN MALAMUTE	–	–	–	–	–	–	–	40
ANATOLIAN SHEPHERD DOG	–	–	–	–	–	–	–	59
BEARDED COLLIE	–	–	–	–	–	56	86	238
BELGIAN SHEPHERD (GROENENDAEL)	–	–	–	–	–	–	37	122
BELGIAN SHEPHERD (TERVUEREN)	–	–	–	–	–	–	–	135
BERNESE MOUNTAIN DOG (1938)	–	–	–	–	–	–	–	190
BORDER COLLIE	–	–	–	–	–	–	–	184
BOUVIER DES FLANDERS	–	–	–	–	–	–	–	60
BOXER	–	–	–	10	194	359	211	174
BRIARD	–	–	–	–	–	–	–	95
BULLMASTIFF	–	–	–	75	65	109	80	117
COLLIE (ROUGH)	–	–	–	–	128	394	249	337
COLLIE (SMOOTH)	–	–	–	–	13	42	34	88
COLLIE	157	–	100	118	–	–	–	–
DOBERMANN	–	–	–	–	15	145	188	253
GERMAN SHEPHERD DOG	–	–	127	255	369	595	435	164
GIANT SCHNAUZER	–	–	–	–	–	–	–	73
GREAT DANE	–	83	53	152	184	147	227	187
HUNGARIAN PULI	–	–	–	–	–	–	–	62
LANCASHIRE HEELER	–	–	–	–	–	–	–	47
MAREMMA SHEEPDOG	–	–	–	–	16	–	–	42
MASTIFF	55	24	9	96	–	26	36	79
NEWFOUNDLAND	78	33	16	77	–	60	52	169
NORWEGIAN BUHUND	–	–	–	–	–	–	26	65
OLD ENGLISH SHEEPDOG	70	78	45	104	52	112	160	145
PYRENEAN MOUNTAIN DOG	–	–	–	–	81	141	169	102
ROTTWEILER	–	–	–	–	41	47	45	235
ST BERNARD	207	100	41	75	76	103	78	104
SAMOYED	–	–	26	111	96	99	104	180
SHETLAND SHEEPDOG	–	–	15	106	101	346	271	236
SIBERIAN HUSKY	–	–	–	–	–	7	–	75
SWEDISH VALLHUND	–	–	–	–	–	–	–	59
TIBETAN MASTIFF	–	–	–	3	–	–	–	–
WELSH CORGI (CARDIGAN)	–	–	–	48	56	85	86	58
WELSH CORGI (PEMBROKE)	–	–	–	182	325	373	284	120

TOY GROUP

	1891	1902	1920	1936	1948	1965	1971	1990
AFFENPINSCHER	–	–	–	–	–	–	–	40
AFFENSCHNAUZER	–	–	–	19	–	–	–	–
AUSTRALIAN SILKY TERRIER	–	–	–	–	–	–	–	31
BICHON FRISE	–	–	–	–	–	–	–	114
CAVALIER K C SPANIEL	–	–	–	–	59	239	252	255
CHIHUAHUA (LONGCOAT)	–	–	–	–	–	151	223	165
CHIHUAHUA (SMOOTHCOAT)	–	–	–	–	–	318	227	95
CHINESE CRESTED	–	–	–	–	–	–	–	98
ENG. TOY TERRIER (BLACK & TAN)	9	–	–	42	36	42	57	24
GRIFFONS BRUXELLOIS	–	4	40	72	36	92	74	89
ITALIAN GREYHOUND	5	4	–	–	–	55	54	42
JAPANESE CHIN	–	–	23	20	45	45	59	94
KING CHARLES SPANIEL	–	–	–	59	29	69	59	94
LOWCHEN (LITTLE LION DOG)	–	–	–	–	–	–	–	47
MALTESE	7	12	13	8	45	61	73	54
MINIATURE PINSCHER	–	–	–	–	–	84	65	73
PAPILLON	–	–	–	67	41	106	124	129
PEKINGESE	–	–	113	359	264	459	334	178
POMERANIAN	46	130	129	201	97	106	95	147
PUG	120	72	43	65	81	208	166	114
TOY SPANIEL	108	45	34	–	–	–	–	–
YORKSHIRE TERRIER	34	8	24	49	68	206	206	228

Appendix 4

CUPS, TROPHIES & SPECIAL PRIZES 1990

THE KEDDEL MEMORIAL TROPHY	Best Exhibit in Show
CRUFTS TROPHY	Best Exhibit in Show
KENNEL CLUB CUP	Reserve Best Exhibit in Show
SEND GOLD VASE	Best of Hound Group
CRUFTS SALVER	Best of Hound Group
THE THEO MARPLES SPORTING TROPHY	Reserve Best of Hound Group
SEND GOLD VASE	Best of Gundog Group
CRUFTS SALVER	Best of Gundog Group
GIRALDA CHALLENGE TROPHY	Reserve Best of Gundog Group
THE 'COUNTRY LIFE' CHALLENGE TROPHY	Best Gundog in Show
SEND GOLD VASE	Best of Terrier Group
CRUFTS SALVER	Best of Terrier Group
CUP	Reserve Best of Terrier Group
SEND GOLD VASE	Best of Utility Group
CRUFTS SALVER	Best of Utility Group
TRAYSHILL CHALLENGE BOWL	Reserve Best of Utility Group
SEND GOLD VASE	Best of Working Group
CRUFTS SALVER	Best of Working Group
THE THEO MARPLES NON-SPORTING TROPHY	Reserve Best of Working Group
WELLCOME CHALLENGE TROPHY	Best Utility or Working Exhibit
SEND GOLD VASE	Best of Toy Group
CRUFTS SALVER	Best of Toy Group
HELEN PILKINGTON CHALLENGE CUP	Reserve Best of Toy Group
THE B KESWICK MEMORIAL TROPHY	Best Cavalier King Charles Spaniel
THE KENNELAC PERPETUAL CHALLENGE CUP	Best Long Coat Chihuahua

Appendix 5

CRUFTS OBEDIENCE WINNERS

Crufts became an Obedience Championship Show in 1955

1955
Homan's Ob.Ch. Shepherdon Spun Gold German Shepherd Dog
Spencer's Ob.Ch. Della of Gipton German Shepherd Dog
Mr George Sly
1956
Shackleton's Ob.Ch. Dash Border Collie
Foreman's Ob.Ch. Amaryllis of Helmdon German Shepherd Dog
Mr R M Montgomery
1957
Shackleton's Ob.Ch. Dash Border Collie
Jones's Ob.Ch. Copyright of Rozavel German Shepherd Dog
Mr K Butler
1958
Howes's Ob.Ch. Amphion of Palermo German Shepherd Dog
Pearce's Ob.Ch. Megan of Monkswood Border Collie
Mrs M Porterfield
1959
Needs's Ob.Ch. Castelnau Pizzicato Golden Retriever
Randall's Ob.Ch. Rafina Schone German Shepherd Dog
Mrs Beryl Langley
1960
Davies's Ob.Ch. Iliad of Tollhurst German Shepherd Dog
Shackleton's Ob.Ch. Zena Working Collie
Mr D Churchman
1961
Coult's Ob.Ch. Black Cloud German Shepherd Dog
Shackleton's Ob.Ch. Zena Working Collie
Mrs R M Montgomery
1962
Homan's Ob.Ch. Glyn of Rigi Border Collie
Pearce's Ob.Ch. Megan of Monkshead Border Collie
Mr F W Ratcliffe
1963
Homan's Ob.Ch. Glyn of Rigi Border Collie
Bates's Ob.Ch. Amanda of Jumaral German Shepherd Dog
Mr N H Haydock
1964
Ob.Ch. Holmfiow Rebel German Shepherd Dog
Pearce's Ob.Ch. Megan of Monksmead Border Collie
Mr L Pagliero

1965
Homan's Ob.Ch. Glyn of Rigi Border Collie
Westgate's Lowenbourne's Penny Border Collie
Mr W J Spencer
1966
Duncan's Ob.Ch. Flak of Ardgye German Shepherd Dog
Pearce's Ob.Ch. Megan of Monksmead Border Collie
Mr C V Butler
1967
Makinson's Ob.Ch. Dirk of Twistwood Working Sheepdog
Warren's Ob.Ch. She's Tiffin Sheepdog
Mrs B V Hill
1968
Faulconbridge's Ob.Ch. Tam II Border Collie
Reeve's Ob.Ch. Ing Shah of Westonvale German Shepherd Dog
Mr J Kenworthy
1969
Bellamy's Ob.Ch. Blaze of Sealight Working Collie
Sivyer's Ob.Ch. Moss Border Collie
Mrs M Pearce
1970
McMillan's Ob.Ch. Micklyn Shandy Cross Breed
Holme's Ob.Ch. Merrye Border Collie
Mrs V M Jones
1971
Smith's Ob.Ch. Jass Border Collie
Jordon's Ob.Ch. Shepdine Bonnie of Sealight Working Sheepdog
Mr W H Shackleton
1972
Hamilton's Ob.Ch. Tevis Border Brett Working Sheepdog
Collin's Ob.Ch. Kinder Syde Raven German Shepherd Dog
Mr L A Pearce
1973
Burdett's Ob.Ch. Golden Gift Golden Retriever
Snook's Ob.Ch. Daintree Debutante of Hallomas German Shepherd Dog
Mr N Braithwaite
1974
Herman's Ob.Ch. Moss Of Thornymoor Border Collie
Standfiled's Ob.Ch. Mischief of Tamerrye Border Collie
Mr N Hills
1975
Bellamy's Ob.Ch. Rogue of Sealight Border Collie
Pykett's Ob.Ch. Jan of Strad Border Collie
Mr N H Haydock
1976
French's Ob.Ch. Tannasg Tweed Border Collie
Hill's Ob.Ch. Greyvalley Honey German Shepherd Dog
Mr G Rowland
1977
Simpson's Ob.Ch. Stengahari Cyclop's German Shepherd Dog
Howell's Ob.Ch. Louville Tanzy Working Sheepdog
Mr W Gore
1978
Naylor's Ob.Ch. Flete of Tamerrye Border Collie
Smith's Ob.Ch. Lowella of Great Meadows Working Sheepdog
Mrs J Seal

1979
Iggulden's Ob.Ch. Springfarm Myth Working Sheepdog
Herring's Ob.Ch. Cindy of Frobisher Working Sheepdog
Mr N Stephens
1980
McKenzie's Ob.Ch. Crest of Muirside Working Sheepdog
Smith's Ob.Ch. Lowella of Great Meadows Working Sheepdog
Mr C M Wyant
1981
Stephens' Ob.Ch. Sharrobin Dai Working Sheepdog
Russell's Ob.Ch. Rintilloch Gingham German Shepherd Dog
Mr R Bate
1982
Knight's Ob.Ch. Triclen Duke of Great Meadows Working Sheepdog
Andrew's Ob.Ch. Pollzack Purdey of Kenstaff Working Sheepdog
Mr F Jones
1983
Cooper's Ob.Ch. Gemmadean Sheppie Working Sheepdog
Hunts' Ob.Ch. Shepdine Briar Working Sheepdog
Mrs P Bellamy
1984
Smith's Ob.Ch. Jay Jade Working Sheepdog
Abram's Ob.Ch. Sian Trooper Working Sheepdog
Mr J Anderson
1985
Stapley's Ob.Ch. Domino Double Working Sheepdog
Waite's Ob.Ch. Kingsfold Cass Border Collie
Mr K Pykett
1986
Patrick's Ob.Ch. Mac Belan Working Sheepdog
Allcock's Ob.Ch. Sealight Becky Border Collie
Mrs M McKenzie
1987
Orme's Ob.Ch. Fransmit Ken Working Sheepdog
Cregg's Ob.Ch. Kentygern Katastrophe Working Sheepdog
Mrs V Dale
1988
Farrington's Ob.Ch. Twistie of Challysfar Working Sheepdog
Bishop's Ob.Ch. Pajawi Crystal Gail German Shepherd Dog
Mrs P Beeton
1989
Hughe's Ob.Ch. Woughstock Wisdom Working Sheepdog
White's Ob.Ch. Darlodge Fen Border Collie
Mrs K Griffiths
1990
Ray's Ob.Ch. Red Hot Toddy Border Collie
Gavin's Ob.Ch. Ladygessler of Bryan Dobermann
Mr R Page

Index